W9-AUQ-621

BAR TARTINE

BAR TARTINE

TECHNIQUES & RECIPES

Nicolaus Balla and Cortney Burns

Photographs by Chad Robertson

CHRONICLE BOOKS

SAN FRANCISCO

Design by Juliette Cezzar

Editorial assistance by Jan Newberry

Typesetting by DC Typography

Food and prop styling by Nicolaus Balla, Cortney Burns, and Chad Robertson

Library of Congress Cataloging-in-Publication Data available.

ISBN 978-1-4521-2646-3

Manufactured in China

10 9 8 7 6 5 4

Chronicle Books LLC
680 Second Street
San Francisco, California 94107
www.chroniclebooks.com

CLEVELAND, 1950

Dark outside, I sit at the table,
the kitchen quiet, its cold black window
framing winter, and night, timelessly still.

Except away, beyond the horizon,
derricked above some radio station
one small red point blinks steadily on.

Grandparents sleep. I still feel the hum
of their Slovak and Hungarian,
syllables echoing like that beacon.

I speak but English. Do those Old World sounds
specially bear rosaries, currants, palm fronds,
gooseberries, crucifixes, and goose down?

I don't know yet about the stone streets of Pest,
poets Kosztolányi, Ady, Attila József,
or the coffeehouse nights that they blessed.

I don't know the garden hills of Buda
– like Istenhegy, on Diana utca,
where grew Radnóti's hexameter stanzas.

But an old language, I feel, I can guess,
yet throbs, like that red light, saying yes, yes,
as if memory pulsed in accents, accents.

– PHIL BALLA, 1977

CONTENTS

PART TWO: RECIPES

SOUPS

SALADS

SHARED PLATES

HARVEST PARTY

SWEETS

FOREWORD

I first met Nick Balla in his dive-y izakaya on Mission Street a few blocks from Tartine Bakery on a warm late summer day. Among the check-cashing storefronts, pawn shops, and a Foot Locker, the last thing I expected was to be served an elegant *suimono* (Japanese clear soup). That day's iteration was an array of carefully peeled, perfectly ripe, air-dried heirloom tomatoes along with chrysanthemum greens, purslane, mouse melons, okra, and sugar snap peas in a transcendent dashi broth finished with Nick's own house-made bottarga shavings. After that first visit, Liz (my wife and Tartine co-chef/owner) and I quickly settled into a routine of eating at Nick's place a couple of nights per week on our way home from the bakery. Nick made onigiri rice kits to occupy our daughter, Archer, while Liz ordered the ever-changing seasonal articulation of suimono and I dug into the heartier side of the menu—grilled tripe, spicy chicken wings, and rare beef heart with bonito and raw onions. I still remember a Buddha's hand sorbet so intensely flavored it left our mouths happily numb. In making bread, contrast is one of the chief goals I'm always striving for. Nick's menu was a study in contrasts, in extremes, really, of the most flavorful kind. Nick's

food spoke to us, referencing a language of flavors that was at once familiar, yet altogether new.

Liz and I opened Bar Tartine in 2005 and, along with the many chefs who collaborated with us during the first six years, we established a solid reputation for the restaurant. Initially envisioned as a sort of West Coast bistro to reflect the places we loved when we were apprenticing in France, the food changed along with whoever was cooking, but remained solidly in the Euro comfort zone. In our business, young chefs move on every few years. When the cycle of change was last upon us, we learned that Nick too was moving on from his Japanese gig at the end of the year, and wondered if he might be interested in working with us. Nick, it turned out, was interested, but wanted to take a break from the modern izakaya boom he had helped pioneer in the Bay Area. He had a deeper exploration in mind, one that had begun in the old town of Budapest when he was a kid in high school. We were game. Nick and I traveled to Budapest. After a week there, with a stop in Copenhagen to taste the zeitgeist, we returned to San Francisco with a new perspective and a lot more questions than answers.

In early 2011, Nick officially began to lead what would become the next evolution for Bar Tartine, and a few months later, Cortney Burns came in one day to help butcher a goat . . . and then never left. Cortney was in the restaurant from early morning until way past the end of dinner service; she was always working. Her first title was Chef of Special Projects. We didn't really know what else to call her in the beginning. She could do anything and everything, and better than anyone else. In charge of making huge batches of fresh cheese, yogurt, bubbling kefirs, buckets of fermenting vegetables, fresh misos, and cured meats, Cortney was regularly showing the rest of the staff how to break down every sort of whole animal and running the line at service. She quickly became co-chef with Nick and, with the two of them together driving the vision of Bar Tartine, a catalytic culinary curiosity began to take shape that could only be described as a universe in constant rapid expansion.

For one long session, Bar Tartine was a hothouse of culinary social experimentation as the restaurant was transformed each Monday evening by an exploration and melding of different culinary traditions. There were so many remarkable meals: a multicourse venture into the world of dashi with the famed masters of koji and kanbutsu, Laotian family-style dinners, Okinawan street food, and the surprising dovetail of Hokkaido and Jutland. Many of our friends were invited to collaborate in the kitchen with Nick and Cortney to celebrate their own book releases while collectively amplifying creativity.

This extraordinary period was followed by a strong pull to focus, refine, and define the clearest expression of the food at Bar Tartine. What resulted is an exceedingly personal type of California cuisine that concentrates the flavors of our local bounty, using ancient techniques with a modern approach. There are no luxury ingredients in the pantry at Bar Tartine. The entire repertoire is built on everyday staple foods: potatoes, onions, peppers, beets and other root vegetables, fresh herbs and garden greens, cured meats, and preserved foods of all types supplied by local farmers and ranchers. "Staple foods of all types" is a wildly inclusive phrase at Bar Tartine—the larder is huge. And yet that larder is as practical as it is aspirational. If you pick only five key ingredients and techniques from this book—and learn to utilize them—the outsized flavors you will be able to achieve cannot be overstated. The truly remarkable approach to cooking presented in this book is that it shows you how to transform everyday foods into something far more than the sum of their parts; this is an introduction to culinary wizardry.

The food of Bar Tartine is firmly grounded in the commonalities within traditional preservation and processing techniques across the globe. This layering of flavors—ones that naturally complement each another in technique or origin, even as they are culled from different cultures—is the key to unlocking long forgotten depths of flavor. Consequently, there is a certain concentration of experiences in the dishes at Bar Tartine that so often imprints flavors into one's memory.

How many times have I been asked how Nick, Cortney, and their team make the potatoes taste so good? Smoking is one of the ways, and one that we are all familiar with. Add to that a dozen more traditional flavor-concentrating techniques and ingredients, and you have a royal snack. This recipe is just one of the many you'll find here, all from the searching minds of two chefs who have been quietly influencing, in profound, far-reaching ways, how we source and eat.

—CHAD ROBERTSON

INTRODUCTION

This book is a snapshot of the menu at Bar Tartine from mid-February 2011, when our tenure as chefs of the restaurant began, through February 2014, when we turned in the manuscript for this book. While the food and discoveries are ever evolving, our guiding convictions remain the same now as they were at the beginning: serve things that we want to eat, that are fun to make, and that satiate us. The menu and this book are the product of our collaboration.

THE FOOD

One day, a dishwasher brought a bag of black paste to work to make a late-night staff meal. It looked and tasted like hatcho miso, a thick, black tarlike substance that originated in the area around Nagoya and is now famous throughout Japan. It was delicious, smoky, sweet, and full of concentrated flavor. The Mayans called it *chimole* and it is essentially a paste made from burnt vegetables. The discussion in the kitchen turned to, "How can we use this on the menu, and what if we try to make it with burnt bread? Hatcho miso is great with clams, so what about chimole with clams?" For us, these moments are life changing because a newly discovered ingredient can be the influence for a dish or entire menu.

Our goal, above all else, is to create an environment where such discoveries can occur organically, and often. We want to work in a space where collective creativity thrives. Everyone here has something to contribute, and no single person can take responsibility for the results. The food at Bar Tartine is an accumulation and melding of experiences and ideas garnered from the entire staff.

The dishes that we develop are always based on something we love to eat. A dim sum lunch that included green onion cakes influenced us to make a similar savory cake with celery root and toasted rice flour. Chile oil–covered cucumbers at a local Sichuan restaurant inspired us to pour our bright red paprika oil over long-aged mustard greens. We consider authenticity a slippery concept, as something that exists to evolve and be interpreted.

There's no one formula or strategy we use for coming up with new dishes. Our only rule is that what we make must be delicious. Peasant flavors influence us more than refined ones. We place a high value on secrets learned from grandmothers and on sampling strange Russian pickles or Taiwanese condiments brought to us by a friend. We like animal fat, hot chiles and smoke, funk, and agrodolce—flavors most commonly found in neighborhood ethnic restaurants or street-food stalls.

THE RESTAURANT

We dread the question, "What do you serve at Bar Tartine?" California cuisine is the simple answer, as we source most of what we cook from nearby. The term *fusion* could also be used, though it unfortunately evokes memories of dishes that marry kiwifruit, wasabi powder, and mashed potatoes.

Another answer is that we serve the food we want to eat. Family influences are our strongest inspiration. Collectively, we are Hungarian, eastern European Jewish, Japanese, Irish, Polish, German, Filipino, Slovak, Laotian, Mexican, and Mayan. The foods of these cultures are what we grew up with, what is in our blood, and what we have the strongest connection to.

The best answer to what we serve, however, is the food itself. Most of the ingredients used at the restaurant are made from scratch. That includes everything from garlic powder, dried apricots, and cured fish roe to almond milk, chile oil, and rice vinegar. Recipes for making these ingredients and scores of others can be found in Part One: Techniques.

Most of the recipes in this book are relatively simple and none requires expensive equipment. Many of them can be made in just minutes and some in just a couple hours; others can take upward of a year. There is a recipe here for any occasion: the sweltering summer day when you don't want to move, let alone cook (Chilled Buttermilk and Cucumber Soup → 156); the cold winter weekend when you don't want to leave the house (Black Garlic and Lentil Soup → 168); or the celebratory dinner that can engage and bring together the whole family (Harvest Party → 298).

This cookbook gives you the opportunity to choose your own adventure.

HOW WE EAT

So many of our favorite meals require nothing more than a bowl and spoon. The recipes in the Soups and Salads chapters are the most personal ones in the book, and the ones we are most likely to make when we're not at work.

These are the dishes we have made again and again, meals that we serve to our families and guests. We serve them because they link us to our past, to our parents and our grandparents, and remind us who we are. More important, we serve them because they are what we want to eat.

PART ONE

TECHNIQUES

INSIDE THE PROJECT KITCHEN

Fate is a powerful agent of creativity. Fate lives on the highest shelves of storerooms, in the back corners of refrigerators, at the market, and on delivery trucks with the wrong paperwork. Fate shows her hand when we purchase too much produce, need to use up something quickly, or unearth a bin of brined vegetables from the previous year. We have what we call "projects" in every nook and cranny of the restaurant. On any given day, spices are drying, cheeses aging, pickles bubbling, sprouts growing, and meats curing. Our larder is a jumping-off point. Eventually that sour cherry syrup, tomato jam, dried zucchini, sambal powder, or goat cheese will inspire new dishes. Fate brings things together, in time.

This techniques section is a collection of recipes from our project kitchen. It is not a comprehensive guide to fermentation, culturing dairy, or making spices. It is here as a reference for how to make the staple items used for the recipes in this book.

HOW TO USE THIS SECTION

This section covers a multitude of techniques, and we've provided several different types of recipes and formulas. For curing meats and fish we use percentages. These percentages demonstrate a relationship of two quantities, so for every specific amount of meat you use, you season with a proportional quantity of salt and spice. For example, if you are curing 2 lb/910 g of tuna loin, you will add 2 percent kosher salt, or 18 grams. Working with a digital scale allows you a tremendous amount of precision, and makes these ratio formulas easy to execute.

Some of these recipes and ratios require carefully calibrated weights and cooking times, whereas others are more freeform. For example, dry mounds of fennel flowers if you have them, but use the correct ratios to ferment vegetables. Most of the techniques here are templates, recipes that we created at the restaurant to fit our needs.

Although making everything from scratch is rewarding, it is not necessary in order to cook from this book. High-quality store-bought ingredients, from buttermilk to fennel pollen and dried chiles to cured fish roe can be used in place of many of the home-made ingredients here.

UTILIZE THE GLUT At some point in every season, a fruit or vegetable reaches its peak. This is when the flavor is best, the harvest abundant, and the price low enough to warrant bulk purchase. It's at this point that we encourage mass processing.

BUILD A LARDER Choose your favorite items from this section to make and stock your pantry so you'll always have them on hand to inspire a new dish or to add a layer of flavor to an old favorite.

RECIPE BY RECIPE You can turn to the recipes in Part Two and work your way through the book one dish at a time, taking on projects from Part One as you encounter them. When you decide to make a recipe, read through the ingredients list first. That way, you can check to see which of them may need to be prepared in advance.

A NOTE ON SALT Different types and brands of salt vary in density and salinity. We use Diamond brand kosher salt in this book for consistency. It does not include any additives and is free of aromas, which is not the case with some other salts. Diamond weighs about half as much as an equal volume of Morton brand kosher salt, and about one-third as much as an equal volume of common table salt. If you use another brand and/or type of salt, adjust the amounts called for accordingly. At the restaurant, we use sea salt or pink Himalayan salt for seasoning. If you choose to use a different salt than Diamond kosher brand, find the conversion rate from the producer or taste until the food is seasoned as you like.

Many recipes in this book call for finishing salt. This refers to coarse salt, such as flaked sea salt. This provides texture, not just seasoning. We use Jacobsen flaked salt, from Oregon, for finishing.

DRYING

Dehydration is more than just a method for preserving food. Extracting the bulk of the water from fruits, vegetables, meats, and fish concentrates flavors and changes textures. It's one of our most important tools for building flavor.

Drying in a Dehydrator

If you want to get into drying your own food in a bigger, more systemized way, a dehydrator is a good addition to your culinary arsenal. At the restaurant, we use dehydrators to process the majority of our dried foods. They maximize airflow exposure and yield consistent results.

Oven-Drying

Dried foods have been around far longer than any gadget, so there's no need to invest in special equipment for many of the projects in this section. A gas oven warmed only by its pilot light is an excellent tool for drying food. An oven with a convection setting works especially well, mimicking a dehydrator fan.

Sun-Drying

Drying foods in the sun requires a few specific conditions. Warm days that reach 85°F/29°C with relative humidity of below 60 percent are perfect; air movement is helpful, too. Very moist ingredients such as tomatoes should be halved, apples should be cut into wedges, and stone fruits halved and pitted. Arrange produce on a rack to allow air to circulate. A screen balanced between two cinder blocks works well. Cover the food with cheesecloth or another screen to keep flies and other insects out. Turn the produce at least once a day, and bring it indoors at night if necessary to protect it from moisture. Taste a little each day to decide when the process is complete.

Air-Drying

Hanging food to dry in a cool, ventilated area is one of the easiest ways to preserve certain ingredients. Take into account both density and water content when choosing foods to hang-dry. Herbs → 30 and peppers → 42 are excellent choices, but tomatoes would likely spoil. Meat and fish are also good candidates for air-drying, but only in situations where the humidity and temperature can be carefully controlled → 61.

Storing Dried Foods

Opaque containers and cool, dark cupboards are ideal for storing dried foods. It is important to keep the food away from light, which can cause both colors and flavors to fade. Generally, dried spices retain aroma and color for at least 6 months at room temperature, or longer if frozen. Use your judgment; if the aroma or color fade, start a new batch. Some dried ingredients have specific storage requirements; these will be noted, when applicable.

Toasting Dry Spices

Spices are most fragrant just after toasting, so toast in small batches as needed. Preheat the oven to 325°F/165°C. Spread the spice in an even layer on a sheet pan and toast just until fragrant, 7 to 10 minutes. Alternatively, warm a dry pan over medium-high heat, add the spice to the pan, and toast, tossing occasionally as it heats, just until fragrant. Timing will depend on the spice; most will take 5 to 7 minutes. Allow to cool completely before grinding.

Grinding Dried Ingredients into Flakes and Powders

Use a spice grinder or mortar and pestle to pulverize dried ingredients. Freeze the grinder bowl for at least 15 minutes to keep foods from overheating, which can deplete essential oils. If you're making a fine powder, sift and regrind any larger pieces for a uniform texture.

BAY LAUREL

HERBS, FLOWERS & SEEDS

Although the delicate flavors of fresh herbs become more intense when dried, their volatile oils dissipate quickly when exposed to high heat. To best preserve their fragrance, dry tender leaves and blossoms soon after picking at a very low temperature. Seeds take longer to dry than the more fragile parts of the plant, so it is best to process them separately.

When herb plants mature and start to flower or seed, they are usually discarded. At this stage they are still useful, and often more flavorful than when young and tender. Drying flowers and seeds captures their aromas, making it possible to utilize their individual characteristics in teas, sodas, pastries, and spice mixes. Lavender, yarrow, citrus blossoms, elderflower, coriander, calendula, geranium, and rose are some of our favorites. Try making your own herbal tea mixes; there are many possible combinations. Seeds are easy to dry for your spice shelf, to salt like capers → 115, or to use fresh in recipes such as tomato jam → 126.

Dried herbs can act as a substitute for fresh in many recipes. Use one-third the amount of dried herbs when substituting for fresh.

Air-Drying Herbs, Flowers, and Seeds

Tie the plants in a bunch; hang in a well-ventilated, dry location free of direct sunlight. Herbs and flowers should dry quickly, within 24 hours. Seeds may take another 8 to 12 hours. After the leaves, flowers, or seeds are dry, shake or pick them from the stem and store in a sealed container. Plants dried in this manner will keep for up to 6 months.

DILL FLOWERS

CORIANDER
SEEDS

CILANTRO
POWDER

CILANTRO
FLOWERS

Drying Herbs, Flowers, and Seeds with a Dehydrator

For fresh, stemmed leafy herbs such as **basil, celery leaf, chervil, cilantro, dill, lemon balm, marjoram, oregano, mint, parsley,** and **tarragon:** Dehydrate at 95°F/35°C until brittle to the touch but still brightly colored, 6 to 8 hours.

For heartier herbs such as **fir tips, lemon verbena, rosemary, bay leaf, sage, eucalyptus,** and **thyme:** Dehydrate at 95°F/35°C until brittle to the touch but still brightly colored, 8 to 12 hours.

For flowers such as **fennel, cilantro (coriander), elder-flower, chamomile, calendula, lavender,** and **hops:** Pluck the flower heads, discarding the stems or putting them to another use. Dehydrate at 95°F/35°C until brittle to the touch but still brightly colored, 2 to 6 hours.

To dry seeds such as **celery, coriander (cilantro), dill, fenugreek,** and **fennel:** Remove the seeds from the flower stems. Dehydrate at 120°F/48°C for 12 to 24 hours, until dry all the way through. Check by cracking a couple of them open.

Chamomile

This mild but distinct flower grows on a large bush and blooms in midsummer. It is easiest to harvest all at once when most of the buds are open, so we often have a few days a year of constant chamomile processing. It is great

for adding aroma to kefir and vinegar, or as an herbal tea, cordial, or tisane. We use it to flavor the custard in rhubarb soup → 330.

Cilantro

These flowers are reminiscent of citrus and pine. We like to use them fresh but since they are so fragile we dry them so we can have them around a bit longer. You can use them whole or crumble them into spice mixes.

ELDERFLOWERS

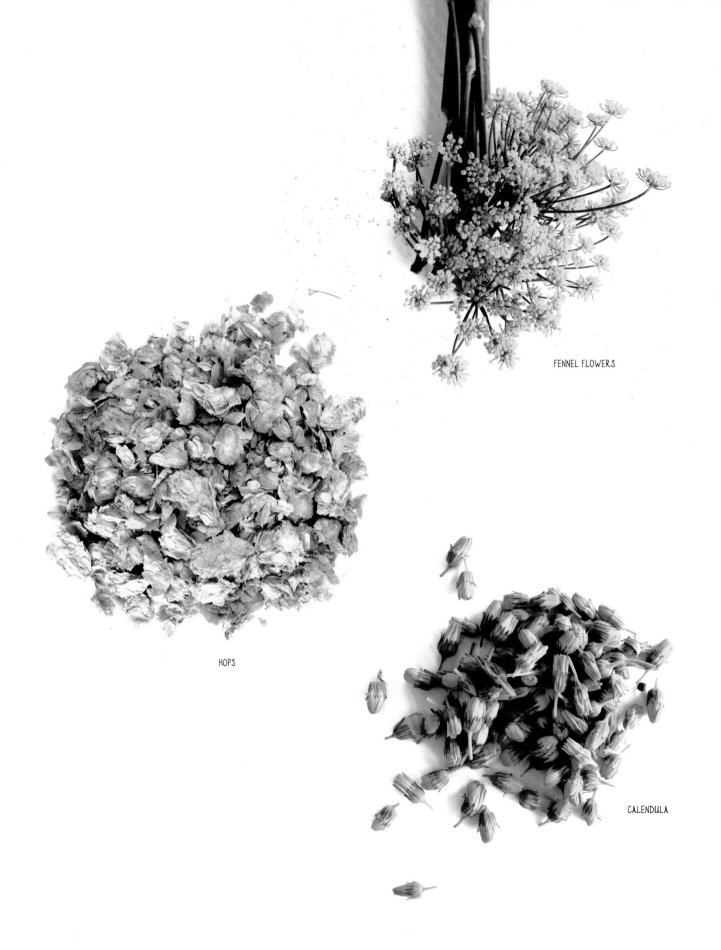

FENNEL FLOWERS

HOPS

CALENDULA

CHAMOMILE

DILL SEEDS

Elderflowers

We make cordials, vinegars, and tisanes with fresh elderflowers, and we also dry them to use in teas, sodas, jams, and pastries. The stems are mildly toxic, so either pick the flowers prior to drying or shake them free of the stems after drying.

Hops

The bitter, mastic aroma of hops demands that they be used sparingly. We like to add them to our shichimi togarashi → 53 in place of the hemp seeds that are often found in traditional Japanese versions.

Fennel Flowers

With its licorice-like flavor, fennel blurs the line between savory and sweet. Crumble dried fennel flower heads into a bowl, turning them into a powder. Including a bit of stem is okay, but using as little as possible is ideal, as dried stems have less flavor. Sift through a fine-mesh sieve to remove any stems. The powder adds a bright anisette aroma to Grilled Tripe with Paprika and Fennel → 290 and Chilled Apricot Soup → 152.

PINK PEPPERCORNS

ALLIUMS

Adding dried alliums to food is a simple way to layer in flavor. Dried onions and garlic can transform sour cream into a delicious dip; raw alliums could never have the same effect. We use lots of dried alliums in dressings, spreads, sauces, and soups.

Sweet White Onion Powder

We use onions labeled as "sweet" for this, as they are less pungent than most onion varieties. Sweet onion powder is particularly good in Liptauer Paprika Cheese Dip → 222, pickled mushrooms → 103, or buttermilk dressing → 186.

Peel the onion, cut in half lengthwise, remove the butt end and core, and thinly slice. Dehydrate at 125°F/52°C until brittle, about 18 hours. Grind the large dried pieces in a food processor to coarse flakes to expose more surface area and return the flakes to the dehydrator. Continue drying them at 125°F/52°C for 8 to 12 hours longer, until all of the moisture is removed and the flakes powder without clumping together when processed in a spice grinder. Pass the powder through a fine-mesh sieve. Store in an airtight container in a cool, dark spot.

Smoked Onion Powder

This powder makes it possible to add a gentle wood smoke flavor to food without having to fire up the smoker every time you need it. It can be added to dressings and dips, such as the English Pea and Goat Cheese Dip → 220.

Peel the onion, leave whole, remove the butt end and core, and cut into ¼ in/6 mm rounds. Soak a handful or two of hardwood chips in water to cover for at least 1 hour.

IF USING A SMOKER: Following the manufacturer's instructions, smoke the onion rings at 160°F/70°C until dark brown, 2 to 4 hours depending on the strength of your smoker.

IF USING A GAS GRILL: Light one burner to medium. Put a smoker box over the lit burner, add some of the soaked wood chips to the box, and close the grill. Adjust the heat as needed to keep the temperature between 160°F and 180°F/71°C and 82°C. The wood chips should begin to smolder and release a steady stream of smoke. Put the onion rings on the grate opposite the lit burner. Cover the grill and smoke, adjusting the heat as needed to maintain the temperature. Check every 45 minutes or so and add more soaked chips as necessary to keep the smoke level constant. Rotate the onions, flipping as needed if one side is coloring faster than the other, until darkened and smoky tasting, about 3 hours.

IF USING A CHARCOAL GRILL: Fill a chimney starter with charcoal. Light it and let burn until the coals are covered with a thin layer of ash. Pour the hot coals on one side of the grill. Put some of the soaked wood chips next to the hot coals, and put the grate on the grill. Put the onion rings on the grate opposite the fire. Cover the grill, positioning the vent on the lid on the side opposite the fire. Stick a thermometer through the vent and heat the grill to between 160°F and 180°F/71°C and 82°C. Smoke the onions, adjusting the fire as needed to maintain the temperature. Check every 45 minutes or so and add more soaked chips as necessary to keep the smoke level constant. Rotate the onions, flipping as needed if one side is coloring faster than the other, until darkened and smoky tasting, about 3 hours.

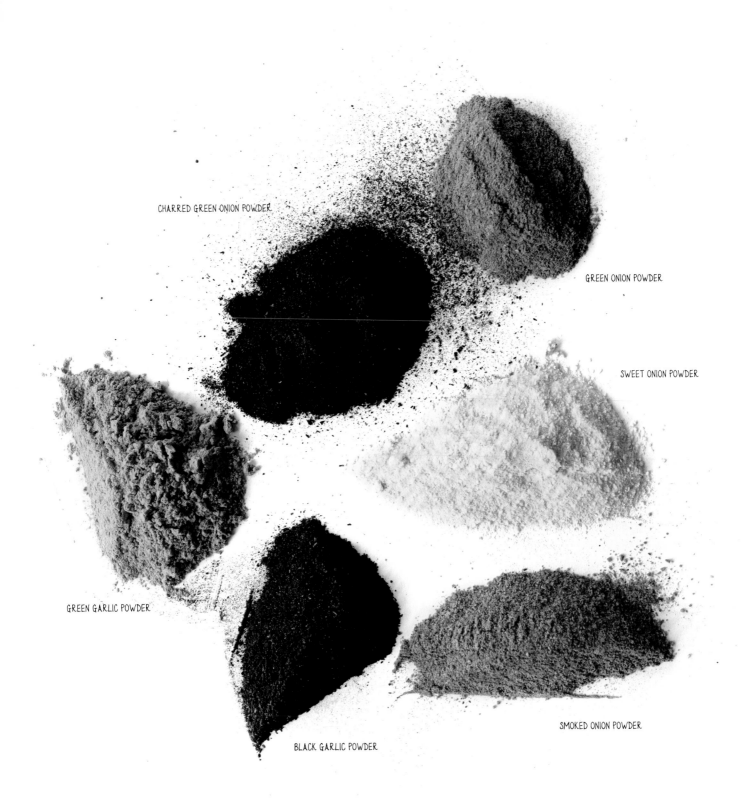

CHARRED GREEN ONION POWDER

GREEN ONION POWDER

SWEET ONION POWDER

GREEN GARLIC POWDER

BLACK GARLIC POWDER

SMOKED ONION POWDER

DRIED AND
SMOKED ONIONS

DRIED ONIONS

To process smoked onion powder, dehydrate at 125°F/52°C until brittle, about 18 hours. Grind the large dried pieces in a food processor to coarse flakes to expose more surface area and return the flakes to the dehydrator. Continue drying them at 125°F/52°C for 8 to 12 hours longer, until all of the moisture is removed and the flakes powder without clumping together when processed in a spice grinder. Pass the powder through a fine-mesh sieve. Store in an airtight container in a cool, dark spot.

Green Onion Powder

This is a great way to use the tops from green onions and leeks. It can also be made with the whole green onions, including the roots, or with just the tops. This bright green powder may be used much like sweet onion powder. Mix it into compound butters and yogurt sauces, and use to season the lentil croquettes **→ 240**.

Trim the roots from whole green onions and wipe with a towel to remove any dirt. Halve the green onions lengthwise from the white bottom all the way to the green top and cut crosswise into 1-in/2.5-cm pieces. Dehydrate at 125°F/52°C until brittle, about 12 hours. Grind the large dried pieces in a food processor to coarse flakes to expose more surface area and return the flakes to the dehydrator. Continue drying them at 125°F/52°C for 8 to 12 hours longer, until all of the moisture is removed and the flakes powder without clumping together when processed in a spice grinder. Pass the powder through a fine-mesh sieve. Store in an airtight container in a cool, dark spot.

Charred Green Onion Powder

This potent black powder is a great way to add a charred flavor to food. It is different than the aroma of wood smoke—here the sugars in the onions themselves are browning, adding a depth of flavor reminiscent of campfire cooking. Use in the pistachio dip **→ 216**.

Trim the roots from whole green onions and wipe with a towel to remove any dirt. Heat a cast-iron skillet over high heat. Add the green onions and cook until charred and blackened, but still moist inside, about 10 minutes. (Alternatively, grill on a charcoal or gas grill.) Coarsely chop the charred onions. Dehydrate at 125°F/52°C until brittle, about 12 hours. Grind the large dried pieces in a food processor to coarse flakes to expose more surface area and return the flakes to the dehydrator. Continue drying them at 125°F/52°C for 8 to 12 hours longer, until all of the moisture is removed and the flakes powder without clumping together when processed in a spice grinder. Pass the powder through a fine-mesh sieve. Store in an airtight container in a cool, dark spot.

Garlic Powder

Garlic, like onions, tastes sweeter when dried. It loses its sharp bite but keeps its characteristic flavor. We rely on this mellow powder to layer garlic flavor into Liptauer Paprika Cheese Dip → 222, pickled mushrooms → 103, and buttermilk dressing → 186. When garlic is dried, it can become quite hard, so use caution when grinding.

Peel the cloves, remove the hard stem end, and cut into very thin slices. Dehydrate at 125°F/52°C until brittle, about 12 hours. Grind the large dried pieces in a food processor to coarse flakes to expose more surface area and return the flakes to the dehydrator. Continue drying them at 125°F/52°C for 8 to 12 hours longer, until all of the moisture is removed and the flakes powder without clumping together when processed in a spice grinder. Pass the powder through a fine-mesh sieve. Store in an airtight container in a cool, dark spot.

Green Garlic Powder

Green, young garlic begins to appear in the early spring, and the entire plant can be used. These tender shoots are somewhat milder

CHARRED GREEN GARLIC

BAR TARTINE

than the bulbs and are slightly herbaceous while still retaining a potent garlic aroma. They can be used in most recipes that call for mature garlic.

Trim the roots from the green garlic and wipe with a towel to remove any dirt. Halve the garlic lengthwise and cut crosswise into 1-in/2.5-cm pieces. Dehydrate at 125°F/52°C until brittle, about 12 hours. Grind the large dried pieces in a food processor to coarse flakes to expose more surface area and return the flakes to the dehydrator. Continue drying them at 125°F/52°C for 8 to 12 hours longer, until all of the moisture is removed and the flakes powder without clumping together when processed in a spice grinder. Pass the powder through a fine-mesh sieve. Store in an airtight container in a cool, dark spot.

Black Garlic

Holding garlic at a constant temperature of 130°F/55°C for 2 to 3 weeks renders the cloves as black as tar. All of the characteristic sharpness disappears and is replaced with a molasses-like sweetness and an aroma reminiscent of licorice. As the garlic is blackening it can be somewhat fragrant. This is one of many

BLACK GARLIC CLOVES

projects that have yielded a visit from a manager at the restaurant next to ours to ask, "What is the smell wafting through the walls?" We use these blackened cloves in our Black Garlic and Lentil Soup → 168, in smoked potatoes → 226, and in chile pastes.

You can use a dehydrator, rice warmer, or slow cooker to make black garlic. Use whole unpeeled garlic heads.

If using a dehydrator, wrap the garlic heads in plastic wrap. This traps humidity and prevents the garlic from drying out. Then wrap the heads in several layers of aluminum foil. Hold at 130°F/55°C until the heads are soft and black, about 3 weeks.

If using a rice warmer or slow cooker, set it to the warm setting (not the cook setting), place the whole garlic heads in the unit,

and leave on until the cloves are soft and black, about 2 weeks.

Store in an airtight container in the refrigerator for up to 6 months. Peel the cloves before using.

Black Garlic Powder

Peel blackened garlic cloves and cut into thin slices. Dehydrate at 125°F/52°C until brittle, about 12 hours. Grind the large dried pieces in a food processor to coarse flakes to expose more surface area and return the flakes to the dehydrator. Continue drying them at 125°F/52°C for 8 to 12 hours longer, until all of the moisture is removed and the flakes powder without clumping together when processed in a spice grinder. Pass the powder through a fine-mesh sieve. Store in an airtight container in a cool, dark spot.

MISCELLANEOUS VEGETABLES

Just about any vegetable can be dried, but each requires a different technique depending on moisture content, density, and how it will be used.

Dried Mushrooms

Mushrooms, like most vegetables, don't have to be beautiful to be flavorful. Ugly mushrooms are perfect for drying and adding to salads, stocks, sauces, vinegars, and infused oils.

Wipe the mushrooms with a damp cloth until clean. Cut the mushrooms in half lengthwise if they are large and remove tough stems, as they usually have less flavor than the flesh. Dehydrate at 120°F/48°C until the mushrooms are completely dry and not at all pliable, 18 to 24 hours. Mushrooms are porous and dry easily, but moisture content, variety, and size can affect the length of time it will take to process them. Store in an airtight container at room temperature for up to 6 months.

Dried Tomatoes

Dried tomatoes have a lot of flavor, acidity, and sweetness and, like

DRIED BUTTONS

DRIED PORCINI

SHIITAKE

DRIED CANDY CAP

DRIED BLACK TRUMPET

onion powder, are an easy way to make a bland broth or sauce taste delicious. We dry them to preserve and concentrate their flavor.

Bring a large pot of water to a boil. Prepare an ice bath. Using a paring knife, core the tomatoes, then score an X in the skin on the blossom end. Boil a few at a time, just until the skins begin to loosen, 10 to 15 seconds. Using a slotted spoon, transfer the tomatoes immediately to

the ice bath and repeat with any remaining tomatoes. Remove from the ice bath and peel away the skins.

Dehydrate the peeled tomatoes, stem-side down, at 130°F/55°C for the desired time. Timing will vary depending on the size and variety of the tomatoes. For 4 to 8 oz/ 115 to 225 g tomatoes, dehydrate for 8 to 10 hours for a jammy and moist consistency (thin skin and soft interior), or for about

DRIED TOMATOES

dried zucchini, a classic ingredient in Oaxacan stews. We started experimenting with it immediately. Drying zucchini makes it sweeter, almost tropical in flavor. Zucchini are a dime a dozen in the summer, cheap and abundant. A jar of preserved zucchini in the winter, however, is a delicacy. Try them in the Rooster Boil → 302. We use it sliced thin in winter salads or as an addition to broth dishes, where it rehydrates and becomes tender.

Cut the zucchini in half lengthwise and lightly salt the cut side. Dehydrate at 120°F/48°C until completely dry, about 24 hours. Store in an airtight container at room temperature for up to 6 months.

18 hours for a partially dry texture (thicker skin and a taffy-like consistency). For a classic sundried tomato texture, dehydrate for 36 to 48 hours, until fully dry and shelf stable. Store the jammy tomatoes for up to 1 week in the refrigerator; for the partially dried tomatoes, refrigerate for up to 4 weeks. Store the fully dry tomatoes in an airtight container in a cool, dry place for up to 6 months.

Dried Zucchini

A friend and visiting Mexican chef saw our shelves of dried vegetables and asked why we didn't have

DRIED ZUCCHINI

PEPPERS

We have spent many hours and weeks and used many thousands of pounds of peppers trying to re-create a paprika powder that is similar to those from Hungary. There is so much essential oil in good paprika that it can permanently stain the bag or jar it is stored in with its fluorescent red color. Peppers need long, hot summer days to sweeten their flesh and cool nights to produce the flavors that match the rich, oily peppers found in Hungary. Juston and Mindy Enos of Full Table Farm now grow peppers in quantity for us from seeds that we sourced from a prized Hungarian paprika variety. After picking, they hang them to dry at their property in Yountville, California. It has yielded the closest thing we can find to the true staple Hungarian spice.

Sweet and Hot Paprika

Many types of peppers can be smoked, dried, flaked, and ground into powder. The best for making red paprika powders have thin to medium thick flesh and are dark red, sweet, and very aromatic. Taste the peppers for spice before choosing which ones to dry or smoke. Note that spiciness increases with moisture loss. Always start with flavorful peppers, as bland fruit will never yield a delicious powder. Red paprika is featured in a number of recipes in this book, including the Rooster Boil → 302, Fisherman's Stew with Paprika and Egg Noodles → 178, and Beef Gulyas with Marrow Toast → 172.

Besides red paprika peppers there are a number of others that we dry every year in the late summer and early fall. Red jalapeños are used to make chipotles, and green Hatch and padrón peppers are dried for a spicy green chile powder. Hatch chiles, named for the valley in New Mexico where they are grown, are certainly one of our favorites. In the summer, large, fire-fueled drum roasters are set up in parking lots across New Mexico, and the air across the state is thick with the smell of roasting peppers. During the short season, the prep room at Bar Tartine smells a lot like those parking lots. The kitchen will be piled high with burlap sacks full of these fragrant chiles as we rush to dry, ferment, and roast them for dips and stews. Because we preserve so many, we enjoy their flavor nearly year-round in dishes such as pistachio dip → 216 or Fisherman's Stew with Green Chile and Collards → 176. There are an overwhelming number of pepper varieties and possible ways to preserve them. Most years we have 20 or 30 varieties of dried and otherwise preserved peppers in our pantry. There are good uses for all of them.

Drying Peppers with a Dehydrator

Do not attempt to dry red paprika peppers in a dehydrator that can't be set below 95°F/35°C. Temperatures above this will cause the peppers to cook from the inside. Before drying, poke a few holes in the flesh where the stem meets the top of the pepper. Dry for 48 to 72 hours on dehydrator racks with enough space that air can flow between the peppers. They are done when they can be crumbled with your hands but are still slightly pliable. Be careful not to leave the peppers in the dehydrator for too long. Overdrying removes essential oils that contain flavor and color.

Drying Peppers without a Dehydrator

The best way to process peppers is by hanging them to air-dry. In Hungary, the sight of drying peppers is iconic. The breeze that blows off of the Danube is said to be perfect for retaining the oils and flavors in the fruit, making

Hungarian paprika among the best in the world.

To hang them, keep the stems intact. Using a long sewing needle, poke through the stem near the top of the pepper. Sew one pepper after another, tying a knot after each and leaving at least ½ in/12 mm of space between them. Hang in a well-ventilated area away from direct sunlight, which can destroy the pigment of the peppers. Be careful of temperatures above 95°F/35°C as the peppers can begin to cook. They are done drying when they can be crumbled with your hands but are still slightly pliable.

Grinding and Storing Dried Peppers

Paprika powder is freshest when ground from whole dried peppers or from flakes. Powders lose aroma, color, and flavor more quickly because they have more surface area exposed to the light and the air. Use a food processor to turn the whole peppers into flakes, removing the seeds beforehand. Use a spice grinder to grind the flakes into powder as needed. Heat affects the quality of the paprika powder, so don't let the grinder overheat while processing. We usually freeze our grinder bowl before powdering. Store the dried

CHIPOTLES

peppers in an airtight container in a dry, cool place. Dried peppers will keep for up to 1 year.

Smoked Peppers

In mid-fall, when our farmers have their last pepper harvest before plowing the plants under for the winter, we process large quantities of smoked peppers for the year. They bring us all of the soft, red, ripe fruit that missed previous harvests and we dry the jalapeños

for chipotles (smoke-dried jalapeños). We use chipotles in our Black Garlic and Lentil Soup → **168**, and Sauerkraut Soup → **170**.

Cut the peppers in half lengthwise. Keep the seeds and ribs intact if you don't mind the spice. We usually remove them from sweet peppers before smoking but leave them in jalapeños. Soak a large handful or two of hardwood chips in water to cover for at least 1 hour or up to overnight.

DRIED
PADRÓN PEPPERS

IF USING A SMOKER: Following the manufacturer's instructions, set up and smoke the peppers at 160°F/70°C until dark and smoky tasting, 2 to 4 hours.

IF USING A GAS GRILL: Light one burner to medium. Put a smoker box over the lit burner, add some of the soaked wood chips to the box, and close the grill. Adjust the heat as needed to keep the temperature between 160°F and 180°F/71°C and 82°C. The wood chips should begin to smolder and release a steady stream of smoke. Put the peppers on the grate opposite the lit burner. Cover the grill and smoke, adjusting the heat as needed to maintain the temperature. Check every 45 minutes or so and add more soaked chips as necessary to keep the smoke level constant. Rotate the peppers, flipping as needed if one side is coloring faster than the other, until darkened and smoky tasting, about 3 hours.

IF USING A CHARCOAL GRILL: Fill a chimney starter with charcoal. Light it and let burn until the coals are covered with a thin layer of ash. Pour the hot coals on one side of the grill. Put some of the soaked wood chips next to the hot coals, and put the grate on the grill. Put the peppers on the grate opposite the fire. Cover the grill, positioning the vent on the lid on the side opposite the fire. Stick a thermometer through the vent and heat the grill to between 160°F and 180°F/71°C and 82°C. Smoke the peppers, adjusting the fire as needed to maintain the temperature. Check every 45 minutes or so and add more soaked chips as necessary to keep the smoke level constant. Rotate the peppers, flipping as needed if one side is coloring faster than the other, until darkened and smoky tasting, about 3 hours.

Dehydrate at 125°F/52°C until brittle, about 12 hours. At this point the peppers can be removed and stored whole or in flakes.

Charred Chiles

Although these chiles have a subtle aroma of smoke, the flavor is very different from wood-smoked peppers. These are cooked at a higher temperature for a shorter amount of time, scorching the outside, browning the natural sugars, and leaving the inside sweet. We use them in the Pistachio Dip → 216.

Prepare a medium fire for direct-heat cooking in a charcoal or gas grill. Set the chiles on the grate directly over the fire and cook, turning occasionally, until well charred on all sides, about 15 minutes.

Dehydrate at 125°F/52°C until brittle, about 12 hours. At this point the chiles can be removed and stored whole or in flakes.

ASSORTED POWDERS

Just about any ingredient can be transformed into a powder. The trick is figuring out how to best process it. The density, water content, sugar content, and texture of a food can greatly affect how it will dry. We are constantly experimenting to find new powders, and the results often inspire new dishes.

Huitlacoche Powder

A delicacy in Mexico, huitlacoche is a fungus that attacks corn kernels, leaving a black "corn mushroom" in its place. It has a sweet, earthy flavor, deep, inky color and loamy aroma. Use it in the charred eggplant spice mix → 51.

Remove the huitlacoche from ears of corn. Dehydrate at 95°F/35°C until it crumbles when rubbed between your fingers, 12 to 24 hours depending on how moist it was to start and the size of the kernels. Just before using, process to a fine powder in a spice grinder. Pass through a fine-mesh sieve if needed. Store in an airtight container in a cool, dry place for up to 6 months.

DRIED HUITLACOCHE

CHARRED CHILES

HUITLACOCHE POWDER

Yogurt Powder

We make this powder with our house-made, whole-milk yogurt, but low-fat or nonfat works as well. Use this powder when you want to boost the acidity and flavor of yogurt in a dish. We like it as a garnish for Kale Salad with Rye Bread, Seeds, and Yogurt → 188, and we add it to the batter for Crepe Cake with Apple Butter, Farmer's Cheese, and Pecans → 342.

Spread undrained plain yogurt → 74 in a shallow heatproof tray in a layer no more than 1 in/2.5 cm thick. Dehydrate at 125°F/52°C, stirring every 12 hours, until the yogurt feels dry to the touch, 24 to 36 hours. Transfer to a food processor and pulse to process it into small pieces. Return the pieces to the dehydrator until completely dry throughout, about 12 hours longer. Store in an airtight container in a cool, dry place for up to 4 months.

Just before using, process to a fine powder in a spice grinder. Pass through a fine- mesh sieve if needed.

Rice Powder

We typically use California-grown short-grain white rice for making this powder, which we use in place of white rice flour. Toasting the rice adds a subtle nutty aroma that we like better than that of plain rice flour in many recipes. We use this powder to set the Steamed Celery Root Cake → 244 and the Farmer's Cheese Dumplings → 234.

Preheat the oven to 350°F/180°C. Spread the rice in a shallow, even layer on a sheet pan and toast, stirring every 5 minutes, until very lightly browned, about 20 minutes. Let cool completely, then store in an airtight container at room temperature for up to 3 months. Just before using, process to a fine powder using a spice grinder. Pass through a fine-mesh sieve if needed.

Rice Koji Powder

The level of natural sugars that develop in rice koji allows us to eliminate additional sweeteners from desserts, such as the steamed parsnip cake → 346. You will need to make the rice koji first → 123, which takes about 5 days. Or, you can purchase it from many Asian markets.

Dehydrate rice koji → 123 at 100°F/38°C, stirring every 6 hours to ensure even drying, until you can crack the grains in half between your fingers, 12 to 24 hours. Store in an airtight container in a dry, cool place for up to 3 months.

Just before using, process to a fine powder using a spice grinder. Pass through a fine-mesh sieve if needed.

Burnt Bread Powder

We use lots of bread at Bar Tartine and therefore sometimes end up with leftovers. One of our favorite uses is this powder. We grill the bread, burning it black to give it the primal, earthy aroma of char and smoke, then we dehydrate and powder it. We add it to spice mixes and burnt bread sauce → 224. Use

YOGURT
POWDER

BURNT BREAD

BURNT BREAD POWDER

it in any dish you think might taste better with a little bit of smoke and char.

Makes 1 pt/345 g

1 lb/455 g crusty, plain country-style bread, cut into slices ½ in/12 mm thick

Toast the bread over an open flame, on a grill, in a toaster, or in a conventional oven until it is burnt and blackened.

Dehydrate the bread at 110°F/43°C until dried all the way through, about 8 hours. Let cool. Crumble into large pieces and transfer to an airtight container. Store in a dry, cool place for up to 1 month. Just before using, process to a fine powder using a spice grinder.

PARSNIP POWDER

DRIED PARSNIPS

Kale Powder

We use kale powder much like we would powdered nori seaweed. Its grassy aroma and bright green hue make it a good addition to spice mixes. In Japan, powdered nori is used in spice mixes, and over rice, sushi, noodles, and omelettes, among other things. We use kale powder in our shichimi togarashi → 53 and furikake → 54.

Remove the kale stems and discard. Tear the leaves into large pieces and dehydrate at 115°F/45°C until completely brittle, 8 to 10 hours. Store in an airtight container in a cool, dark spot for up to 6 months. Just before using, process to a fine powder using a spice grinder. Pass through a fine-mesh sieve if needed.

Parsnip Powder

Fresh parsnips are very sweet, and when dried they are almost like sugar. We use parsnip powder on desserts in place of the more classic garnish of confectioners' sugar. Try it on the steamed parsnip cake → 346 and on the carob semifreddo → 324.

Peel the parsnips, cut in half lengthwise, and cut crosswise into half-moons ¼ in/6 mm thick. Dehydrate at 125°F/52°C until completely dry, about 24 hours. Store in an airtight container in a cool, dark spot for up to 3 months. Just before using, process to a fine powder using a spice grinder. Pass through a fine-mesh sieve if needed.

Sauerkraut Powder

Sauerkraut powder can act as a substitute for salt when seasoning dishes, also adding a layer of acidity. Use it to garnish just about anything; it can go on the smoked potatoes → 226 instead of the black garlic vinaigrette, or on fresh tomatoes, onions, or grilled fish. Three cups/550 g drained packed sauerkraut yields about ½ cup/65 g sauerkraut powder.

Dehydrate sauerkraut at 120°F/48°C, stirring every 12 hours, until evenly dry, 36 to 48 hours. Store in an airtight container in a dry, cool place for up to 6 months. Just before using, process to a fine powder using a spice grinder.

CHARRED EGGPLANTS

SPICE MIXES

Our spice shelf began with onion and pepper powders and over time has grown to include lots of dried oddities. Any ingredient that is flavorful and can be powdered may find a home in our larder. Kale, burnt bread, and flaxseeds work well in spice mixes, often ending up blended with chiles, dried citrus, mushrooms, and seaweed. We are inspired by mixes from around the world, recreating them using our local ingredients.

Charred Eggplant Spice

Eggplant has a subtle flavor and absorbent texture that soaks up the aroma of fire like a sponge. Here we combine charred eggplant with chiles, huitlacoche, and green onion to make a seasoning mix that tastes like the pure flavor of earth and smoke.

Makes ½ pt/115 g

8 fresh árbol chiles, stemmed
6 Japanese eggplants or 2 large globe eggplants
2 tbsp charred green onion powder → 36
2 tbsp huitlacoche powder → 47
2 tsp kosher salt

In a cast-iron skillet over medium-high heat or on a grill over a medium-hot fire, char the chiles on all sides until evenly blackened, about 3 minutes. Burn the eggplants on all sides over a very hot flame on a grill or on a roasting rack set over a gas flame until the skin is completely blackened and a white-grey ash begins to form, 10 to 12 minutes. At this point, the eggplants will be soft in the middle with a layer of burnt skin and flesh on the outside. Remove from the grill carefully; they may break and will be very hot. Let cool to room temperature.

Chop the charred chiles and eggplants into large pieces, place in a shallow pan, and dehydrate at 120°F/48°C until they crumble easily, 12 to 24 hours. Let cool

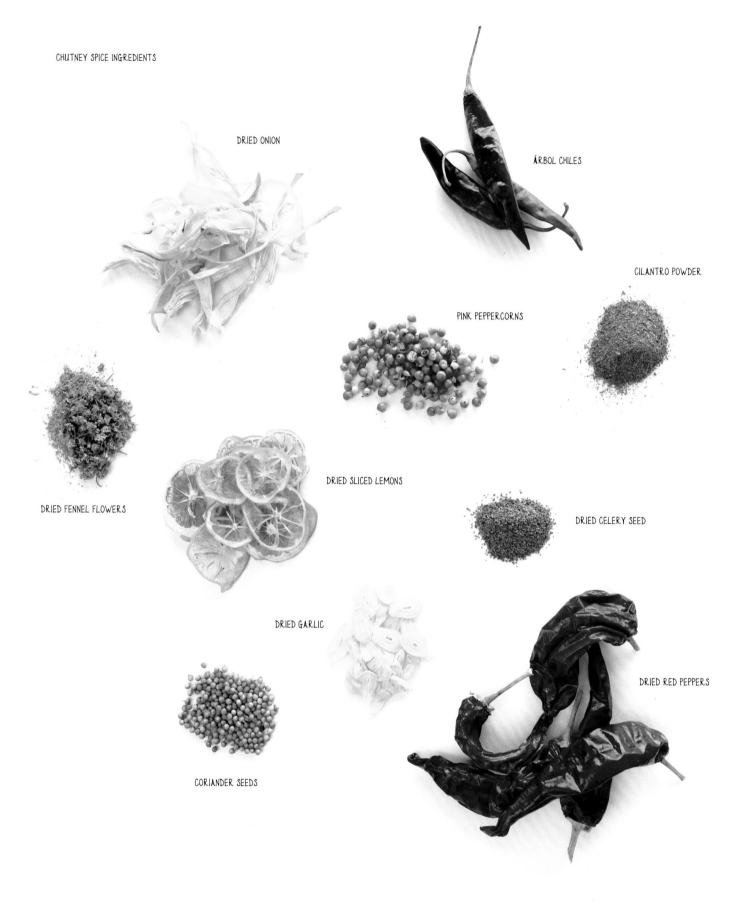

CHUTNEY SPICE INGREDIENTS

DRIED ONION

ÁRBOL CHILES

CILANTRO POWDER

PINK PEPPERCORNS

DRIED SLICED LEMONS

DRIED CELERY SEED

DRIED FENNEL FLOWERS

DRIED GARLIC

DRIED RED PEPPERS

CORIANDER SEEDS

BAR TARTINE

completely. In a spice grinder, process the chiles and eggplants to a fine powder and transfer to a medium bowl. Add the green onion powder, huitlacoche powder, and salt and stir to combine. Store in an airtight container in a cool, dry place for up to 2 months.

Chutney Spice

This ode to Middle Eastern chutney spice makes an excellent seasoning for grilled meats and vegetables. We make it using only ingredients we process in house. Add this mix to the sunflower tahini → 188 or to season roasting carrots → 224.

Makes ½ cup/65 g

2 tbsp garlic powder → 37

3 tbsp sweet onion powder → 34

6 slices dried citrus, ground → 57

1 tbsp coriander seeds, toasted and ground → 31

1 tbsp dried cilantro, powdered → 31

½ tsp dried celery seeds → 31, ground

1 tbsp fennel flowers, powdered → 33

1 tsp árbol chile powder → 42

2 tsp ground pink peppercorns → 30 or black peppercorns

1 tbsp sweet paprika → 42

2 tsp kosher salt

Combine all of the ingredients in a small bowl and mix well. Store

CHUTNEY SPICE

in an airtight container at room temperature for up to 2 months.

Shichimi Togarashi

A popular condiment in Japan, shichimi togarashi is traditionally a combination of seven ingredients, usually hemp seeds, citrus peel, togarashi pepper (a Japanese hot red pepper), seaweed, sesame seeds, sansho (a Japanese herb), and ginger or shiso. Our riff on the traditional blend calls for ingredients grown in Northern California. We use citrus peel, sometimes yuzu, sometimes lemon or bergamot. Instead of hemp seeds, we use beer hops. We add wild nori seaweed from Mendocino and toasted sushi nori. Sunflower seeds, kale, green onions, and red peppers—all

from local farms—give the mix a unique flavor.

This spice mix is the perfect condiment. Keep it on your dining table next to the salt and pepper and use it freely to season grilled meats, vegetables, noodles, and rice dishes.

Makes 1½ cups/115 g

½ cup/20 g wild nori

8 sheets sushi nori

2 tsp dried hops → 31

3 tbsp sunflower seeds

¼ cup/20 g sweet paprika flakes → 42

2 tbsp hot paprika flakes → 42

3 tbsp green onion powder → 36

3 tbsp kale powder → 50

1 tbsp lemon peel powder → 57

1 tsp kosher salt

Preheat the oven to 300°F/150°C. Spread the wild and sheet nori (even if the package says "toasted" it will need to be toasted again in this recipe), and hops in a single layer on a sheet pan. On a separate pan, spread out the sunflower seeds. Warm both pans in the oven until fragrant, about 5 minutes. Let cool to room temperature.

Process the wild and sheet nori, hops, and sweet and hot chile flakes in a spice grinder or coffee grinder to a coarse powder. Transfer to a small bowl; add the green onion powder, kale powder, lemon powder, and salt; and stir to combine. Pulse the sunflower seeds in the grinder just until broken into coarse pieces. Add to the bowl and stir to mix. Transfer to an airtight container and store at room temperature for up to 1 month.

Furikake

Furikake, a rice seasoning, usually contains seaweed, sesame seeds, and often dried fish. It can be used dry or mixed with soy sauce and sweetened sake or mirin wine. The moistened version is often stuffed into the rice-ball snack called onigiri, the most popular snack in all of Japan. We like it on vegetable dishes, over grilled or steamed fish, and for a garnish on salads or snacks (see English Pea and Goat Cheese Dip → 220).

SHICHIMI TOGARASHI

Makes 1¼ cups/120 g

½ cup/20 g wild nori and/or
   dulse seaweed
8 sheets sushi nori
3 tbsp sunflower seeds
2 tbsp black sesame seeds
2 tbsp white sesame seeds
10 small dried anchovies
   (optional)
3 tbsp kale powder → 50
1 tsp kosher salt

Preheat the oven to 300°F/
150°C. Spread the wild and
sheet nori (even if the package
says "toasted" it will need to
be toasted again in this recipe)
in a single layer on a sheet pan.
On a separate pan, spread out
the sunflower seeds and black

and white sesame seeds. Warm
both pans in the oven until fragrant, about 5 minutes. Let cool
to room temperature.

Process the dried anchovies (if
using) and wild and sheet nori in
a spice grinder to a coarse powder. Transfer to a small bowl, add

the kale powder and salt, and stir
to combine. Pulse the sunflower
seeds and sesame seeds in the
grinder just until broken into
coarse pieces. Add to the bowl
and stir to mix. Transfer to an airtight container and store at room
temperature for up to 1 month.

FURIKAKE

FRUITS

Dried fruit takes the place of sugar in much of our cooking. Whenever possible we try to sweeten with ingredients such as dried fruits that have inherent aroma, instead of with refined ingredients such as white sugar, which have no flavor.

Dried Apricots

Fresh apricots, already wildly sweet, become more concentrated when dried. We take advantage of that concentration by using them when making the rye porridge → **334** and sauerkraut soup → **170**.

Using your hands or a knife, split the apricots in half and remove the pits, reserving them for noyaux → **84**. Dehydrate the fruits at 120°F/48°C until dense and chewy, 24 to 32 hours.

Let cool completely. Store in an airtight container in a cool, dry place for up to 1 month.

Citrus

During the height of citrus season, in December and January, we process citrus for the entire year. We make jams and syrups, but the dried fruit is the most important for us. Combine dried citrus → **57** with dried flowers → **31** and/or herbs → **31** to make your own tea blends. Our favorite use for smoked blood orange peels is to steep them with pu-erh tea to create a beverage reminiscent in aroma of Lapsang souchong.

Lemon rounds pair well with lemon balm or verbena; the bergamot with grated ginger. Kaffir lime is great for spicy soups, and citron infuses alcohol with a strong aroma. We use the citrus peel powders in spice mixes and in desserts. It is useful for adding concentrated citrus aroma without any liquid.

APRICOTS PREPPED FOR DRYING

Sliced and Dried Citrus

Using a sharp mandoline slicer or a knife and extreme caution, slice lemons, limes, oranges, yuzu, or bergamot into rounds about ⅛ in/3 mm thick and remove the seeds. Dehydrate at 115°F/46°C until completely dry, 18 to 24 hours. Store in an airtight container in a dry, cool place for up to 9 months.

Citrus Peel Powder

Peel any citrus and reserve the flesh for another use. Bring a large saucepan filled with water to a boil, add the peel, and boil for 1 minute. Drain and rinse under cold running water. Repeat this step twice more, using fresh water each time.

Dehydrate the citrus peels at 125°F/52°C until completely dry, 18 to 24 hours. Store in an airtight container in a dry, cool place for up to 9 months. Just before using, process to a fine powder using a spice grinder. Pass through a fine-mesh sieve if needed.

Smoked Blood Orange Peels

Peel blood oranges and reserve the flesh for another use. Bring a large saucepan filled with water to a boil, add the peel, and boil for 1 minute. Drain and rinse

under cold running water. Repeat this step twice more, using fresh water each time.

Soak a large handful or two of hardwood chips in water to cover for at least 1 hour or up to overnight.

IF USING A SMOKER: Following the manufacturer's instructions, set up and smoke the blood orange peels at between 160°F and 180°F/71°C and 82°C until darkened and smoky tasting, about 2 hours.

IF USING A GAS GRILL: Light one burner to medium. Put a smoker box over the lit burner, add some of the soaked wood chips to the box, and close the grill. Adjust the heat as needed to keep the temperature between 160°F and 180°F/71°C and 82°C. The wood chips should begin to smolder and release a steady stream of smoke. Put the orange peels on the grate opposite the lit burner. Cover the grill and smoke, adjusting the heat as needed to maintain the temperature. Check every 45 minutes or so and add more soaked chips as necessary to keep the smoke level constant. Rotate the orange peels, flipping as needed if one side is coloring faster than the other, until darkened and smoky tasting, about 2 hours.

SLICED AND DRIED CITRUS

CITRUS PEEL POWDER

SMOKED BLOOD ORANGE PEELS

IF USING A CHARCOAL GRILL: Fill a chimney starter with charcoal. Light it and let burn until the coals are covered with a thin layer of ash. Pour the hot coals on one side of the grill. Put some of the soaked wood chips next to the hot coals, and put the grate on the grill. Place the citrus peels on the grate opposite the fire. Cover the grill, positioning the vent on the lid on the side opposite the fire. Stick a thermometer through the vent and heat the grill to between 160°F and 180°F/71°C and 82°C. Smoke the orange peels, adjusting the fire as needed to maintain the temperature. Check every 45 minutes or so and add more soaked chips as necessary to keep the smoke level constant. Rotate the orange peels, flipping as needed if one side is coloring faster than the other, until darkened and smoky tasting, about 2 hours.

Dehydrate the smoked peels at 125°F/52°C until completely dry, 18 to 24 hours. Store in an airtight container in a dry, cool place for up to 9 months.

Dried Sour Cherries

The season for sour cherries is short, so process them as soon as they are available. Drying concentrates their acidity and sweetness. We use them in soups such as Sauerkraut Soup → 170, in granola, or simply as a snack. Plan on 2 qt/1.2 kg fresh cherries yielding 1 pt/1.1 g dried cherries.

Arrange pitted cherries in a single layer in a pan 2 in/5 cm deep and dehydrate at 120°F/48°C until soft and chewy like a raisin but not too wet or hard, 12 to 16 hours. Store in an airtight container in a dry, cool place for up to 6 months.

Dried Strawberries

Makes 2 lb/910 g

5 lb/2.3 kg strawberries, hulled
2 qt/2 L apple juice

Arrange strawberries in single layers in roasting pans and pour the apple juice over. Dehydrate at 120°F/48°C until soft and chewy like raisins, 24 to 36 hours. Store in an airtight container in a cool, dry place for up to 6 months.

Hoshigaki

Unripened Hachiya persimmons are so loaded with tannins that they are essentially inedible until they've ripened to an almost custardlike state or they've been dried, as they are here. Instead of loading the fruits into a dehydrator or spreading them on a screen in the sun, we dry them in the traditional Japanese style, hanging the fruits from their stems with a string and gently massaging them over the course of several weeks. They are wonderful eaten on their own, with a cheese plate and sake, or in salads.

You'll want to find persimmons with the stems still attached, so you can tie strings to them. If the stem is T shaped, that job will be even easier.

HOSHIGAKI PREPARATION

With a paring knife, carefully trim the peel from the top of each fruit by slicing from the outside of the fruit toward the stem and turning the fruit in a circle to score the entire top. Cut a slit in the loose ring, and pull it from the fruits leaving the stem intact. Peel the fruits. Tie each one by its stem to a length of string. Repeat until all of the fruits are ready to hang. Select a moderately cool space (no warmer than 65°F/18°C) with good ventilation and hang them where they won't be disturbed. When the surface of the fruits begins to look slightly dry, after 3 to 5 days, gently massage the fruits to coax the sugars to the surface, break down fibers, and eliminate any internal air pockets where mold might grow. Continue massaging the fruits every 3 days until their surface is frosted with a white, sugary bloom. Dry them until they feel like a leather wallet full of cash, about 1 month. Cut the persimmons from their strings and put them on a work surface. Using a rolling pin, gently roll the fruits to flatten the flesh to an even thickness, further ensuring that there are no air pockets for mold to grow as they are stored. Transfer to an airtight container and store in a cool, dark place for up to 6 months.

Dried Stone-Fruit Leaves

The leaves from stone-fruit trees—apricot, peach, nectarine, plum, and cherry—have a bitter almond aroma, much like that of noyaux **→ 84**. To take advantage of this special fragrance, steep the dried leaves in teas or in custards **→ 330**. Roll the leaves with a rolling pin to break down the cell walls, as is done for tea leaves. This will ensure you get more aroma from the leaves as they dry.

Dehydrate the stone-fruit leaves at 110°F/43°C until completely dry, about 12 hours. Alternatively, hang to dry, following the directions for air-drying **→ 30**. Store in an airtight container at room temperature for up to 9 months.

HOSHIGAKI

COD BOTTARGA

HERRING BOTTARGA

DRIED TUNA LOIN

DRIED ABALONE

DRIED BEEF

GREY MULLET BOTTARGA

MEAT & FISH

Preserving meat and fish gives us the opportunity to change the texture and flavor of the proteins without cooking them. Like the other items in this section, we are removing moisture from a product, concentrating and building flavors.

When curing meat and fish, a natural white mold often forms on the surface. This is a sign of healthy aging; however, if the mold starts to turn dark green or black, wipe with a towel moistened with vinegar and water. Most molds are harmless, but black molds should be avoided. Controlling the flow of air and humidity will help to abate unwanted mold growth. You can also purchase beneficial molds to inoculate your curing chamber. These will propagate and take over so every batch of meat or fish you cure will be inoculated with the proper spores.

Dry-Cured Meat or Fat

Fish and meat can be cured in just about any place that you can keep protected while maintaining a temperature between 55°F/12°C and 62°F/16°C (with a relative humidity between 65 and 75 percent). If you can't find a spot with the proper conditions, a curing box may be a good investment. An old refrigerator can easily be outfitted with a thermostat, humidity sensor, humidifier, and a small fan to keep the air flowing.

The following technique for dry meat that can be grated can be used for whole pieces of meat or fat. It works well for dried tuna loin, which we grate over Brussels sprouts → 274, and pork fatback, which we grind and spread on toast → 306. The dried beef that we cure is reminiscent of Italian bresaola, though ours is a bit drier, like the northern European versions. This recipe contains curing salt #2 (sodium nitrate) to help protect the product. We often cure with only salt, sometimes adding parsley and celery, which contain naturally occurring nitrates.

One 2 lb/1 kg piece of beef eye of round or pork fatback
2 percent kosher salt
0.3 percent curing salt #2
0.4 percent freshly ground black pepper
0.5 percent caraway seeds

Weigh the meat or fat; then, using the percentage given for each of the remaining ingredients, calculate the amount by weight of kosher salt, curing salt, pepper, and caraway seeds. Combine the dry ingredients in a small bowl and mix well. Rub the mixture on the meat or fat, coating it evenly, then transfer to a container, cover tightly, and refrigerate. Rotate once daily for 10 days.

Drain off any liquid that has accumulated in the container. Using heavy cotton butcher's twine, truss the meat or fat, making a knot at one end from which to hang it.

Select a cool, dry location (55°F/13°C) with 65 to 75 percent humidity and a fan to keep the air moving. If you are curing meat, hang until it feels firm to the touch and its weight is reduced by about 50 percent, 60 to 90 days. The fat won't lose much weight (only 10 to 15 percent), as it has a much lower water content than the meat. It will be slightly drier than when it began curing, the seasoning will have penetrated throughout, and you will be able to grate it. Wipe any excess seasoning from the outside and store, tightly wrapped or Cryovac-bagged, in a refrigerator for up to 3 months.

If you have a meat slicer, you can slice the dried meat thinly, or grate it with a coarse Microplane. Alternatively, you can invest in a katsuobushi shaver and slice the meat into thin ribbons as we do at the restaurant. The beef shavings are often used on vegetable dishes—see gai lan with air-dried beef → 286. The fat can be sliced thin and served with a charcuterie spread or processed in a food processor into a spreadable paste to have on toast with paprika and onion → 306.

Karasumi/Bottarga

Nick's uncle fishes grey mullet off the coast of Florida. Grey mullet roe is one of the best in the world for making bottarga that is similar to the excellent Italian grey mullet bottarga. We cure a few large batches each year. When the roe has dried to the point that it has lost about 30 percent of its original weight, it is called *karasumi* and is usually served sliced thin with sake or beer in Japan. Much of the roe harvested in Florida goes to Asia to make this delicacy. When it is dried even longer, losing up to 50 percent of its weight, it is known as *bottarga* and is finely grated over dishes for an added briny flavor. We use this same process for abalone and tuna loin; it can also be used with fresh roe from cod, herring, or tuna. We use a brine called *solé* to cure these delicate items. *Solé* is a term used to describe a fully saturated brine

usually made with Himalayan pink salt. Submerging in brine distributes salt throughout the item during the curing phase; the pink salt is high in beneficial trace minerals and has a pleasant flavor. Any pure salt will work.

To make the solé, combine 30 percent Himalayan or sea salt by weight of the water in a large, nonreactive container. Allow it to rest for 24 hours for the salt to dissolve. If the salt has fully dissolved, add more until some crystals remain on the bottom of the container. This indicates that the brine has become fully saturated.

Pull all visible veins from the roe, being careful not to damage the membrane, and wipe the sacs with a damp towel to remove any blood or stains. Separate the roe sacs; there are usually two in each fish. About one in every

fifteen sacs will be joined at one end. These cannot be completely separated without tearing the sacs. Leave them intact; they will still produce a good product. Place the roe in a nonreactive container and completely submerge in solé, weighted with a small plate to keep the roe below the surface of the liquid. Let stand at room temperature for 2 hours to cure. The roe will firm up a bit but will still be soft and should be handled carefully.

Remove the roe and discard the brine. To make karasumi, place the roe sacs on a perforated rack, at 55°F/12°C and 75 percent humidity, until dry but still slightly pliable and reduced in weight by about 30 percent, about 3 weeks. To make bottarga, continue drying until firm throughout, and reduced in weight by about 50 percent, 5 to 7 weeks total.

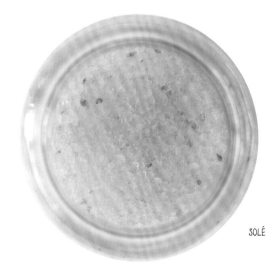

SOLÉ

BAR TARTINE

DRIED FISH

After the initial drying it's best to let the roe sacs continue to cure in the refrigerator for 1 to 2 months before using. This seems to mellow the flavor of the fish, and remove the slight bitterness that the roe has just after curing. If you have a vacuum-sealing system we recommend bagging your roe at this point. If not, hold in plastic bags with as much air pressed out of them as possible. The cured roe can be stored, refrigerated, for up to 1 year if the humidity in the refrigerator is not above 65 percent. Watch for mold if your refrigerator has a higher humidity; if you see any forming, wipe it off with a towel moistened with vinegar and water.

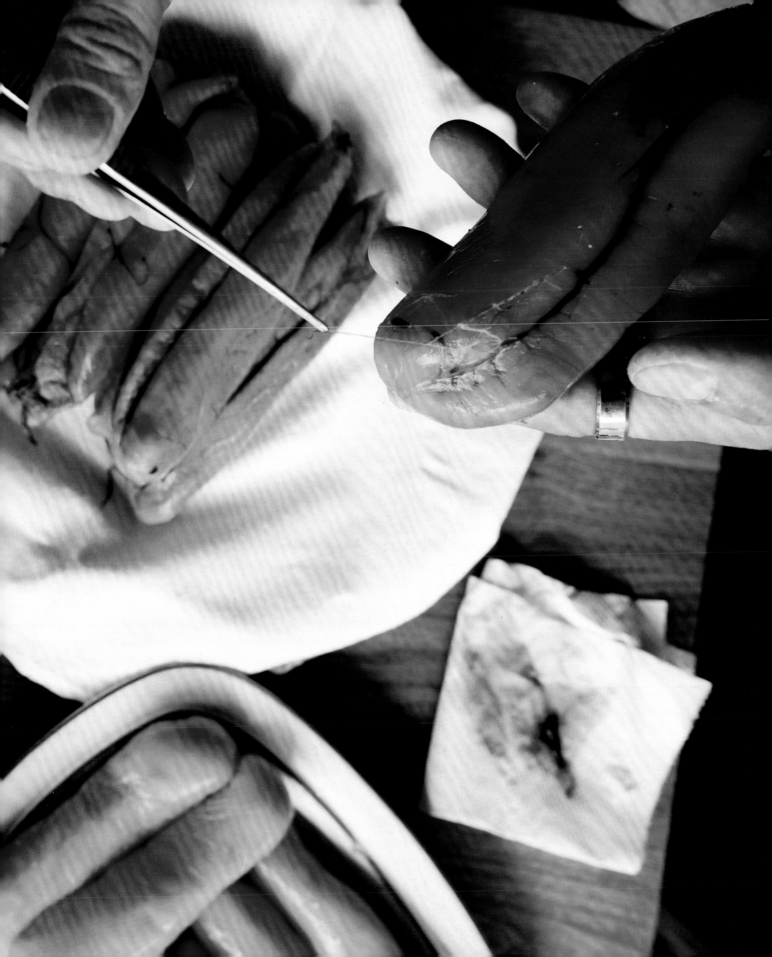

DAIRY

Our dairy program began humbly—with yogurt, sour cream, and kefir—and evolved to include all the products we currently use: blue cheese, pepper Jack, gouda, triple creams, feta, and fresh cheeses such as mozzarella, goat cheese, and farmer's cheese.

Making cheese at home does not have to be a daunting undertaking. Although you can get everything you need to make farmer's cheese and yogurt at the grocery store, other recipes here, like the ones for sour cream and goat cheese, require special cultures. Don't be intimidated by the laboratory-like names aroma B and MT1. These cultures are easy to use and will give you a quality product.

Whey

The thin liquid left over after you drain the curd mass in cheese making is known as whey. There are two kinds: sweet whey and sour whey. Sweet whey still has lactose present. We get our sweet whey from making farmer's cheese → 67, goat cheese → 68, and other rennet-set cheeses. We make a version of *brunost* (or *geitost*, if using goat's milk whey), the brown cheese popular all over Norway, by reducing sweet whey. We also use sweet whey in sauces, for soaking nuts, for fermenting vegetables, and for baking.

Sour whey is the result of lactic acid coagulation rather than rennet coagulation. We get ours from making yogurt → 74. We use most of our sour whey in our lacto-fermented sodas → 132 to add natural acidity to the base of sweet fruit juices.

Both sweet and sour whey can be stored in an airtight container in the refrigerator for up to 1 week.

Farmer's Cheese

Known as *turó* in Hungary, farmer's cheese is similar to ricotta but is naturally acidified without using added cultures. We use this cheese in sauces, for farmer's cheese dumplings → 234 and farmer's cheesecake → 348.

Makes 1½ lb/680 g

9 cups/2.1 L whole milk
3 cups/710 ml heavy cream

In a 3-qt/3-L nonreactive oven-proof dish, combine the milk and cream, cover, and let stand at room temperature, between 67°F/19°C and 72°F/22°C, for 60 to 72 hours, until the whey is visible along the sides of the curd mass. Try not to move the container much during this time, as movement can break the curd, and we've noticed it doesn't curdle well if jostled too much. When the whey is visible, the base is ready to go in the oven to set the curds.

Preheat the oven to 300°F/150°C. Place the covered dish in the oven. After 30 minutes, check to see if curds have begun to coagulate. Use caution when removing the lid, as the butterfat on the surface of the cheese can be hot.

When the cheese has fully separated into curds, and the whey starts to become clear, remove the dish from the oven and let cool for at least 15 minutes prior to straining.

Line a colander with cheesecloth and place over a container large enough to hold the whey. Transfer the curds to the prepared colander and let drain at room temperature. If you are making Warm Farmer's Cheese → 232, strain for 30 minutes and serve immediately. At this point most of the whey will have drained off but enough will remain that the butterfat is still floating with the curds. To make the Farmer's Cheese Dumplings → 234 or Farmer's Cheesecake → 348, strain for 2 hours until there is almost no whey remaining in the colander with the cheese. The cheese will keep in an airtight container, refrigerated, for up to 1 week. Store the whey as directed → 67.

Goat Cheese

This classic goat cheese can be used as a dip, a spread, or in sauces. We add a bit of cow's cream to the goat's milk to add butterfat, and thus richness.

Makes 2 lb/910 g

4 cups/960 ml goat's milk
¼ cup/60 ml heavy cream
¼ tsp aroma B or equivalent
    powdered mesophilic culture
⅛ tsp liquid calcium chloride,
    diluted in 1 tbsp cold water
⅛ tsp single-strength rennet,
    diluted in 1 tbsp cold water

GOAT CHEESE

In a large stainless-steel pot, warm the goat's milk and cream over low heat to 86°F/30°C. Distribute the aroma B over the surface of the milk and let stand undisturbed for 5 minutes, then whisk for 1 minute. Add the diluted calcium chloride and stir for 30 seconds to incorporate fully. With a whisk or spoon, mix in the diluted rennet for 45 seconds with a gentle up-and-down chopping motion to gently incorporate.

Cover the pot and let rest undisturbed at a temperature between 67°F/19°C and 72°F/22°C until the curds form a mass that pulls away from the sides of the pot to reveal the translucent whey, 8 to 12 hours.

Line a colander with cheesecloth and place over a medium bowl. Transfer the curds to the prepared colander and let drain at room temperature until there is almost no whey remaining in the colander with the cheese, about 2 hours. The cheese will keep in an airtight container in the refrigerator for up to 1 week. Store the whey as directed <u>→ 67</u>.

Cottage Cheese

Both of us recall this cheese from the Midwestern meals of our childhoods, where it was often served alongside half a grapefruit and garnished with curly parsley. We serve this exact dish at the restaurant for brunch, only we make our own large-curd, rennet-set cheese to complete the memory.

Although the instructions may at first seem difficult, once you get the hang of the process, it will become an easy, go-to fresh cheese to make at home. We stir sour cream into ours, but you can use yogurt or buttermilk instead.

Makes 1½ lb/680 g

4 qt/960 ml whole milk
¼ tsp aroma B or equivalent powdered mesophilic culture
¼ tsp liquid calcium chloride, diluted in 2 tbsp cold water
¼ tsp single-strength liquid rennet, diluted in 2 tbsp cold water
1 tsp kosher salt
1 cup/240 ml sour cream <u>→ 71</u>, kefir cream <u>→ 76</u>, or kefir buttermilk <u>→ 76</u>

In a large stainless-steel pot, warm the milk over very low heat, stirring as it warms, to 80°F/27°C. Distribute the aroma B over the surface of the milk and let stand undisturbed for 5 minutes, then

whisk to incorporate. Add the diluted calcium chloride and stir for 30 seconds to incorporate fully. Mix in the diluted rennet for 45 seconds with a gentle up-and-down chopping motion to incorporate. Be careful not to disturb the curds.

Cover the pot and let rest undisturbed at room temperature until the curds form a mass that pulls away from the sides to reveal the greenish whey in a thin layer on top of the mass and all around it, about 6 hours, or until you have a clean break.

Check for a clean break by plunging your finger into the milk and lifting it back up, hooking into the curd. If a piece of curd moves away and greenish liquid pools in its place, it is ready. If it's still quite loose, wait 30 minutes more and try again. When ready, use a long, thin knife or cake spatula to make a series of parallel cuts through the mass, spacing them ½ to ¾ in/12 mm to 2 cm apart. Then make an equal number of cuts perpendicular to the first cuts to form small cubes. Let stand for 10 minutes, then stir continually for 5 minutes.

Return the pot to the stove top over very low heat and warm the curds to 115°F/45°C, taking care that the temperature does not increase by more than a few degrees every 5 minutes. Stir the curds gently every 5 minutes to expel more whey and to ensure they are not sticking to the bottom of the pot. The curds should reach the target temperature in 15 to 20 minutes.

The curds should now be cooked through and reveal a slight resistance when you squeeze them. Allow the mixture to settle for 10 minutes, then spoon off the whey from the surface until the curds are visible. Reserve the whey for another use → 67.

Line a colander with cheesecloth and place over a container large enough to hold the whey without the strainer sitting in it. Drain for about 15 minutes. Fill another bowl, large enough to hold the colander, with cold water. Set the colander inside the bowl, immersing the curds completely in the chilled water, and breaking them up to the size of your thumbnail as they cool. After 10 minutes, lift the colander out of the water and add ice to the bowl of cold water. Place the colander of curds back over the bowl. Chill to at least 40°F/4°C, about 20 minutes.

Set the colander over an empty bowl and let the chilled curds drain for 1 hour. Transfer the curds to a bowl and toss with the salt. Add as much of the sour cream as desired, making the cheese as creamy or as dry as you like. Taste and adjust the seasoning with salt, then transfer to an airtight container and refrigerate for up to 7 days. Loosen curds with a couple spoonfuls of buttermilk for a thinner consistency.

Cheese in the Style of Feta

This brined cheese is made to replicate the aroma and texture of feta. The salinity of this cheese makes it a natural choice to use in sweet potato salad → 208 or whipped feta → 190.

Yields 2 lb/905 g

Lipase
2 gl/7.5 L whole cow's or
   goat's milk
¼ cup/60 ml heavy cream
¼ tsp feta culture such as
   Danisco Feta A or B
½ tsp liquid calcium chloride,
   diluted in 2 tbsp cold water
¼ tsp single-strength rennet,
   diluted in 2 tbsp cold water
2¾ cups/730 g kosher salt
½ tsp liquid calcium chloride,
   diluted in 2 tbsp cold water
1½ qt/1.3 L filtered grapeseed oil

Aromatics such as: lemon
   rounds, pink peppercorns,
   lavender, sage, rosemary,
   or bay leaves

Dip a skewer into the lipase, transferring 2 tips worth to a small bowl containing 1 tbsp cold water. Let rest for 20 minutes to activate. It will give your cheese the aroma of goat or sheep that is so often associated with this style.

In a large heavy-bottomed 12-qt/11.5-L pot over medium heat, bring the milk and cream to 89°F/31°C. Evenly distribute the feta culture over the top and allow to sit for 5 minutes to hydrate. Add the lipase and the diluted calcium chloride. Stir for 30 seconds to incorporate fully. Allow to rest, maintaining the temperature for 30 minutes. After 30 minutes check your temperature; it should be 89°F/31°C. If not, rewarm over low heat until it reaches 89°F/31°C.

Take the mixture off of the heat. Add the diluted rennet with an up-and-down chopping motion to gently incorporate. Continue chopping for 30 seconds. Cover the pot and leave to set for 1 to 2 hours, or until you have a clean break. Check this by plunging your finger into the milk and lifting it back up, hooking into the curd. If a piece of curd moves away and greenish liquid pools in its place, it is ready. If it's still quite loose, wait 30 minutes more and try again.

When ready, use a long, thin knife or cake spatula to make a series of parallel cuts through the mass, spacing them 1 in/3 cm apart. Then make an equal number of cuts perpendicular to the first cuts to form small cubes. Rest for 15 minutes, stir gently for 5 to 7 minutes, then allow to rest an additional 15 minutes.

Set up a cheesecloth-lined colander or well-perforated forms (such as green plastic berry baskets) over a container that is deep enough to catch the draining whey. Remove the whey down to the level of the cheese curds. Ladle the curds and remaining whey into the colander or forms. After 1 hour, turn the cheese, flipping over, releasing the mass so the bottom is now the top. Turn again after 3 hours. Continue draining for 8 hours more, covered, at room temperature (68°F to 72°F/ 20°C to 22°C).

In a nonreactive container, make a saturated brine by dissolving the salt in 4 qt/3.75 L cold water. Add the calcium chloride to balance the pH. Submerge the

cheese in the brine for 2 hours. Remove the cheese and set aside.

Discard 1½ qt/1.4 L of the brine, adding 1½ qt/1.4 L cold, unsalted water to the remaining 2½ qt/ 2.3 L brine. Return the cheese to the brine to age and cure, storing at 55°F/12°C for 1 month. You can use your cheese at this stage.

If you wish to marinate your cheese in oil, remove it from the brine. Discard the brine and allow the cheese to drain in a perforated container for 30 minutes. Pour the grapeseed oil into a nonreactive container, submerge the cheese in the oil, and add the desired aromatics. Allow it to infuse in the refrigerator at 41°F/5°C for at least 1 week and up to 3 months.

The brined cheese is ready after a month, but benefits from aging. If you do not have a wine refrigerator or a cool cellar, it's fine to age in the refrigerator.

Sour Cream

We put sour cream on almost everything. Some people are reluctant to use it, but our suggestion is to use it liberally. We stand behind our belief that wholesome foods, regardless of fat content, are the best things to eat. This recipe includes added cultures that take over the environment in the

SOUR CREAM

cream, consistently giving it the flavor, acidity, and thickness that we desire. MT1 is a feta cheese culture that makes the sour cream extra tart.

Makes 2 qt/2 L

2 qt/2 L heavy cream
1 tsp aroma B or equivalent powdered mesophilic culture
¼ tsp MT1 or more for added tartness

BAR TARTINE

In a large stainless-steel pot, warm the cream over very low heat, stirring as it warms, to 89°F/32°C. Add the aroma B and the MT1 and let sit for 15 minutes to hydrate. Whisk to evenly blend. Immediately transfer the mixture to sterile jars or other heat-proof containers. The sour cream can be stored in these containers after culturing.

Place the jars in a spot with a constant temperature of 89°F/32°C for 12 hours. An unheated oven with a pilot light, a dehydrator set to 89°F/32°C, or a slow cooker with a water bath at constant temperature would all work. After 12 hours, the cream should be noticeably thicker. Stir the cream and move to a kitchen counter or pantry with a temperature of between 67°F/19°C and 72°F/22°C to complete the thickening and souring process.

After 12 hours more, stir again and refrigerate overnight to cool completely and allow the cream to thicken further. Store in an airtight container in the refrigerator for up to 2 weeks.

Yogurt

We purchased a Greek yogurt starter years ago and we have used it ever since. As long as we feed it fresh milk at least once a week, the culture stays healthy and propagates indefinitely.

You can make yogurt at home using a small amount of commercial yogurt if you don't want to have to manage your own starter culture. You'll need to start with fresh plain yogurt each time you make a new batch, but you'll be saved the responsibility of keeping the culture alive.

Makes 8 cups/2 L undrained yogurt, or 3 cups/ 720 ml drained yogurt

2 qt/2 L whole milk
¼ cup/60 ml self-propagating yogurt starter or store-bought full-fat plain yogurt

In a large stainless-steel pot, warm the milk over very low heat to 110°F/43°C. Whisk in the starter. Transfer the mixture to canning jars or other nonreactive containers and cover gently with a lid. Culture the yogurt in an unheated oven with a pilot light, in a slow cooker, or in a warm-water bath set at 110°F/43°C until the milk thickens to the consistency of store-bought yogurt, about 6 hours. Store in an airtight container and refrigerate for up to 2 weeks.

For a thicker, Greek-style texture, line a colander with cheesecloth or a coffee filter and set over a bowl. Spoon the yogurt into the prepared colander and drain, refrigerated, until quite thick,

about 24 to 48 hours. The clear liquid at the bottom of the bowl is the sour whey.

Making Kefir

Dairy kefir is best known as a thick, effervescent beverage. The white plastic bottles ubiquitous in Russian markets have made their way into major grocery chains. The grains are colonies of healthy bacteria and yeast that feed on lactose, converting it to lactic acid. During this process, a wide range of bioavailable probiotics are produced. Since the microbes in grains eat lactose, kefir-based dairy products can often be enjoyed by people who are sensitive to cow dairy. We use the grains to culture cream, which we use as the base for our cultured butter.

Kefir grains are alive and need a constant food source to stay healthy. Water kefir grains eat table sugar/sucrose (they can be trained to eat many sugar sources), and dairy kefir grains feed on the lactose sugar in milk. Each needs to be cared for a bit differently, but, if you keep them healthy, they will grow and proliferate indefinitely. When your grains begin to reproduce, give away some of the excess or freeze them for up to 1 month. You can also spread the grains on unbleached parchment paper and let stand at room

temperature until completely dry, 2 to 3 days. Transfer the dried grains to a resealable plastic bag or to an airtight glass or plastic container and store in a cool, dry place for up to 6 months. Bring them back to life and keep them activated by rehydrating in fresh milk.

You can pause the kefiring process by storing the grains in fresh milk and refrigerating.

For storing kefir grains: Store dairy kefir grains in fresh milk with a ratio of 1 tbsp kefir grains to 2 qt/2 L milk. Refrigerate in an airtight container for up to 4 weeks. Drain and add fresh milk every 7 days.

Milk Kefir

Milk kefir provides a great base to layer flavors into. A few of our favorites are white coffee, bergamot, and cardamom, or Fig Leaf Syrup → 129. Use it any time you would use milk—on cereal, in smoothies, or in salad dressings or soups—or drink it plain.

Makes 2 qt/2 L

2 qt/2 L whole milk
1 tsp dairy kefir grains

Pour the milk into a 3-qt/2.8-L nonreactive container. Add the kefir grains, allowing them to float freely. Cover and let stand between 67° and 72°F/ 19° and 22°C until gently soured and noticeably thicker, 24 to 36 hours.

Strain the kefir through a nylon-mesh sieve placed over a pitcher or bowl, capturing the grains in the sieve. (Be sure to use a nylon sieve, as kefir grains can be sensitive to metal.) Transfer the kefir to an airtight container, filling it only two-thirds full to allow room for carbon dioxide buildup. Cover and refrigerate for up to 1 week. Open the container occasionally to release the carbon dioxide. It is ready to drink immediately.

KEFIR GRAINS

Kefir Cream

Cream cultured with kefir grains thickens like sour cream. We use it to garnish desserts (see parsnip cake → 346), in savory dishes (see lentil croquettes → 240), and to make our cultured butter. It is not quite as thick as our cultured sour cream → 71, but works well as a substitute in most recipes.

Makes 2 qt/2 L

2 qt/2 L heavy cream
1 tsp dairy kefir grains

Pour the cream into a 3-qt/3-L nonreactive container. Wrap the kefir grains in cheesecloth, tie securely, and add the bundle to the cream. This will make it possible to fish them out when the culturing has ended. Cover and let stand at between 67° and 72°F/19° and 22°C until gently soured and noticeably thicker, 24 to 36 hours.

Remove the bundle of kefir grains and reserve the grains → 74 for future batches. Transfer the kefir to an airtight container, filling it only two-thirds full to allow room for carbon dioxide buildup. Cover and refrigerate for at least 12 hours to thicken. It can be held in a refrigerator for up to 2 weeks.

Kefir Butter and Buttermilk

Cream that is cultured with kefir grains can be processed into cultured butter as is often done with crème fraîche. Regular whipping cream can be used to make butter, but we choose to culture ours first to add flavor and probiotics. The buttermilk that remains after churning the butter is just as useful and delicious as the butter itself. We use it in soups, salad dressings, and sauces. Chad uses it to make his sprouted rye bread.

Makes 8 oz/225 g butter and 3 cups/720 ml buttermilk

1 qt/960 ml chilled kefir
    cream → 76
Kosher salt (optional)

Prepare an ice bath with a colander in it. Place the kefir cream in the bowl of a stand mixer fitted with the whisk attachment and tent the bowl with plastic wrap to prevent the cream from splattering. Whisk the cream on low speed until it begins to froth. Increase the speed to medium and continue beating until it has thickened to a solid mass and separated from the buttermilk.

Place a fine-mesh sieve over a bowl and drain the butter into it. Transfer the buttermilk to an airtight container and refrigerate for up to 2 weeks.

Transfer the butter to the ice bath to wash off the excess whey. Using your hands, squeeze the butter to press out any remaining liquid; this makes it less prone to spoilage. When the liquid runs clear, season the butter with salt, if desired, by kneading it into the mass with your hands. Transfer the finished butter to a sealed container. Refrigerate for up to 1 month.

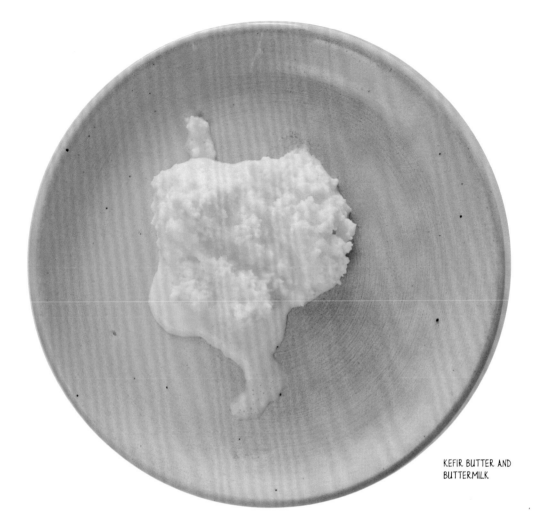

KEFIR BUTTER AND
BUTTERMILK

Brown Butter

Browning butter toasts the milk solids, giving the butter a nutty aroma that lends itself well to savory and sweet dishes. We brown our kefir butter, yielding a slightly acidic flavor and a more complex aroma than uncultured butter. Adding lemon juice at the end of cooking gives flavor to the butter and prevents the solids from burning. During this step, the butter may foam up a bit so be sure you have a pot size that can accommodate a rapid increase in volume.

Yields 2 cups/480 ml

1 lb/455 g unsalted kefir butter
  → 76, unsalted sweet cream
  butter, or unsalted cultured
  butter
1 tsp kosher salt
½ tsp fresh lemon juice

In a 4-qt/3.8-L heavy pot, melt the butter with the salt over medium heat. At first, the butter will foam up and then the foam will dissipate. After 3 to 5 minutes, the milk solids will begin to brown, leaving some brown specks in the bottom of the pot. Once you detect the specks and the butter smells nutty, remove the pot from the heat, add the lemon juice, and let the butter cool, stirring constantly. Refrigerate for up to 3 months.

BAR TARTINE

SPROUTING & SOAKING

Sprouting awakens dormant nutrients in seeds, nuts, legumes, grains, and grasses. It is an easy way to incorporate fresh ingredients into your cooking during the winter months, when access to produce can be limited. In the restaurant, we sprout a wide variety of foods for use in breads and to garnish and flavor dishes. We appreciate both the health benefits of sprouting and the flavors and textures they provide. When we sprout, we are mimicking nature by providing water, which starts the growing cycle.

They are several techniques for sprouting the seeds of legumes, grasses, and nuts. Soaking is the first stage of sprouting. It tenderizes the seeds and releases the nutrients and enzymes that lie dormant when the seeds are dry. While technically sprouted, soaked seeds have no visible tails growing from them, which is why they are referred to as "soaks." Some seeds are sprouted until they develop short tails; this generally takes 2 to 3 days and requires rinsing and draining. Others sprout for longer, from 8 to 12 days, either because they are slow growing or because we want to grow long sprout tails. Some seeds we sprout to short tails and plant in soil to grow greens.

For sprouting, you'll need a container that allows air to circulate and water to drain. This can be a commercial sprouting tray, a simple canning jar fitted with a screen, or even a bowl with a sieve. We use 4-qt/3.8-L containers covered with cheesecloth for draining the water and keeping unwanted things out. Always check for stowaway rocks in your seeds before sprouting. Make sure that the seeds you are using are raw, never heated or seasoned.

Bean Sprouts

A wide variety of dried beans are easily sprouted. We often use **mung bean, lentil, chickpea**, and **fenugreek**.

Yield: 1:2 dry to finished sprouts

Time: 12 hours to soak, 2 to 4 days to sprout

Put the beans in a clean sprouting container and cover with 3 parts cold water to 1 part bean, stirring to ensure an even soak. Soak at room temperature, between 68° and 72°F/20° and 22°C for 12 hours. The beans will have expanded from the water, but sprouts won't be visible yet. Drain the water by inverting your container, making sure to use cheesecloth, a screen, or a sieve to catch the contents.

Let the drained beans stand at room temperature for 8 hours, then rinse them with cold water three times a day. When all of the beans have grown small tails, they are finished. This can take 2 to 3 days, more if the room is colder, less if it is warmer. Give the sprouts a final rinse, dry them quickly on a clean towel, transfer to a sealed container, and refrigerate for up to 1 week until ready to use. We often cook the sprouts at this point as well.

Seed Sprouts

Sprouting **dill, caraway, radish,** and **onion seeds** is a bit different from sprouting legumes. Each type of seed has its own idiosyncrasies. These take a long time to sprout but are so flavorful that they are worth the wait. We like to let them grow long tails, and they're great in salads (Beet and Blue Cheese Salad → **192**).

Yield: 1:4 dry to finished sprouts

Time: no soaking, 14 to 16 days to sprout

Rinse the seeds in cool water, transfer them to a clean sprouting container, and place out of direct sunlight at room temperature, between 68° and 72°F/ 20° and 22°C. Rinse the seeds once a day for 6 days, draining well after each rinse. After the sixth day, rinse every other day until they have grown greens. On the tenth day, move the sprouting container close to a light source to bring out the leaves. When the seeds all have little leaves 1 in/ 2.5 cm in length, they are done. This will take 14 to 16 days total sprouting time. Give the sprouts a final rinse, then use a small salad spinner to remove excess moisture, transfer to a sealed container, and refrigerate until ready to use, up to 1 week.

Sunflower or Pumpkin Seed Soaks

We soak hulled **sunflower** and **pumpkin seeds** before using them in most recipes. We let them dry again before toasting to make sunflower tahini to garnish Kale Salad → **188**. For the recipes in this book that call for toasted sunflower or pumpkin seeds, the seeds may be soaked first if you choose, but it is not mandatory. Use hulled, raw sunflower or pumpkin seeds.

Yield: 1:1.5 dry to finished sprouts

Time: 2 hours

Place the sunflower or pumpkin seeds in a clean sprouting container and cover with 3 parts water to 1 part seed, stirring to ensure an even soak. Soak at room temperature, between 68°and 72°F/20° and 22°C, for 2 hours. They will have expanded in the water, but sprouts will not be visible. Drain the water by inverting the container, making sure to use cheesecloth, a screen, or a sieve to catch the contents.

The seeds can now be dried in a low oven or a dehydrator to make them shelf stable, toasted for immediate use, or covered and refrigerated for up to 1 week. Use for milks and butters → **83**.

Pseudocereals

Amaranth, **buckwheat**, and **quinoa** are pseudocereals: high-protein, gluten-free ancient broadleaf plants that are considered whole grains. Like true cereals, which are grasses, we use them as flours, as breakfast cereals, or in salads (Sunchoke Custard with Sunflower Greens → **248**). We often soak and cook these as we would the unsprouted grains.

Amaranth or Quinoa Sprouts

These sprouts can be eaten raw 48 hours after soaking. They'll develop tails and at this point they are ready to eat. They will get soft if they grow longer.

Yield: 1:1.5 dry to finished sprouts

Time: 30 minutes to soak for cooking; 2 to 3 days to sprout

Place the amaranth seeds in a clean sprouting container and cover with 3 parts cold water to 1 part amaranth, stirring to ensure an even soak. Soak at room temperature, between 68° and 72°F/20° and 22°C, for 30 minutes. The amaranth will have expanded in the water, but sprouts will not be visible. Drain the water by inverting the container, making sure to use cheesecloth, a screen, or a sieve to catch the contents.

Leave the drained amaranth for 8 hours, and then rinse with cold water three times a day. When all of the seeds have grown small tails, they are finished. This can take 2 to 3 days total, more if the room is colder, less if it is warmer. Give the sprouts a final rinse, dry quickly on a clean towel, transfer to a sealed container, and refrigerate for up to 1 week.

SOAKING SEEDS BEFORE SPROUTING

Buckwheat Sprouts

Pseudocereals are still in their raw form after an initial 30-minute soak. After soaking, they can either be cooked immediately or sprouted for a couple of days to grow tails and make them palatable in a raw state. We soak hulled buckwheat groats for the buckwheat dumplings → **236** to activate them before cooking.

Yield: 1:1.5 dry to finished sprouts

Time: 30 minutes to soak for cooking; rinse 3 times a day, 2 to 3 days to sprout for eating raw

Place the buckwheat groats in a clean sprouting container and cover with 3 parts water to 1 part buckwheat, stirring to ensure an even soak. Soak at room temperature, between 68° and 72°F/20° and 22°C, for 30 minutes. The buckwheat will have expanded in the water, but sprouts will not be visible. Drain the water by inverting the container, making sure to use cheesecloth, a screen, or a sieve to catch the contents. You will want to rinse these a few times after the soak as they are quite slimy.

Leave the drained buckwheat for 8 hours, and then rinse with cold water three times a day. When all of the groats have grown small tails, they are finished. Sprouting may take 2 to 3 days total, more if the room is colder, less if it is warmer. Give the sprouts a final rinse, dry quickly on a clean towel, transfer to a sealed container, and refrigerate for up to 1 week.

Microgreens

Microgreens are often planted in soil, allowed to photosynthesize, and then harvested soon after their first leaves appear. We tend to grab a handful or two every time we pass the trays, so we have a hard time keeping them in stock.

To grow microgreens, you must first soak the seeds, then rinse them for 2 days so they begin to sprout, and finally plant them in a thin layer of moist soil. The yield is roughly equivalent to the amount of seeds you sow.

Pea and Sunflower Greens

Place the peas or unhulled sunflower seeds in a clean sprouting container and cover with 3 parts cold water to 1 part seeds, stirring to ensure an even soak. Soak at room temperature, between 68° and 72°F/20° and 22°C, for 12 hours. The peas or sunflower seeds will have expanded in the water, but sprouts will not be visible. Drain the water by inverting the container, making sure to use cheesecloth, a screen, or a sieve to catch the contents.

Leave the drained peas or sunflower seeds for 8 hours, and then rinse with cold water three times a day. When all of the peas or sunflower seeds have grown small tails, they are ready to

plant. This can take 2 to 3 days total, more if the room is colder, less if it is warmer. Give the sprouts a final rinse and drain.

Fill a shallow seed tray with moist potting soil and spread the seeds in an even layer over the soil. It's fine if they are touching; we plant our trays pretty densely. Cover the tray with a lid and store at room temperature in low light until the seeds begin to grow vertical shoots. Water a few times a day by spraying them, or by gently pouring water over the entire surface of the soil. Once they are rooted, remove the cover and place on a window-sill or under a grow lamp and continue to add water as needed to keep the soil moist. Begin using the microgreens when their first green leaves unfold, in about 14 days. The sunflowers will shed their seeds as they sprout, but some hold tight to them. Just squeeze them between your fingers to release them before cutting.

Nuts

It's our habit to soak all nuts before we use them. Nuts are technically soaks because they do not grow tails, although you will often hear them referred to as sprouted. Water helps release the enzyme inhibitors that keep the nutrients dormant. Adding salt to the soaking water neutralizes the enzymes and releases the phytic acid.

Nuts add texture, flavor, fat, and nutrients to many of our dishes, such as Hazelnut Cookies → 354, Krumcake → 312, and Slow-Roasted Carrots with Burnt Bread and Almond Milk → 224. You can use the soaked nuts raw as a snack, blended into smoothies, or to thicken sauces. Note that when nuts get soaked it kickstarts their metabolism and they begin feeding on their own fat. Soaked nut butters are therefore less creamy than non-soaked.

Soaked Nuts

Yield: 0.75:1 dry to soaked nuts

Time: 48 hours

Put dry shelled **almonds, hazelnuts, walnuts,** or **pistachios** in a clean sprouting container and cover with 3 parts cold water to 1 part nuts. Add ¼ **tsp salt per 1 qt/1 L of water.** Soak at room temperature for 24 hours.

Drain the water by inverting the container, making sure to use cheesecloth, a screen, or a sieve to catch the contents. Cover with fresh cool water and continue to soak for 24 hours longer. After 48 hours, the nuts can be drained and refrigerated, covered, for up to 1 week. They make a great raw snack. The recipes throughout the book call for nuts to be soaked before using, but it is not mandatory.

Toasted Sprouted Nuts

Toasting sprouted nuts renders them shelf stable and makes them more aromatic. They can also be processed into toasted nut butters.

Preheat the oven to 300°F/150°C. Drain the nut soaks and spread them on a rimmed baking sheet. Toast until they are dry and have turned a very light golden brown, 25 to 30 minutes. Remove from the oven and let cool. Transfer to an airtight container and store at room temperature for up to 1 month or in the freezer for up to 6 months.

Dried Sprouted Nuts

This is a good method for storing sprouted nuts if you want to save them for later use, or for eating raw. They are also ready to process into nut butters.

Place the nuts in a dehydrator set at 100°F/38°C until completely dry, about 24 hours. Transfer to an airtight container and store at room temperature for up to 1 month.

Sprouted Nut or Seed Milk

You can use nearly any type of nut or seed to make milk. Toasting the nuts or seeds is optional and gives the milk a darker color and richer flavor.

Line a fine-mesh sieve with cheesecloth and place over a medium bowl. Working in batches, combine the nuts or seeds with equal parts fresh water and purée until very smooth, about 3 minutes. Pour into the prepared sieve. Alternatively, use a nut-milk bag, allowing the milk to drain in the refrigerator overnight. Gather the edges of the cheesecloth with your hands and twist to squeeze out as much liquid as possible from the pulp. Transfer to an airtight container and refrigerate, covered, for up to 3 days.

Sprouted Nut or Seed Butters

Our recipes all include nuts and seeds that have been sprouted and toasted. If your butter seems dry, add a bit of neutral vegetable oil or coconut oil to achieve the desired consistency.

CASHEW BUTTER

WALNUT BUTTER

PEANUT BUTTER

HAZELNUT BUTTER

Using a nut-butter machine, a juicer capable of making nut butters, a food processor, or a blender, process the nuts or seeds according to the manufacturer's instructions. The texture of the end product depends on both the equipment and the nuts or seeds you use; we usually start by using a juicer and then blend our nuts in a blender to make the paste very smooth. Using a blender or food processor alone, you will render a more rustic butter. Softer nuts, such as cashews, will yield a smoother paste, whereas harder nuts, such as almonds, will yield a more granular paste. Transfer to an airtight container and refrigerate for up to 1 month.

Noyaux

Crack the pit of any stone fruit, from cherries to peaches to apricots, and you'll find an edible seed inside. Known as noyaux, they have an aroma of orange peel and amaretto. Use them to flavor liqueurs, syrups, custards, or ice cream; grind them to make a flour to use in cakes and pastries; or use them as a garnish for Chilled Apricot Soup → 152. The noyaux can be soaked before toasting, but it is not mandatory. Once the meat has been extracted, we toast the noyaux a second time to intensify their aroma and to eliminate the small amount of prussic acid present in them. (When consumed in large amounts, prussic acid can be toxic.)

Yield: 1:1.25 fresh to soaked weight

Time: 24 hours to soak

Spread the pits in a single layer on a flat, sturdy surface. Lay a towel over them to keep the shells from scattering. With a hammer or mallet, crack the pits, taking care not to break the inner seeds. Pull the seeds out of the shells.

Put the noyaux in a clean sprouting container and cover with 3 parts cold water to 1 part noyaux. Add a pinch of salt, stirring to ensure an even soak. Soak at room temperature, between 68° and 72°F/20° and 22°C for 24 hours. Drain the water by inverting the container, making sure to use cheesecloth, a screen, or a sieve to catch the contents. See dried sprouted nuts → 83.

To toast noyaux, preheat the oven to 300°F/150°C. Drain the noyaux and spread them on a rimmed baking sheet. Toast until they are dry and have turned a very light golden brown, 10 to 15 minutes. Remove from the oven and let cool. Transfer to an airtight container and store at room temperature in a cool place for up to 1 month.

OILS & ANIMAL FATS

Infused oils, filtered oils, unfiltered oils, and animal fats have distinct roles in our cooking.

Infused oils begin with neutral filtered oils that we flavor with herbs or vegetables. Chile oil, parsley oil, and sunchoke oil are examples. They are almost always used as a garnish to give a dish aroma and a bit of fatty texture. An infusion of sunchoke transforms a light, filtered oil into a rich, flavorful finishing oil with a weight similar to that of extra-virgin olive oil.

Filtered oils are useful for cooking, in vinaigrettes, or for frying. There are many of these in most grocery stores, many of which we would not recommend using. They are often made from questionable ingredients in a questionable manner. We use filtered grapeseed, rice bran, and sunflower oils in the recipes throughout this cookbook because we think they are the purest and cleanest-tasting available. It is always best to look for organic varieties when shopping for these.

We use two key techniques for making these oils: cold processing for delicate herbs to preserve their flavor and bright color and heat processing for studier ingredients.

Unfiltered oils are useful for garnishing and adding a lot of flavor and texture. Pistachio, sunflower, pumpkin, grapeseed, and extra-virgin olive oils are some of the most common that are available unfiltered. These don't last as long on a shelf because of the residual sediments left over from pressing. Keep refrigerated after opening to prevent them from developing a rancid flavor.

Animal fats are useful for cooking, flavoring, as components in recipes, and, in some cases, just for eating. They garnish vegetables, such as our Gai Lan with Air-Dried Beef → **286**, and they give texture and flavor to buckwheat dumplings → **236**, and to dishes like steamed celery root cake → **244**.

Cold-Processed Infused Oils

Cold infusing is best for delicate ingredients like herbs or flowers that can lose quality with long exposure to heat. These are often quickly blanched and shocked in water to set their color, but not long enough to be detrimental to the integrity of the ingredient.

Herb Oil

Herb oils offer an extra bit of herbaceous flavor in liquid form. They are a way for us to take a neutral base such as filtered grapeseed or sunflower oil and give it vibrant color and flavor.

Makes 2 cups/480 ml

3 bunches fresh herbs, such as flat-leaf parsley, cilantro, chives, basil, tarragon, carrot tops, marjoram, or dill, large stems removed

2 cups/480 ml filtered grapeseed or sunflower oil

Chill a blender beaker in the freezer for at least 15 minutes.

Line a fine-mesh sieve with cheesecloth or a coffee filter and set over a medium bowl.

Prepare an ice bath. Bring a large pot of water to a boil, add the herbs, and boil for 10 seconds. Immediately transfer the herbs

TOP TO BOTTOM:
TALLOW, SCHMALTZ, LARD

PINE OIL

to the ice bath to preserve its bright green color. When cool, squeeze out all of the water.

In the chilled blender, combine the herbs and oil and blend on high speed just until the oil turns bright green. Do not overblend or the oil will heat up, which can destroy the aroma and the color. Pour the oil into the prepared sieve and immediately refrigerate the setup. Leave the oil in the refrigerator to strain slowly, about 3 hours. You can press the last bit out by tightening down on the cheesecloth to release the moisture.

Discard any solids and transfer the oil to an opaque container. (Light can cause green oils to lose their color, so keep them chilled and store in an opaque container.) Refrigerate for up to 1 week.

Pine Oil

Makes 2 cups/480 ml

1 cup/25 g packed young fir tips
2 cups/480 ml filtered grapeseed
   or sunflower oil

Chill a blender beaker in the freezer for at least 15 minutes.

Line a fine-mesh sieve with cheesecloth or a coffee filter and set over a medium bowl.

CHILE OIL

Rinse the fir tips well and then thoroughly dry them.

In the chilled blender, combine the fir tips and oil and blend on high speed just until the oil turns light green. Do not overblend or the oil will heat up, which can destroy the aroma and the color. Pour the oil into the prepared sieve and immediately refrigerate the setup. Leave the oil in the refrigerator to strain slowly, about 3 hours.

Discard any solids and transfer the oil to an opaque container. Refrigerate for up to 1 month.

Hot-Processed Infused Oils

Some ingredients release their aroma into oil best when gently heated. Peppers only truly show their full potential when cooked in oil or fat. Chile oil made from dried peppers is so flavorful that it is almost more of a sauce than a garnish. Be careful that the temperature is not too high, as this can compromise the flavor and color of the oil. The ideal temperature to infuse the ingredients into the oil in these recipes is 175°F/80°C. If you are concerned that even at the lowest setting the heat is too high, slip a heat diffuser under the pan.

Caraway Oil

Makes 1 cup/240ml

1 cup filtered grapeseed or
  sunflower oil
2 tbsp caraway seeds, toasted
  and ground → 30

Line a fine-mesh sieve with cheesecloth or a coffee filter and set over a medium bowl.

Add the oil to a medium pan on the stove top. A gentle pilot light on a gas stove should provide enough heat, or turn the burner to the lowest setting. Heat until the oil reaches 175°F/80°C. Hold at this temperature for 10 minutes and then remove from the heat. Add the caraway seeds. Let the oil cool to room temperature.

Strain the oil through the prepared sieve and discard the solids. Transfer the oil to an airtight container and refrigerate for up to 1 month.

Sweet or Spicy Chile Oil

Makes 2 cups/480 ml

½ cup/90 g hot or sweet paprika
  flakes, depending on the
  amount of spice you like → 42,
  toasted
6 garlic cloves, crushed
2 cups/480 ml filtered grapeseed
  or sunflower oil

FENNEL
OIL

the oil to an airtight container and refrigerate for up to 1 month.

Fennel Oil

Makes 2 cups/480 ml

1 fennel bulb, fronds reserved, bulb julienned

2 tbsp fennel seeds, toasted and ground → 31

2 cups/480 ml filtered grapeseed or sunflower oil

2 tbsp dried fennel flowers, powdered → 33

Preheat the oven to 175°F/80°C, or use an induction burner. In a medium baking dish, or a small pot if using an induction burner, combine the fennel fronds and julienned bulb, fennel seeds, and oil, distributing the ingredients evenly. Cover and cook until the oil is aromatic and infused with the flavor of the fennel, about 4 hours. Remove from the heat and stir in the fennel powder. Let the oil cool to room temperature.

Line a fine-mesh sieve with cheesecloth or a coffee filter and set over a medium bowl.

Strain the oil through the prepared sieve and discard the solids. Transfer the oil to an airtight container and refrigerate for up to 1 month.

Add the paprika flakes, garlic, and oil to a medium pan on the stove top. A gentle pilot light on a gas stove should provide enough heat, or turn the burner to the lowest setting. Heat until the oil reaches 175°F/80°C. Hold at this temperature for 10 minutes and then remove from the heat. At this point the paprika and garlic should be aromatic. Let the oil cool to room temperature.

Line a fine-mesh sieve with cheesecloth or a coffee filter and set over a medium bowl.

Process the oil with the paprika flakes and garlic in a blender at high speed until puréed. Strain the oil through the prepared sieve and discard the solids. Transfer

Sunchoke Oil

Makes 2 cups/480 ml

5 lb/2.3 kg sunchokes, grated
2 cups/480 ml filtered grapeseed
  or sunflower oil

Preheat the oven to 175°F/80°C, or use an induction burner. In a medium baking dish, or a small pot if using an induction burner, combine the sunchokes and oil, distributing the sunchokes evenly. Cover and cook until the oil is aromatic and infused with the flavor of the sunchokes, about 12 hours. Let the oil cool to room temperature.

Line a fine-mesh sieve with cheesecloth or a coffee filter and set over a medium bowl.

Strain the oil through the prepared sieve and discard the solids. Transfer the oil to an airtight container and refrigerate for up to 1 month.

Pork Fat Chile Oil

Makes 2 cups/480 ml

1 cup/240 g lard → 93
1 cup/240 ml filtered grapeseed
  or sunflower oil
¼ cup/45 g Hatch chile flakes
  → 42 or green padrón flakes
6 garlic cloves, crushed

Add the lard, oil, chile flakes, and garlic to a medium pan on the stove top. A gentle pilot light on a gas stove should provide enough heat, or turn the burner to the lowest setting. Heat until the chile flakes release their flavor and color, about 25 minutes. Let the oil cool to room temperature.

Line a fine-mesh sieve with cheesecloth or a coffee filter and set over a medium bowl.

Strain the oil through the prepared sieve and discard the solids. Transfer the oil to an airtight container and refrigerate for up to 1 month. Bring to room temperature before using.

Garlic Oil

Makes 2 cups/480 ml

20 garlic cloves, crushed
2 cups/480 ml filtered grapeseed
  or sunflower oil

Add the garlic and oil to a medium pan over low heat and warm gently until the garlic is tender, about 30 minutes. Let the oil cool to room temperature.

Line a fine-mesh sieve with cheesecloth or a coffee filter and set over a medium bowl.

Strain the oil through the prepared sieve, reserving the garlic cloves for another use. Transfer the oil to an airtight container and refrigerate for up to 1 month.

GARLIC OIL

BAR TARTINE

Animal Fats

Over the past couple of generations, animal fats, like schmaltz (rendered chicken or goose fat) and lard (rendered pork fat), became symbols of gluttony and the epitome of unhealthful eating. They are coming back into fashion, and their reputations have been restored as good-for-you, flavorful ingredients. Rightly so.

Schmaltz (Rendered Poultry Fat)

Our appreciation for schmaltz is probably related to Cortney's fond memories of her mother making chopped liver with her grandmother's hand-cranked meat grinder. To get the process rolling, her mom would make schmaltz and *gribenes* (onions and crisp chicken skin) to give the chopped liver its flavor. Schmaltz is a delicious cooking fat, making it a good choice for frying onions, wilting greens, or adding to a soup.

Makes about 1 cup/225 g

1 lb/455 g chicken, goose, or duck fat and skin, chopped with a knife or coarsely ground in a meat grinder

¼ cup/60 ml water

In a cast-iron skillet or heavy-bottomed saucepan over low heat, combine the fat and skin with the water. Cook just until the fat begins to melt, about 15 minutes. Increase the heat to medium-low and continue to cook until the fat has rendered and the liquid is clear, about 2 hours. Any bits of chicken left in the pan should not brown, as the fat will take on a burnt flavor if it cooks at too high of a temperature. (If they start to brown, add a bit more water and lower the heat.)

Line a fine-mesh sieve with cheesecloth or a coffee filter and set over a medium bowl.

Strain the fat through the prepared sieve, reserving the solids for another use. Let cool, then transfer to a jar with a tight-fitting lid and refrigerate for up to 1 month.

Lard (Rendered Pork Fat)

Mangalitsa, a curly haired pig raised primarily for the production of lard, is a Hungarian favorite. They are so fatty, it's not uncommon for a 250-lb/115-kg animal to yield just 65 lb/30 kg of lean meat. We sometimes get Mangalitsa pigs from George and Gar House, Hungarian-American hog farmers who also grow walnuts just a few hours east of San Francisco, near the town of Winters.

Most homes in Hungary have a lard pot in the cupboard, keeping it supple and spreadable. You can do the same, leaving small amounts at room temperature so you are at the ready for that warm slice of bread just waiting to be slathered with pork fat. We use this in the Celery Root Cake → 244 and for the Pork Fat Chile Oil → 91.

Makes 1½ cups/340 g

1 lb/455 g pork fat, chopped with a knife or coarsely ground in a meat grinder

¼ cup/60 ml water

In a cast-iron skillet or heavy-bottomed saucepan over low heat, combine the fat with the water. Cook just until the fat begins to melt, about 15 minutes. Increase the heat to medium-low and continue to cook until the fat has rendered and the liquid is clear, about 2 hours. Any bits of pork left in the pan should not brown, as the fat will take on a burnt flavor if it cooks at too high of a temperature. (If they start to brown, add a bit more water and lower the heat.)

Line a fine-mesh sieve with cheesecloth or a coffee filter and set over a medium bowl.

Strain the fat through the prepared sieve, reserving the solids.

Let cool, then transfer to a jar with a tight-fitting lid and refrigerate for up to 1 month.

Whipped Cured Pork Fatback

In Hungary, whipped or rendered lard is spread on toast and served with onions and paprika powder → 306. *Zsíros Kenyér*, as it is called, is one of Hungary's most popular snacks. We like to cure pork fatback with salt to develop its flavor, and later we whip it before spreading it on toast.

Makes 2 cups/445 g

1 lb/455 g slab of cured pork fatback (→ 61), chopped with a knife or coarsely ground in a meat grinder

Bring the fat to room temperature, transfer to a food processor, and whip to a smooth paste. Pass the whipped fat through a fine-mesh sieve to remove any sinew. Transfer to an airtight container and refrigerate for up to 1 month.

Tallow (Rendered Beef Fat)

The beauty of rendered beef fat, or tallow, is its ability to make vegetables taste meaty without adding actual animal protein. We particularly like tallow for any dish with a beef component: for the sauce that accompanies our beef tartare → 282, for frying potatoes and wilting greens to accompany steak, for cooking mushrooms and eggs, and for poaching cabbage for pairing with corned beef. In our gai lan with air-dried beef → 286, we pour tallow over the vegetable just before serving.

Makes 1½ cups/335 g

1 lb/455 g fresh beef fat, chopped with a knife or coarsely ground in a meat grinder

¼ cup/60 ml water

In a cast-iron skillet or heavy-bottomed stockpot over low heat, combine the fat with the water. Cook just until the fat begins to melt, about 15 minutes. Increase the heat to medium-low and continue to cook until the fat has rendered and the liquid is clear, about 2 hours. Any bits of beef left in the pan should not brown, as the fat will take on a burnt flavor if it cooks at too high a temperature. (If they start to brown, add a bit more water and lower the heat.)

Line a fine-mesh sieve with cheesecloth or a coffee filter and set over a medium bowl.

Strain the fat through the prepared sieve. Let cool, then transfer to a jar with a tight-fitting lid and refrigerate for up to 1 month.

VINEGARS

Almost anything that contains convertible sugars can be made into vinegar. It is the process of turning sugar into alcohol and alcohol into acetic acid.

The following is what you will need to get started making your own vinegars, accompanied by recipes for some of our favorites.

We make our vinegar in flip-top bottles, canning jars, or 5-gl/19-L carboys. Use the size that suits your needs, keeping in mind that all containers must be nonreactive and airtight.

Vinegar Starter

There are several options for starting a fresh batch of vinegar. You can purchase a vinegar starter or culture, known as a "mother," from a home brew shop; you can use raw (unpasteurized, unfiltered) vinegar; or you can use vinegar saved from a previous batch. Sometimes we forgo the starter altogether and let nature take its course. This usually works just as well.

Making Vinegar

Vinegar always begins with a base of alcohol. There is the option to start with a pre-fermented base of wine, beer, spirits, or sake. Alternatively, the alcoholic base can be made instead of purchased by using juice, sugar, fruit scraps, beer mash, or sake mash and then allowing it to ferment.

To turn an alcoholic base into vinegar, pour the mixture into a wide-mouthed container, filling it three-fourths full. If using a vinegar starter, add it at this stage. Cover the open rim with cheesecloth; oxygen is vital for this part of the fermentation. Leave the top uncapped, as it needs oxygen to sour. Let stand in a dark spot at room temperature, between 68° and 72°F/20° and 22°C, tasting every week or so, until the vinegar is acidified to your liking, 2 to 4 months. When the acidity is where you like it, cap the bottle and continue to age at room temperature to mellow the acidity, about 6 months or so, before using. The vinegar will keep at room temperature indefinitely. If a mass forms, discard it; it is a harmless by-product of the fermentation process. Always start with good-quality ingredients. Bad wine and bland fruit do not make delicious vinegar. The same is true with beer; we avoid hoppy beers as hops can inhibit the fermentation process.

Fruit Scrap Vinegar

Makes 1 qt/960 ml

3 tbsp fermented honey → 121
   or honey
4 cups/960 ml warm water
1 to 2 lb/455 to 910 g fruit scraps,
   peels, and cores
2 tbsp vinegar starter (optional)

Dissolve the honey in the water and add the fruit scraps. Put the mixture into an airtight container with an airlock and let stand at cool room temperature (60° to 68°F/16° to 20°C) until it ferments and tastes tangy and slightly alcoholic, 5 to 10 days. if you don't have a container with an airlock, use a canning jar and release the pressure by opening the lid a couple times a day.

Strain the solids and return the liquid to the container. To turn an alcoholic base into a vinegar, proceed as directed.

Apple or Pear Cider Vinegar

Apple and pear vinegars are easy to make and ever useful to have around the kitchen. Start with tart, sweet, and aromatic fruit for the best end results.

Makes 1 qt/960 ml

4 cups/ 960 ml apple or pear
   juice (see Juicing → 129)
¼ cup/60 ml vinegar starter
   (optional)

Put the juice into an airtight container with an airlock and let stand at cool room temperature (60° to 68°F/16° to 20°C) until it ferments and tastes tangy and slightly alcoholic, 5 to 10 days. If you don't have a container with an airlock, use a canning jar and release the pressure by opening the lid a couple times a day. At this point, the juice will have become semi-soft cider.

To turn an alcoholic base into a vinegar, proceed as directed.

Wine Vinegar

Makes 1 qt/960 ml

4 cups/960 ml red, white, or
   fortified wine
2 tbsp vinegar starter (optional)

To turn an alcoholic base into a vinegar, proceed as directed.

DILL FLOWER
VINEGAR

Rice Vinegar

You can make rice vinegar from sake or, if you're feeling ambitious, you can make your own fermented rice beverage using rice koji as the base → **123**.

Makes 1 qt/960 ml

4 cups/ 960 ml sake
2 tbsp vinegar starter

To turn an alcoholic base into a vinegar, proceed as directed → **95**.

Infused Vinegars

Rice vinegar has a neutral flavor and mild acidity that's ideal for making infusions. Infused vinegars can be stored indefinitely in sealed containers at room temperature or in the refrigerator.

Marjoram Vinegar

Use vibrant young marjoram to capture the sweet nuances of the herb.

Makes 2 cups/480 ml

2 cups/480 ml rice vinegar → **98**
Leaves from 2 bunches fresh marjoram

Malt Vinegar

Buy a beer you like to drink and allow it to sour. It's a simple way to experiment with many different beers to see the difference in flavors you can create.

Makes 1 qt/960 ml

4 cups/960 ml unhopped or
lightly hopped beer
2 tbsp vinegar starter (optional)

To turn an alcoholic base into a vinegar, proceed as directed → **95**.

In a 1-qt/960-ml jar, combine the vinegar and marjoram. Cover and let stand at cool room temperature until the vinegar has taken on the flavor of the herb, about 3 weeks.

Strain through a fine-mesh sieve, transfer to an airtight container, and store at room temperature indefinitely.

Dill Flower Vinegar

Just before dill plants go to seed, they are flush with vibrant yellow flowers. The blossoms have the bright flavor that we associate with dill and a hint of caraway aroma.

Makes 2 cups/480 ml

2 cups/480 ml rice vinegar → **98**
2 to 3 handfuls of dill
    flower clusters

In a 1-qt/960-ml jar, combine the vinegar and flowers. Cover and let stand at cool room temperature until the vinegar has taken on the flavor of the herb, about 3 weeks.

Strain through a fine-mesh sieve, transfer to an airtight container, and store at room temperature indefinitely.

Elderflower Vinegar

Elderflowers make a beautiful yellow vinegar with floral and fruity flavors—a great "drinking vinegar." The stems of the flowers are mildly toxic, so be sure to use only the blooms. For a refreshing beverage, sweeten the vinegar with fermented honey → **121** or fig leaf syrup → **129** to taste. Add ¼ cup/60 ml sweetened vinegar to 1 cup/240 ml sparkling water and serve over ice.

Makes 2 cups/480 ml

2 cups/480 ml rice vinegar → **98**
2 to 3 handfuls of
    elderflower clusters

In a 1-qt/960-ml jar, combine the vinegar and flowers. Cover and let stand at cool room temperature until the vinegar has taken on the flavor of the flowers, about 3 weeks.

Strain through a fine-mesh sieve, transfer to an airtight container, and store at room temperature indefinitely.

Mushroom Vinegar

We first made this vinegar in an attempt to layer even more earthy flavor into our Smoked Potatoes → **226**.

MUSHROOM VINEGAR

Yield 2 cups/480 ml

3 cups/620 ml rice vinegar → **98**
1 cup/25 g assorted dried
    mushrooms, such as porcini,
    chanterelle, shiitake, black
    trumpet, and/or white button

In a small saucepan over low heat, combine the vinegar and mushrooms. Bring to a simmer, cover, and steep gently for 20 minutes. Remove from the heat and let stand covered at room temperature to infuse for 24 hours.

Strain through a fine-mesh sieve. Discard the mushrooms or reserve to use in a salad or stew. Transfer the vinegar to an airtight container and store at room temperature indefinitely.

PICKLES & PRESERVES

We use two basic pickling mediums, salt brine and vinegar brine. The vegetables we preserve in salt brines are soured naturally by lactic acid fermentation, a process that begins immediately and continues until no sugar remains to be converted, producing flavorful, probiotic-rich, raw pickles. Foods preserved by vinegar rely on acetic acid alone, created in a previous fermentation, and can be ready to eat within an hour. Both techniques result in delicious but very different products.

The Basics

Just about any glass or ceramic container can be used as a fermentation crock or for storing vinegar pickles. Food-grade plastic vessels are good, too. Avoid metal containers, however, as they can react with the salt and acid that are present. Most pickles can be stored in a refrigerator indefinitely. Textures and flavors will change slightly as the pickles age.

When filling the jars for aging in the refrigerator, it is best to fill them as close to the top as possible. The less air in the top of the jar, the less chance mold will form. A simple setup of a plate and a weight will keep them submerged.

Brine Ferments

We use a basic ratio of 1 tbsp salt to 1 cup/240 ml water. For dry salting, we start with 2.5 percent salt by weight. Some vegetables need more salt after a bit of time in the fermenter; you'll just have to taste them to know if more should be added. The vegetables should seem slightly salty at first. As time passes, that salinity will wane and the flavors will mature.

At the restaurant, we use 8-gl/30-L beer fermenters fitted with airlocks to keep the oxygen out while allowing the carbon dioxide to escape, and ceramic crocks outfitted with a water-trough or airlock-lid system. Containers with airlocks are not necessary as long as the pickles are monitored closely for mold growth while souring. The less air space at the top of the pickle container the better, so use the smallest pickling vessel possible when brine fermenting.

Brine-fermented foods must be completely submerged in liquid to keep mold from forming, so a weight of some type is necessary. Some specialty crocks come with weights. Otherwise, select a plate that fits snugly in your container and top it with a jar of water, clean rock, or other weight of similar heft. A plastic bag filled with salted water will also do the job, and if the bag breaks, your brine won't be diluted. Once the weight is in place, secure the lid of your container to keep as much oxygen out as possible.

Although it may look unpleasant, mold that forms on the surface of a brine is almost always harmless and can simply be skimmed away with a clean utensil. Molds develop primarily because of too much exposure to oxygen, a too-warm environment, or a brine that's not salty enough. Keeping food submerged in brine helps keep mold to a minimum and makes it easier to skim it off when it appears.

With salt brines, once fermentation gets under way, the brine will change from clear to cloudy, and natural yeasts will settle on the bottom of the vessel. These changes are natural and are not cause for alarm.

We never pour a leftover salt brine down the drain (except for brines used to extract tannins, like the one for pickled green walnuts, → 114). You can use leftover brines to start a new batch of fermented pickles (you might need to add a

bit more salt), or you can add just a splash or two to jump-start the process of a new batch. Leftover salt brine can also be used in salad dressings or to add extra acidity to stewed sauerkraut → **292**.

Vinegar Pickles

We don't use a set ratio for vinegar brines. Each recipe is unique to the ingredient to be processed. Refrigerate in airtight containers. Mold can develop on exposed vinegar pickles.

Pickled Hot Peppers

Nick's family is from Michigan. They all have gardens and they all grow incredible peppers. His uncle Joe in particular makes a large batch of pickled peppers every year, just as his father, John, did. Some of them invariably make their way to San Francisco, where we eat them straight out of the jar. This is a simple vinegar pickle recipe, but there is no better way to preserve peppers when they are good. No matter how many times we try to replicate this recipe in California, our pickled peppers—though delicious— don't taste like those from

Michigan. Sometimes we make these with only green jalapeños, sometimes with hot Hungarian wax peppers. Any pepper will work, so use what is available.

Makes 4 qt/3.8 L

2 cups/480 ml water

4 cups/960 ml distilled white vinegar

7 tbsp/90 g sugar

½ cup/70 g kosher salt

5 lb/2.3 kg hot peppers, stem ends removed

1 tbsp black peppercorns

1 tbsp coriander seeds

1 tbsp mustard seeds

4 bunches dill

12 garlic cloves, crushed

PICKLED MUSHROOMS

In a large nonreactive saucepan, combine the water, vinegar, sugar, and salt over medium-high heat and warm to just under a boil, stirring to dissolve the sugar and salt.

Divide and pack the peppers into two 2-qt/2-L glass canning jars. Divide the peppercorns, coriander seeds, mustard seeds, dill, and garlic evenly between the jars. Pour the hot brine over the peppers and secure the lids. Let cool on a countertop and refrigerate for up to 6 months.

Pickled Mushrooms

We see versions of these pickles in Russian markets and in Italian delis. Both types are equally addictive. We make our version with lots of paprika, which gives it a strong Hungarian accent. The draw of this dish is the combination of the savory garlic-laced paste that coats the outside and the sweet-and-sour, almost-creamy-textured inside of the button mushroom. This pickle is great to have on the table with all kinds of meals and with the Liptauer dip **→ 222**.

Makes 1½ pt/675 ml

1 lb/455 g button mushrooms

2 tbsp filtered sunflower or grapeseed oil

3 tsp kosher salt

¼ cup/60 ml red wine vinegar **→ 95**

2 garlic cloves, minced

1 tbsp chopped fresh flat-leaf parsley

1 tbsp chopped fresh marjoram or 1 tsp dried marjoram **→ 31**

2 tbsp sweet paprika **→ 42**, powdered

1 tbsp light brown sugar

2 tsp sweet onion powder **→ 34**

1 tsp garlic powder **→ 37**

Minced zest of 1 lemon

1 tsp freshly ground black pepper

Preheat the oven to 350°F/180°C. In a large roasting pan, combine the mushrooms with 1 tbsp of the oil and 1½ tsp of the salt and toss to coat. Roast until tender, about 10 minutes.

In a large bowl, combine the vinegar, garlic, parsley, marjoram, paprika, brown sugar, onion powder, garlic powder, lemon zest, pepper, and the remaining 1½ tsp salt and mix well. Add the warm mushrooms and stir and toss to coat the mushrooms evenly. Chill the mushrooms completely in the refrigerator before serving, about 2 hours. Transfer the mushrooms and brine to one or more nonreactive containers and refrigerate for up to 1 month.

Escabeche

This recipe was inspired by the humble taqueria pickles found throughout the Mission district in San Francisco. *Escabeche* is the name for these charred pickled vegetables that you can scoop up yourself from the salsa bar, eating as much as you want. It is usually a mix of carrots, onion, jalapeño, and marjoram, although there are many variations.

Makes 2 qt/515 g

2 cups/480 ml distilled white vinegar

2 cups/480 ml water

5 tbsp/65 g sugar

5 tbsp/45 g salt

4 shallots

8 garlic cloves

2 green serrano chiles, stemmed

1-in/2.5-cm piece fresh ginger, peeled and minced

6 baby carrots, halved lengthwise

1 fennel bulb, cored and cut into wedges

12 baby turnips, trimmed and halved

12 red radishes, trimmed and halved

1 sweet white onion, cut into ¼-in/6-mm rounds

Marjoram oil → 87 for garnish

1 tbsp fresh marjoram leaves for garnish

In a large nonreactive saucepan, combine the vinegar, water, sugar, and salt over medium-high heat and warm to just under a boil, stirring to dissolve the sugar and salt. Let the brine cool to room temperature.

In a blender or food processor combine the shallots, garlic, and chiles with a couple spoonfuls of the brine, just enough to get the mixture moving, and process until a coarse paste forms. Stir the paste and the ginger into the remaining brine. Cover and refrigerate until ready to use.

Heat a cast-iron skillet over medium-high heat. Add the carrots, cut-side down, and top with another heavy pan or

ESCABECHE

OVERGROWN GARDEN PICKLES

Turn to this recipe in late summer when your garden goes into overdrive or when there is a deal on the ugly but delicious vegetables at the farmers' market. It's a simple technique that can be used for almost any vegetable, resulting in a glut of pickles to enjoy well into the winter months.

Makes 3 gl/11.5 L

Enough whole vegetables, such as cucumbers (flower ends removed), summer squash, onions, carrots, beets, green tomatoes, green beans, and/or sunchokes, to fill a 3-gl/11.5-L container

2 cups/280 g kosher salt

8 qt/7.5 L water

8 garlic cloves

4 shallots, peeled

5 serrano or jalapeño chiles, or any hot chiles from the garden, stemmed

2 bunches fresh dill

Fresh herbs sprigs, such as basil, tarragon, parsley, or marjoram, for garnish

Fennel oil → 90 or extra-virgin olive oil for garnish

Put all of the vegetables in a 3-gl/11.5-L nonreactive container. In a separate nonreactive container, dissolve the salt in the water to make a brine. Transfer about 2 cups/480 ml of the

similar weight. Cook until the cut side of the carrots begins to brown lightly, about 60 seconds. Transfer to a flat plate to cool quickly and to stop the cooking process. Repeat with the fennel bulb, turnips, radishes, and onion. Move the cooled vegetables to a nonreactive container and pour in the brine, immersing the vegetables. Cool to room temperature. Marinate for 1 hour before eating.

When ready to eat, transfer the vegetables to a serving bowl with some of the brine. Garnish with the marjoram oil → 87 and fresh marjoram leaves and serve. The escabeche tastes best the day it is made, but it will keep submerged in brine, covered, and refrigerated for up to 1 month.

brine to a blender; add the garlic, shallots, and chiles; and process on high speed until homogenized. Pour the purée into the remaining salt brine and stir to mix well. Add the dill bunches to the vegetables, then pour the brine over them. Top the vegetables with a weight to keep them submerged in the brine. Seal the container, using a lid with an airlock, if you have one. If you have sealed it without an airlock, open the container every few days or so to release carbon dioxide buildup, and check for mold. Place in a clean, well-protected, low-light area with an ambient temperature of 60° to 68°F/16° to 20°C until the pickles taste sour, about 1 month. Refrigerate for up to 1 year.

To serve, slice the pickles into bite-size pieces and return them to the brine. Refrigerate until serving, for up to 1 year. We like to garnish these pickles with torn garden herbs and fennel oil.

Brined Beets

Earthy, sweet, salty, and sour, pickled beets are among our favorite pickles. To serve the beets, cut them into wedges and top with chopped dill, chopped green onion, and sour cream. They are also delicious bathed in buttermilk dressing → 186.

Makes 2 qt/545 g

1 tsp black peppercorns, toasted and ground → 30
1 tsp coriander seeds, toasted and ground → 30
1 star anise pod, toasted and ground → 30
1 tsp brown mustard seeds, toasted and ground → 30
1 tsp fennel seeds, toasted and ground → 30
1 bay leaf
3 lb/1.4 kg red beets, peeled
1 bunch fresh dill
1 cup/140 g kosher salt
4 qt/3.8 L water
6 garlic cloves
1 shallot
1 green serrano chile, stemmed

Place the peppercorns, coriander seeds, star anise, mustard seeds, fennel seeds, and bay leaf in a pouch made of cheesecloth. Add to a 2-gl/7.5-L nonreactive container along with the beets and dill. In a separate nonreactive container, dissolve the salt in the water to make a brine. Transfer about 1 cup/240 ml of the brine to a blender; add the garlic, shallot, and chile; and process on high speed until homogenized. Pour the purée into the remaining salt brine and stir to mix well. Pour over the beets and seasonings and top with a weight to keep the beets submerged in the brine. Seal the container, using a lid with an airlock, if you have

BRINED BEETS

one. If you have sealed it without an airlock, open the container every few days or so to release carbon dioxide buildup, and check for mold. Place in a clean, well-protected, low-light area with an ambient temperature of 60° to 68°F/16° to 20°C until the beets taste sour, about 1 month.

Transfer the beets and brine to one or more nonreactive airtight containers and refrigerate for up to 1 year.

BRINED RAMPS AND CHIVES

Brined Ramps

We believe in the importance of supporting local farms and limiting our menu to ingredients grown close to home. That said, there is a handful of ingredients that we just can't live without: Japanese kombu (kelp), sour cherries and ramps from Michigan, and the roe from grey mullet that Nick's uncle catches in Florida.

Ramps are not cultivated and their season, which is usually in April, is short, so processing time is limited. We love the unique young onion and gentle garlic aroma of these wild onions and ferment mountains of them each year. The flavor is irreplaceable. Most of our ramps now go into the ramp mayonnaise that we serve with our Smoked Potatoes → **226**. If you cannot get ramps, use

Chinese garlic chives, fermenting them in exactly the same manner.

Makes 3 pt/550 g

3 tbsp kosher salt
2 cups/480 ml water
2 lb/910 g ramps, root ends trimmed

In a nonreactive container, dissolve the salt in the water to make a brine. Add the ramps and top with a weight to keep them submerged in the brine. Seal the container, using a lid with an airlock, if you have one. If you have sealed it without an airlock, open the container every few days

or so to release carbon dioxide buildup, and check for mold. Place in a clean, well-protected, low-light area with an ambient temperature of 60° to 68°F/16° to 20°C until the ramps taste sour, 3 to 4 weeks.

Transfer the ramps and brine to one or more nonreactive airtight containers and refrigerate for up to 1 year. Their flavor becomes less intense and more nuanced as they age. We like them best after about 6 months.

BRINED CARROTS

Brined Carrots

The combination of sweet young carrots, green garlic, and late-winter Meyer lemons showcases the transition from winter to spring.

Makes 4 qt/2 kg

4 oz/115 g green garlic, stalks and bulbs, trimmed of any yellow outer leaves

2 Meyer lemons

3 lb /1.4 kg baby carrots, tops trimmed with ½ in/12 mm of the stem attached

½ cup/70 g kosher salt

2 qt/2 L water

Cut the green garlic into small rounds about ¼ in/6 mm thick. Put the garlic slices in a colander and submerge in water to rid them of any sand, dirt, or debris trapped in the layers. Drain the slices and reserve.

Using a vegetable peeler, cut the zest from the lemons in long strips and reserve. Halve the lemons, squeeze out the juice, and reserve the juice.

Place the carrots, garlic, lemon zest, and lemon juice in a 2-gl/ 7.5-L nonreactive container. In a separate nonreactive container, dissolve the salt in the water to make a brine. Pour the brine over the carrots and seasonings and top with a weight to keep the carrots submerged in the brine. Seal the container, using a lid with an airlock, if you have one. If you have sealed it without an airlock, open the container every few days or so to release carbon dioxide buildup, and check for mold. Place in a clean, well-protected, low-light area with an ambient temperature of 60° to 68°F/16° to 20°C until the carrots taste sour, about 3 weeks.

Transfer the carrots and brine to one or more nonreactive airtight containers and refrigerate for up to 1 year.

Brined Mustard Greens

Our sous chef Harry grew up eating pickled mustard greens with beef tendon, which his dad, who was born in Laos, makes by the bucketful. Harry brings some back whenever he goes home to Sacramento for a visit. In this recipe, the mustard greens are brine-pickled and the optional tendon is cooked separately, then added to the already pickled greens, thereby pickling the tendon, too. Serve it with spicy chile oil → **89** or with some sticky rice, chipotle paste → **119**, and grilled sausage.

Makes 4 qt/2.4 kg

BRINED MUSTARD
GREENS

MUSTARD GREENS

6 tbsp/50 g kosher salt

2 cups/480 ml water

4 lb/910 g small Chinese mustard greens, *gai choy*, left whole

1-in/2.5-cm piece fresh ginger, peeled and thinly sliced

4 garlic cloves, grated

2 green serrano chiles, stemmed and minced

BEEF TENDON

1 tbsp kosher salt

4 cups/960 ml beef broth → **142**, or water

8 oz/225 g beef tendon

To ferment the mustard greens: In a nonreactive container, dissolve the salt in the water to make a brine. Add the mustard greens, ginger, garlic, and chiles and top with a weight to keep them submerged in the brine. Seal the container, using a lid with an airlock, if you have one. If you have sealed it without an airlock, open the container every few days or so to release carbon dioxide buildup, and check for mold. Place in a clean, well-protected, low-light area with an ambient temperature of 60° to 68°F/16° to 20°C until the greens taste sour, 3 to 4 weeks.

Transfer the greens and brine to one or more nonreactive airtight containers and refrigerate for up to 1 year. The flavor becomes less intense and more nuanced as the greens age. We like it best after at least 1 month.

To ferment the beef tendon: Once the mustard greens have soured for 3 to 4 weeks, prepare the beef tendon. Preheat the oven to 300°F/150°C. In an oven-proof pot with a lid or a deep baking dish, dissolve the salt in the broth. Add the beef, cover, place in the oven, and braise until very tender, about 5 hours.

Remove the tendon from the broth, reserve the broth for another use, and let the tendon cool, refrigerated, for at least 3 hours, until firm. Cut the tendon into slices ¼ in/6 mm thick.

Mix the tendon into the mustard greens, distributing the slices evenly, and refrigerate for 5 days before using. Taste the beef; it should taste slightly sour and salty. It will keep, refrigerated, for up to 2 weeks.

Brined Green Beans

This pickle came about in an attempt to re-create a pickle we had at a favorite local Chinese restaurant. We immersed the beans in a salt brine with no additional ingredients to mask the flavor and the results were incredible. They have a green, Castelvetrano olive flavor that is great in salads (see Tomato and Pickled Green Bean Salad with Whipped Feta **→ 190**), or served with chile oil **→ 89** and shichimi togarashi **→ 53** as a condiment to eat with steamed rice.

Makes 6 cups/1.2 kg

BRINED GREEN BEANS

3 tbsp kosher salt
3 cups/720 ml water
1 lb/455 g green beans, trimmed and sliced into rings ⅛ in/3 mm thick

In a nonreactive container, dissolve the salt in the water to make a brine. Add the green beans and top with a weight to keep them submerged in the brine. Seal the container, using a lid with an airlock, if you have one. If you have sealed it without an airlock, open the container every few days or so to release carbon dioxide buildup, and check for mold. Place in a clean, well-protected, low-light area with an ambient temperature of 60° to 68°F/16° to 20°C until the beans taste sour, about 3 weeks.

BEEF TENDON WITH BRINED MUSTARD GREENS

Transfer the beans and brine to one or more nonreactive airtight containers and refrigerate for up to 1 year.

Sauerkraut

At Bar Tartine, we process truck-loads of cabbage each year. Each batch of sauerkraut starts with about 300 lb/135 kg of cabbage, which take two people one evening to clean, shred, pound, and pack into buckets, and another couple of months to sour to the point that we like to serve it.

Some batches are soured with caraway and juniper berries. Sometimes we grate in fresh wasabi grown in Half Moon Bay, California, for a spicy condiment. Several times every year we make a batch of red-cabbage kraut, adding locally grown young ginger. Save the outer leaves from the cabbage to brine and use with charred pepper paste → 113.

Makes 1 qt/740 g

7 tbsp/60 g kosher salt
5 lb/2.3 kg cabbage, cored and
    thinly sliced crosswise

In a large bowl, massage the salt into the cabbage. Pack the cabbage into a crock or nonreactive jar. It may take several hours for the cabbage to release enough liquid to submerge the solids.

When the liquid nears the top of the cabbage, top with a weight to keep it submerged in brine. (Some cabbage contains more moisture than others; dryer cabbage may not expel enough liquid to cover the top. In this case add a bit of brine—1 tbsp kosher salt per 1 cup/240 ml water.) Seal the container, using a lid with an air-lock, if you have one. If you have sealed it without an airlock, open the container every few days or so to release carbon dioxide buildup, and check for mold. Place in a clean, well-protected, low-light area with an ambient temperature of 60° to 68°F/ 16°C to 20°C until the cabbage tastes quite sour, about 1 month.

It is up to you as to when you move the cabbage to the refrigerator, which will slow the souring and keep the cabbage crunchier. We often let it sour for more than 2 months before serving. Pack the sauerkraut into jars with lids and refrigerate for up to 1 year.

Sauerkraut-Stuffed Peppers

Stuffed peppers are seen in markets and homes all over Hungary. A summer delicacy, they are often displayed near the front of shop windows, usually among a variety of different-colored pickled vegetables. The Great Market Hall, the large central market of Budapest, is a good place to see them in abundance. Here, we have combined our house-made sauerkraut with vinegar-pickled sweet peppers to yield a pickle that works as a side dish or a snack eaten straight from the jar.

Makes 15 stuffed peppers

4 cups/960 ml distilled white
    vinegar
4 cups/960 ml water
⅔ cup/130 g sugar
⅔ cup/100 g kosher salt
15 small red sweet peppers,
    such as Cherry Bomb or round
    paprika
About 2 cups/275 g drained
    sauerkraut → 111

In a large nonreactive saucepan over medium-high heat, combine the vinegar, water, sugar, and salt and warm to just under a boil, stirring to dissolve the sugar and salt. Let the brine cool to room temperature.

Using a paring knife, cut out the stem from the top of each pepper to make a small opening. Gently scrape out the seeds and ribs, taking care not to tear the peppers. Put them in a non-reactive container with a tight-fitting lid and pour in the cooled brine. Top the peppers with a weight to keep them submerged in the brine, and refrigerate for 24 hours. This step will pickle the

SAUERKRAUT-STUFFED PEPPERS

peppers and make them pliable, and easier to stuff.

Drain the peppers, reserving the peppers and brine separately. Stuff the peppers with the sauerkraut. Return them to the container, pour in the brine, and top the peppers with a weight to keep them submerged in the brine and refrigerate for 2 days before serving.

Transfer the peppers and brine to one or more nonreactive airtight containers and refrigerate for up to 1 year.

Brussels Kraut

Fermenting whole Brussels sprouts preserves them far beyond their season. Our guests are always surprised when we have Brussels sprouts on the menu in July. This recipe gives them a sour flavor and retains their crunchy texture. They are great as a fresh pickle eaten on their own or in a salad, but we like them best cooked into soups (see Warm Beet Soup with Smoked Brisket and Brussels Kraut → 162).

Makes 6 qt/4.46 kg

¾ cup/100 g kosher salt
3 qt/720 ml cold water

2 lb/910 g Brussels sprouts, butts trimmed

In an 8-qt/7.5-L nonreactive container, dissolve the salt in the water to make a brine. Add the Brussels sprouts and top with a weight to keep them submerged. Seal the container, using a lid with an airlock, if you have one. If you have sealed it without an airlock, open the container every few days or so to release carbon dioxide buildup, and check for mold. Place in a clean, well-protected, low-light area with an ambient temperature of 60° to 68°F/16° to 20°C until

CABBAGE LEAVES WITH CHARRED CHILE PASTE

the Brussels sprouts taste sour, about 12 weeks.

Transfer the Brussels sprouts and brine to one or more nonreactive airtight containers and refrigerate for up to 1 year. They are best if left to mature for 2 months before serving.

Cabbage Leaves with Charred Chile Paste

When we make a 300-lb/135-kg batch of sauerkraut → 111, we are left with a large bin of outer leaves from the heads that could not be sliced thinly enough for our fine-cut kraut. We ferment the leaves in brine left over from past batches of sauerkraut, and then rub them

in charred pepper paste. This cabbage pickle is a bit like Korean kimchi, but with a denser texture. Serve the leaves on their own as a condiment, blend them into a marinade, or use them as the base of a pork stew.

Makes 4 qt/2.28 kg

2 qt/2 L sauerkraut brine → 111 plus 2 tbsp kosher salt, or ½ cup/70 g kosher salt dissolved in 2 qt/2 L water

3 lb/1.4 kg cabbage leaves and scraps from making sauerkraut → 111, thinly sliced, or one 3-lb/1.4-kg head green cabbage, cored and thinly sliced crosswise

1 pt/480 ml charred pepper paste → 118

Pour the brine and salt into a 2-gl/7.5-L nonreactive container. Add the cabbage and top with a weight to keep it submerged. Seal the container, using a lid with an airlock, if you have one. If you have sealed it without an airlock, open the container every few days or so to release carbon dioxide buildup, and check for mold. Place in a clean, well-protected, low-light area with an ambient temperature of 60° to 68°F/16° to 20°C until the cabbage tastes sour, about 1 month.

When the cabbage is ready, remove it from the brine, reserve the brine for another use, and rub the cabbage with the pepper paste, coating it evenly, and refrigerate for up to 1 week before serving.

Transfer to one or more nonreactive airtight containers and refrigerate for up to 1 year.

BRINED BABY SAVOY CABBAGE

PICKLED GREEN WALNUTS

Pickled Green Walnuts

Unripened walnuts are wildly astringent and inedible, but once they are pickled, they take on a texture much like dry black olives and a flavor similar to pickled artichokes. Before you begin, be sure your walnuts are truly immature. Cut one open to be sure; if they resist in the center, it's possible they have begun to form the interior shell. Cut further and investigate. If they are too mature, use them to make *nocino*, a digestif made by mixing walnuts with a neutral spirit and sugar.

The walnuts will stain your hands black, so wear gloves as you work with them.

The British traditionally serve pickled walnuts alongside a platter of boiled meats. We like them in our Sweet Potato Salad **→ 208**. They can also be used in place of olives in many recipes and are great with blue cheese.

Makes 3 qt/3 kg

2 lb/910 g green walnuts
2½ cups/350 g kosher salt
8 qt/7.5 L water

1 cup/240 ml fermented honey **→ 121**, or honey
1 qt/960 ml malt vinegar **→ 98**
1 tbsp black peppercorns
1 tsp coriander seeds

With a sharp needle or a thumb-tack, poke each walnut five or six times.

In a large nonreactive container, dissolve 1 cup/140 g of the salt in 4 qt/3.75 L Add the prepared walnuts and top them with a weight to keep them submerged in the brine. Cover with a lid with an airlock, if you have one, and place in a clean, well-protected, low-light area with an ambient temperature of 60° to 68°F/ 16° to 20°C for 7 days. Check daily and if any white mold begins to form, scrape it off. This process will slightly ferment the nuts and leech out some of the astringency.

Drain the walnuts and discard the brine. In the same container, dissolve another 1 cup/140 g of the salt in the remaining 4 qt/ 3.75 L water to make a fresh brine. Add the walnuts and once again top with a weight to keep them submerged. Re-cover with the airtight lid and continue to soak in the same location for 7 days more, checking daily for mold and scraping off any you find. After 7 days, the brine should be bitter and a thin slice from a walnut should not taste overly tannic.

Drain the walnuts, discard the brine, and spread the walnuts in a single layer on a large sheet pan. Let the walnuts stand at room temperature, turning them occasionally, until they oxidize and turn completely black, about 48 hours.

In a large canning jar or ceramic crock, dissolve the honey and remaining ½ cup/70 g salt in the vinegar and stir in the peppercorns and coriander seeds. Add the walnuts and top with a weight to keep them submerged. Cover with the airtight lid and refrigerate for 1 month. Taste a walnut; it should be pickled all the way through. The pickled walnuts are best if left to mature for 3 months before serving, and will keep for up to 1 year.

Pickled Seeds and Green Berries

Capers don't grow in the San Francisco Bay Area, so we look for ways to replicate their briny, salty flavor. The fresh green seeds picked from flowering plants and cured in salt have a texture similar to that of capers but a whole new range of flavors. Use these seeds and berries in salads, as a garnish for soups, or any time you would reach for a jar of capers.

Green dill seeds, green fennel seeds, green elderberries, nasturtium buds, onion buds, and/or green coriander seeds
3 percent kosher salt by weight
20 percent sauerkraut brine
→ 111 by weight

Weigh the seeds and berries, then, using the percentages given, calculate the necessary amount of salt and brine. Combine the seeds and berries, salt, and brine in a small nonreactive airtight container, cap tightly, and shake well. Place in a clean, well-protected, low-light area with an ambient temperature of 60° to 68°F/16° to 20°C for 2 months, turning the container over every 2 days to disperse the liquid evenly. These are done when they are lightly soured.

They will keep in the refrigerator for up to 1 year.

Onion Brine

Many classic meat brines include processed sugar. This recipe uses the natural sweetness of onion instead. We use this brine for many of our meats at the restaurant (see Smoked Brisket → 162, Pork Knuckle → 292, and Rooster Boil → 302).

Makes 4 qt/3.8 L

2 sweet white onions, cut into chunks
1 bunch fresh flat-leaf parsley, coarsely chopped
3.5 qt/3.3 L cold water
½ cup/55 g kosher salt

In a blender or food processor, combine the onions, parsley, and half of the water and process into a smooth purée. Transfer to a large bowl, add the remaining water and the salt, and stir well.

Use right away, or transfer to an airtight container and refrigerate for up to 2 weeks.

Lime Pickle

This is a condiment from Nick's childhood. His mother always had South Indian–style achar lime pickles on the door of the refrigerator. She would often serve them with rice, fish, or chicken and garden vegetables. We've tried to re-create his flavor memory here.

The amount of juice in a lime can vary, and we call for juicing 3 lb/1.4 kg of limes here, which means you may have some lime juice left over. If you can find fresh turmeric we recommend using it, but the recipe is also delicious with powdered. Use these pickles in the marinade for the Whole Grilled Eggplant → 304 and puréed and rubbed on any grilled meats.

TOP ROW: GREEN BEANS, CORIANDER SEEDS, ONION BUDS, WASABI STEMS. BOTTOM ROW: DILL SEEDS, NASTURTIUM SEEDS, GREEN ELDERBERRIES, FENNEL SEEDS.

Makes 2 qt/1.71 kg

5 lb/2.3 kg limes

1 cup/140 g kosher salt

1 tsp caraway seeds, toasted and ground → 30

1 tsp dill seeds, toasted and ground → 30

1 tsp coriander seeds, toasted and ground → 30

2 green serrano chiles, stemmed and minced

4 garlic cloves, minced

1 tbsp fresh ginger, peeled and minced

1 tbsp ground turmeric, or 3 tbsp fresh turmeric juice

Juice 3 lb/1.4 kg of the limes, strain any pulp with a fine-mesh sieve, and set aside. In a small bowl, stir together the salt, caraway seeds, dill seeds, coriander seeds, chiles, garlic, ginger, and ground turmeric (if using turmeric juice, reserve to add later).

Trim the stems from the remaining 2 lb/910 g limes, taking care not to cut into the flesh. Using a paring knife and starting at the stem end, cut each fruit into four wedges, cutting to, but not through, the base. Working with one lime at a time, hold it over a bowl, gently pry it open, and then cover with the salt mixture, capturing in the bowl any of the mixture that fails to adhere.

Pack the salted limes into a sterilized 2-qt/2-L canning jar. If using turmeric juice, pour it into the jar and then pour in the reserved lime juice to cover the limes completely. Seal the jar and place in a clean, well-protected, low-light area with an ambient temperature of 60° to 68°F/16° to 20°C for 3 to 4 weeks, turning the jar upside down occasionally to prevent mold growth. The limes are ready when the peels look

LIME PICKLE

slightly translucent, but are best if left to mature for 3 months before serving.

Transfer the jar to the refrigerator, where the limes will keep for up to 1 year.

Lime Pickle Condiment

Makes 2 qt/1.7 kg

1 qt/875 g limes from lime pickle → 115, strained
¼ cup/60 ml sunchoke oil → 90, garlic oil → 91, or sesame oil
1 onion, thinly sliced
2 cloves garlic, minced
½ serrano chile, finely grated

2 tbsp chutney spice → 53
1 tbsp kosher salt
¼ tsp ground turmeric
¼ cup plus 2 tbsp/90 ml pickle brine from lime pickle → 115
¼ cup/85 ml fermented honey → 121, or honey

Pour water into a steamer pan, place the steamer rack above the water, and put the lime pickle on the rack. Cover the steamer, bring the water to a boil over medium heat, and steam until the limes can be pierced with slight force by a skewer, 10 to 15 minutes. Remove the limes from the steamer, leave till cool

enough to handle, and cut into ½-in/12-mm pieces.

Heat a medium pot over medium heat until a drop of water flicked on the surface sizzles gently on contact. Add the oil and then immediately add the onion, garlic, and serrano, and cook, stirring occasionally, until the vegetables are slightly softened but not browned, about 5 minutes. Mix the chutney spice, salt, and ground turmeric with the reserved pickling liquid and the honey, stirring to dissolve. Add the spice-honey mixture to the pot and bring to a simmer

LIME PICKLE
CONDIMENT

while stirring. Add the limes and cook uncovered until the liquid has reduced everything to a thick paste, about 5 minutes. Let cool. Transfer to small jars, cap tightly, and refrigerate for up to 6 months.

Sweet Pepper Paste

In Hungary, paprika paste is sold in tubes like toothpaste. When Nick was attending high school in Budapest, his favorite after-school snack was a chunk of bread with the paprika condiment and some kolbász (sausage) and cheese. This is our version of the pepper paste. Try it with the Warm Farmer's Cheese → **232**.

Makes 1 pt/480 ml

5 lb/2.3 kg sweet red peppers, stemmed and seeded
4 tbsp/35 g kosher salt

In a blender, combine the sweet peppers and salt and process to a smooth paste. Transfer the paste to a nonreactive container. Place a piece of plastic wrap flush against the paste, pressing to dispel air and deter mold growth, and cover with a tight-fitting lid. Place in a clean, well-protected, low-light area with an ambient temperature of 60° to 68°F/ 16° to 20°C for 1 week. Stir the contents once daily.

After 1 week, the paste should taste gently sour. If you think it needs more time, leave the container at room temperature, stirring and tasting the contents once daily, until the paste tastes mildly acidic.

Pour the fermented pepper paste into a stainless-steel or glass baking dish large enough so the paste is not more than 1 in/2.5 cm thick. Transfer to a dehydrator or oven set at 110°F/43°C and dry until it reaches the consistency of canned tomato paste, 12 to 16 hours. Stir the paste halfway through the drying time so a thick skin doesn't form on top. When the paste is thick, purée in a blender until smooth.

Transfer to small jars and refrigerate for at least 3 months before using. This paste will continue to age and will taste best after 6 months, and keeps indefinitely. To powder, see → **121**.

Charred Pepper Paste

This paste came to be at a harvest party in Napa with our friends Juston and Mindy Enos from Full Table Farm. Juston was kind enough to dig a big hole in his backyard so we could burn mounds of his paprika peppers over walnut shells. The resulting chile paste has a complex flavor from the combination of smoking and charring.

Makes 1 qt/1 kg

1 generous handful walnut shells or alder fruit wood
5 lb/2.3 kg sweet red peppers, stemmed and seeded
8 oz/225 g hot red chiles, such as serrano or jalapeño, stemmed
1 sweet white onion, cut into rings ¼ in/6 mm thick
20 garlic cloves
5 tbsp/45 g kosher salt

Soak the shells in water to cover for at least 1 hour and as long as overnight.

Prepare a medium-hot fire for direct-heat cooking in a charcoal grill. Arrange the peppers, chiles, onion rings, and garlic directly over the fire and grill, turning as needed, until thoroughly and evenly charred on all sides but still soft in the center, about 10 minutes. (You may need to use a grill basket for the garlic cloves to prevent them from

SWEET
PEPPER
PASTE

SAMBAL-STYLE
CHILE PASTE

CHARRED
PEPPER PASTE

CHIPOTLE
PASTE

After 1 week, the paste should taste gently sour. If you think it needs more time, leave the container at room temperature, stirring and tasting the contents once each day, until the paste tastes mildly acidic.

Pour the fermented pepper paste into a stainless-steel or glass baking dish and transfer to a dehydrator or oven set at 110°F/43°C and dry until it reaches the consistency of canned tomato paste, 12 to 16 hours. Stir the paste halfway through the drying time so a thick skin doesn't form. When the paste is thick, purée in a blender until smooth.

Transfer to small jars and refrigerate for at least 3 months before using. This paste will continue to age and will taste best after 6 months, and keeps indefinitely. To powder, see → 121.

Chipotle Paste

This paste is an homage to the cans of chipotle peppers in adobo sauce that make staff meals delicious in restaurants around the world and that our mothers used for enchilada night. It is spicy!

Makes 1 qt/1.05 kg

3 lb/1.4 kg red jalapeño
  chiles, stemmed and halved
  lengthwise with seeds intact

falling through the grate.) The timing will vary depending on the vegetable. When the vegetables are halfway charred, drain the shells and distribute over the coals next to the vegetables and cover the grill. Cook and smoke until evenly charred on the outside but still tender in the middle, about 10 minutes more. Let cool to room temperature.

In a blender or food processor, combine all of the charred vegetables and the salt and process to a smooth paste. Transfer the paste to a nonreactive container. Place a piece of plastic wrap flush against the paste, pressing to dispel air and deter mold growth, and cover with a tight-fitting lid. Place in a clean, well-protected, low-light area with an ambient temperature of 60° to 68°F/16° to 20°C for 1 week. Stir the contents once daily.

2 lb/910 g sweet red peppers, stemmed and seeded

3 large sweet white onions, cut into rings ¼ in/6 mm thick

20 garlic cloves

4 tbsp/35 g kosher salt

Soak a large handful or two of hardwood chips in water to cover for at least 1 hour.

IF USING A SMOKER: Following the manufacturer's instructions, set up and smoke the jalapeños, sweet peppers, onions, and garlic at 160°F/70°C until dark brown, 2 to 4 hours, depending on the strength of your smoker. Let cool.

IF USING A GAS GRILL: Light one burner to medium. Put a smoker box over the lit burner, add some of the soaked wood chips to the box, and close the grill. Adjust the heat as needed to keep the temperature at 160°F/70°C. The wood chips should begin to smolder and release a steady stream of smoke. Put the jalapeños, sweet peppers, onions, and garlic on the grate opposite the lit burner. (You may need to use a grill basket for the garlic cloves to prevent them from falling through the grate.) Cover the grill and smoke, adjusting the heat as needed to maintain the temperature. Check every 45 minutes or

so and add more soaked chips as necessary to keep the smoke level constant. Rotate the vegetables, flipping as needed if one side is coloring faster than the other, until darkened and smoky tasting, about 3 hours. Let cool.

IF USING A CHARCOAL GRILL: Fill a chimney starter with charcoal. Light it and let burn until the coals are covered with a thin layer of ash. Pour the hot coals on one side of the grill. Put some of the soaked wood chips next to the hot coals, and put the grate on the grill. Put the jalapeños, sweet peppers, onions, and garlic on the grate opposite the fire. (You may need to use a grill basket for the garlic cloves to prevent them from falling through the grate.) Stick a thermometer through the vent and heat the grill to 160°F/70°C. Smoke the jalapeños, peppers, and garlic, adjusting the heat as needed to maintain the temperature. Check every 45 minutes or so and add more soaked chips as necessary to keep the smoke level constant. Rotate the vegetables, flipping as needed if one side is coloring faster than the other, until darkened and smoky tasting, about 3 hours. Let cool.

In a blender or food processor, combine all of the smoked vegetables and the salt and process

to a smooth paste. Transfer the paste to a nonreactive container. Place a piece of plastic wrap flush against the paste, pressing to dispel air and deter mold growth, and cover with a tight-fitting lid. Place in a clean, well-protected, low-light area with an ambient temperature of 60° to 68°F/16° to 20°C for 1 week. Stir the contents once daily.

After 1 week, the paste should taste gently sour. If you think it needs more time, leave the container at room temperature, stirring and tasting the contents once each day, until the paste tastes mildly acidic.

Pour the fermented pepper paste into a stainless-steel or glass baking dish large enough so the paste is not more than 1 in/2.5 cm thick. Transfer to a dehydrator or oven set at 110°F/43°C and dry until it reaches the consistency of canned tomato paste, 12 to 16 hours. Stir the paste halfway through the drying time so a skin doesn't form. When the paste is thick, purée in a blender until smooth.

Transfer to small jars and refrigerate for at least 3 months before using. This paste will continue to age and will taste best after 6 months, and keeps indefinitely. To powder, see → 121.

SAMBAL POWDER

Sambal-Style Chile Paste

Hungarians are not genetically linked to Europeans; their roots are Central Asian. So it is not surprising that the spicy sambal, or chile paste, that you find as a condiment in many Asian restaurants and households is nearly the same as what you find on Hungarian tables. We also like to make a powder out of some of the paste. The powder is great on rice, grilled meats, or fried fish. The anchovies, lime, and ginger are optional. If you omit the anchovies, add an additional 1½ tsp kosher salt.

Makes 1 pt/525 g

5 lb/2.3 kg fresh chiles, such as bird's eye, cayenne, or árbol, stemmed

20 garlic cloves, minced

5 salt-cured anchovies, minced

1-in/2.5-cm piece fresh ginger, peeled and minced

Zest of 3 limes, preferably kaffir limes, zested on a fine Microplane

3½ tbsp/30 g kosher salt

In a large bowl, combine the chiles, garlic, anchovies, ginger, lime zest, and salt. Working in batches, purée in a blender. Transfer the paste to a non-reactive container. Place a piece of plastic wrap flush against the paste, pressing to dispel air and deter mold growth, and cover with a tight-fitting lid. Place in a clean, well-protected, low-light area with an ambient temperature of 60° to 68°F/16° to 20°C for 1 week. Stir the contents once daily.

After 1 week, the paste should taste gently sour. If you think it needs more time, leave the container at room temperature, stirring and tasting the contents once each day, until the paste tastes mildly acidic.

Pour the fermented pepper paste into a stainless-steel or glass baking dish large enough so the paste is not more than 1 in/2.5 cm thick. Transfer to a dehydrator or oven set at 110°F/43°C and dry until it reaches the consistency of canned tomato paste, 12 to 16 hours. Stir the paste halfway through the drying time so a skin doesn't form. When the paste is thick, purée in a blender until smooth.

Transfer to small jars and refrigerate for at least 3 months before using. This paste will continue to age and will be best after 6 months, and keeps indefinitely.

To turn paste into powder: Pour the paste into a stainless-steel or glass baking dish large enough so the paste is not more than 1 in/2.5 cm thick. Transfer to a dehydrator or oven set at 110°F/43°C until the paste is completely dry, 24 to 36 hours. Break up the dried paste into pieces, transfer to a blender or spice grinder, and process to a fine powder. Be careful, as the dust and fumes are spicy! Store the powder in an airtight container in a cool, dry place for up to 6 months.

Fermented Honey

Fermenting honey gives it slight acidity and a more complex flavor. Capped honey will not ferment in its natural state of 17 to 18 percent moisture content; it will ferment, however, if it is above 60°F/16°C with greater than 20 percent moisture content. Use this honey as you would any other honey.

FERMENTED HONEY

Makes 1 cup/335 g

1 cup/335 g honey
2 tbsp water

In a small glass jar, stir together the honey and water and cover the jar with cheesecloth. Place in a clean, well-protected, low-light area with an ambient temperature of 60° to 68°F/16° to 20°C for 2 weeks. Stir the contents once daily just until the honey starts to sour very slightly. The flavor will be subtle when the honey is finished fermenting. Cap tightly and refrigerate for up to 1 year.

Creamed Honey

This is an amazingly thick, opaque honey with the texture of meringue. It allows us to introduce honey flavor to various foods without thinning them, such as the crepe filling → 342.

Combine equal parts crystallized honey and uncrystallized honey in the bowl of a stand mixer fitted with the whip attachment. (If you have only crystallized honey on hand, warm half of it gently to liquefy it.) Whip on high speed until the mixture is pale and thick, and no trace of the honey crystals remains, 20 to 30 minutes. Store in an airtight container at room temperature for 1 month. It may need to be rewhipped if it liquefies, which may happen if your room gets too hot. Alternatively, you can keep it in the refrigerator and bring to room temperature 1 hour before using, as it is very stiff right from the fridge.

CREAMED HONEY

Rice Koji

Koji is the fermented medium that is responsible for many of the unique flavors found in Chinese, Japanese, and Korean foods and beverages, such as sake, amazake → 328, miso, and soy sauce. At the restaurant, rice koji goes into our desserts, sauces, and meat marinades.

Koji is made by inoculating cooked grains or legumes with a fungus, most commonly *Aspergillus*

oryzae, producing high quantities of glutamic acid and an appealing flavor and fragrance.

We inoculate various grains to make our own koji. Here, we call for rice, though other grains and legumes can be cultured the same way. You can buy different spore types, depending on your desired end product. We use light koji-kin spores here to produce a sweet koji for things like amazake and white miso.

Makes 2 lb/910 g rice koji

2 lb/910 g short-grain white rice
⅛ tsp koji-kin spores
⅛ tsp rice powder →48, or
    rice flour

Rinse the rice. In a large bowl, cover the rice with cold water. With your hands, agitate the rice in the water, massaging it gently to remove the starches. The water will become opaque and murky. Drain the water and place the rice back in the bowl, covering it again with cold water. Agitate and continue this process four or five times, until the water runs clear. Drain one last time, add cold water to cover by 2 in/5 cm, allowing room for expansion, and let soak in the refrigerator for at least 3 hours, or for up to 18 hours. The rice should absorb water while soaking and increase 20 to 30 percent in weight, which is a good indication that it's ready to steam.

Pour the rice into a colander or large sieve and let drain for 20 minutes to be sure no liquid remains. Pour water into a steamer pan and place the steamer rack above the water. Line the steamer rack with cheesecloth or a tea towel. Bring the water to a boil over medium-high heat, and check to make

RICE KOJI

sure the water is not touching the bottom of the rack. Place the drained rice in the cloth-lined rack, cover, and steam over medium-high heat until the rice is slightly sticky, and the kernels are easy to separate and still have a bit of chew when you bite into one, 40 to 60 minutes. Steamed rice is more opaque than boiled rice when ready.

Remove the rice from the steamer, transfer to a shallow pan large enough to hold the rice in a thin even layer, and let cool to 86°F/30°C. Mix the measured koji-kin with the rice powder. When the rice has cooled, sift the koji-kin–rice powder mixture evenly over the warm rice, then stir and toss to distribute. Place the rice in a layer no more than 3 in/7.5 cm thick in a nonreactive

covered or uncovered container, depending on your warming vessel. Find a warm spot with a temperature between 90° and 95°F/32° and 35°C and 75 to 90 percent humidity, such as the top of your stove, a dehydrator set at 90°F/32°C, or a cooler outfitted with hot-water bottles, to hold the rice at constant temperature to incubate for 48 to 60 hours. Stir the rice every 8 hours to create some airflow and to prevent clumping. The rice is ready when it smells sweet and white mold is covering all of the grains. Be leery of oddly colored molds, as they are a sign of poor airflow, inconsistent temperatures, or the presence of other bacteria that you don't want in your koji. Koji likes airflow, but it also wants a

constant temperature. We culture ours in a dehydrator with a very low-powered fan. We keep it covered because we don't want it to dry out, as it benefits from some moisture when culturing. If you are using a rigged-up cooler, you can leave the rice container uncovered, as you will be creating a humid environment. Whatever setup you use, just be sure to keep a bit of moisture on the rice, either using damp paper towels draped over the rice or a small pan with water placed in the setup.

When the rice is fully blanketed with white, cheesy-smelling mold, use it right away, transfer it to a nonreactive, airtight container and refrigerate for up to 2 weeks, or freeze it for up to 6 months. You can also dry it in a dehydrator set at 95°F/35°C until it is thoroughly dry, 8 to 12 hours, then process it to a flour to use in the parsnip cake → 346.

Salt Koji

Salt koji is produced by fermenting rice koji with water and salt. This causes a slight acidic tang to develop and adds salinity that balances the natural sweetness of the koji. Sold as a paste in jars in many Asian markets, salt koji can be used as a marinade for meats and vegetables or mixed into sauces (see Beef Tartare Toast with Bottarga→ **282**).

Makes 1 qt/1.02 kg

1 lb/455 g rice koji or other
    inoculated grain → **123**
¾ cup/105 g kosher salt
2¾ cups/660 ml filtered water
    at 85°F/29°C

In a food processor, or with a mortar and pestle, pulse the rice koji kernels until they are broken up into small pieces but not powdered. Place the koji in a nonreactive container, add the salt and water, and stir to mix well. Cover tightly and place in a clean, well-protected, low-light area with an ambient temperature of 60° to 68°F/16° to 20°C. Stir once daily until the mixture smells faintly sweet, about 10 days.

In a blender, process the rice to a smooth paste. Transfer to a nonreactive airtight container and refrigerate for up to 2 months.

Candied Beets

This recipe delivers both an unusual and delicious version of candied beets and a sweet beet syrup for adding to mimosas, cocktails, lemonade, or sparkling soda. You can also purée the beets to make a faux jam to use in

CANDIED BEETS AND SYRUP

the candied beet tart → **338** or to spread on toast.

Makes 5 cups/1.2 L syrup and 2½ lb/1.2 kg candied beets

2 cups/480 ml water
2 cups/480 ml fresh lemon juice
3½ cups/840 g fermented honey
    → **121**, or honey
2 tsp salt
3½ lb/1.6 kg red beets, peeled
1 bay leaf
1 tbsp black peppercorns
1 tbsp fennel seeds
1 tbsp coriander seeds
Zest strips of 1 orange

In a large heavy-bottomed pot over medium heat, combine the water, lemon juice, honey, and salt. Bring to a simmer, stirring to dissolve the sugar, and then

add the beets. Wrap the bay leaf, peppercorns, fennel seeds, coriander seeds, and orange zest in cheesecloth, tie securely, and add the bundle to the pot. Simmer until the beets are soft when poked with a skewer but still hold their shape, 1 to 1½ hours. Remove from the heat and let the beets cool in the syrup for about 4 hours.

Discard the cheesecloth bundle. Transfer the beets and syrup to airtight containers and refrigerate for up to 2 months.

Tomato Jam

This savory jam has a bit of spice, lots of agrodolce, and the crunch and citrus flavor of green coriander berries. We make a big batch of this in August, when tomatoes are abundant. It's also at this time that coriander plants have begun to seed. We serve this on sandwiches, as a condiment for charred meats, and with the whole grilled eggplant → 304.

Makes 3 cups/615 g

1 tbsp filtered grapeseed oil

1 red onion, minced

¼ cup/60 ml red wine vinegar → 95

2 green serrano chiles, stemmed and minced

2 tbsp chutney spice → 53

1 tbsp peeled and minced fresh ginger

4 garlic cloves, minced

¼ cup/25 g sweet onion powder → 34

3 tbsp/25 g kosher salt

2½ tsp freshly ground black pepper

5 lb/2.3 kg tomatoes, dried for 18 hours → 40

½ cup/65 g fresh green coriander seeds, or ½ bunch cilantro, leaves picked and minced

TOMATO JAM

Place a medium heavy-bottomed saucepan over medium heat and warm until a drop of water flicked on the surface sizzles gently on contact. Add the oil and onion and cook, stirring often to avoid coloring, until tender, about 10 minutes. Add the vinegar, chiles, chutney spice, ginger, garlic, onion powder, salt, and pepper and simmer for 5 minutes. Stir often to ensure that the mixture is not sticking to the bottom of your pan.

In a food processor, purée the onion mixture with the dried tomatoes until it is the consistency of chunky applesauce.

Taste and adjust the salt. Add the fresh coriander seeds or chopped cilantro. Transfer to a nonreactive airtight container and refrigerate for up to 1 month.

Apple Butter

Any tart apple, such as Honeycrisp, Pink Lady, or Granny Smith, works well here, but we particularly like to make this with Pink Pearl apples. These apples have coral flesh, a sweet-tart flavor, and a brief season, at the tail end of August. One of our favorite ways to capture their flavor and brilliant color is to make this apple butter. Apple peels and seeds are all excellent sources of pectin, so just wash and cut the fruit and don't bother with anything else. A hand-cranked food mill is the best tool for puréeing the apples. It pushes out the pulp while holding back the seeds, stems, and peels. A bit of this apple butter stirred into yogurt is one of our favorite snacks.

Makes 3 cups/520 g

5 lb/2.3 kg tart apples, such as
    Pink Pearl, Honeycrisp, or
    Pink Lady, quartered
1 cup/240 ml water
½ cup/120 ml apple cider
    vinegar → 95

In a large heavy-bottomed pot over medium heat, combine the apples, water, and vinegar. Cook, stirring often, until the apples are tender and begin to fall apart, about 2 hours.

Place a food mill over a medium bowl and pass the apples through the mill, puréeing it directly into the bowl. Pour the apple paste into a stainless-steel or glass baking dish large enough so the paste is not more than 1 in/2.5 cm thick. Transfer to a dehydrator or oven set at 120°F/43°C until it reaches the consistency of canned tomato paste, 12 to 16 hours.

In a blender, purée the apple paste until smooth. Transfer to small jars, cap tightly, and refrigerate for up to 4 months.

APPLE BUTTER

SYRUPS & BEVERAGES

We process all of our non-alcoholic beverages and cocktail infusions mainly because we like to make things. It gives us yet another way to capture and concentrate the flavors of the seasons. Sodas and syrups are easy to make at home and offer a fresh way to layer in flavors and use some of our favorite ingredients.

Juicing

We use a few different pieces of equipment to extract juice—a centrifuge juicer, a masticating juicer, a cold-press juicer, a blender, a manual fruit press, and a steam extractor. After juicing, be sure to pass the juice through a fine-mesh sieve or cheesecloth to remove remaining pulp.

Apples, Pears, and Beets

Cut the fruit into pieces that will fit through the juicer's feed tube. Masticating, centrifuge, manual fruit press, and cold-press juicers work well.

Cherries

Stem and pit the fruit. Masticating, centrifuge, manual fruit press, steam extraction, and cold-press juicers work well.

Ginger

Cut the ginger into pieces that will fit through the juicer's feed tube. Both masticating and centrifuge juicers work well. A blender will also extract juice with a bit of water added to it; be sure to cut the ginger small, as it is fibrous and can stall the blender.

Grapes

Remove the stems. Masticating, centrifuge, manual fruit press, steam extraction, and cold-press juicers work well.

Syrups

Syrups are a prime example of what we call the law of diminishing returns. A large box of tomatoes yields a small jar of syrup. However, the syrup is so concentrated it will last a long time. Sour cherry and apple cider syrups are good in beverages and desserts or as accents for savory dishes. They can be used in place of pomegranate molasses in most recipes. Mushroom syrup is reminiscent of soy sauce—brush it on raw meat or fish as you would with tamari for sashimi.

Sour Cherry Syrup

This syrup has a balance of acidity and sweetness that's not unlike pomegranate molasses, and it has come to be one of the most exciting ingredients in our pantry.

Makes 1 cup/240 ml

4 lb/1.8 kg sour cherries, pitted and juiced → 129, or 6 cups/ 1.4 L sour cherry juice

Pour the cherry juice into a medium heavy-bottomed saucepan and simmer over very low heat, stirring occasionally, until reduced to 1 cup/240 ml, about 5 hours. As it nears the point where it has sufficiently reduced, the bubbles will get very small. Watch closely, particularly as the reduction nears the finishing point, as it can burn quickly. The syrup is ready when it coats the back of a spoon.

Let cool completely, transfer to a nonreactive airtight container, and store at room temperature for up to 1 year.

Fig Leaf Syrup

The herbaceous, subtle coconut flavor of fig leaves makes a delicious pairing with milk kefir, creating an almost coconut milk–like beverage. Fig leaves also behave like a coagulant, which we learned the hard way. After steeping the leaves in milk kefir overnight, we arrived at the restaurant to discover that instead of making a beverage, we had made a coconut-scented fig leaf cheese. To infuse the kefir with the aroma without changing the structure of the milk, we decided to make this fig leaf syrup that we use to flavor and sweeten the kefir. Mix ¼ cup/60 ml of the syrup with 1½ cups/360 ml of the milk kefir and serve chilled on ice or as is.

Makes 7 cups/1.7 L

4 cups/960 ml water
3 cups/720 ml fermented honey
  → **121**, or honey
12 large fig leaves

In a medium heavy-bottomed saucepan over medium heat, combine the water and honey and stir until the honey dissolves. Bring to a simmer and remove from the heat. Put the fig leaves in a large, wide-mouthed heat-proof container and pour the hot syrup over the leaves, submerging them completely. Cover and let stand at room temperature until the syrup is infused with the flavor of the leaves, about 24 hours.

Strain the syrup through a fine-mesh sieve and discard the

SOUR CHERRY SYRUP

leaves. Store the syrup in an air-tight container in the refrigerator for up to 1 year.

Apple Cider Syrup

We decided to make a large batch of apple cider and reduce it to make this syrup. It ended up being tart and flavorful. Pears also work well for this syrup.

Makes 2 cups/480 ml

15 lb/6.8 kg large tart apples, juiced, or 4 qt/3.8 L tart apple juice

Put the apple juice into an air-tight container with an airlock, and let stand at cool room temperature until it ferments and tastes tangy and slightly alcoholic, 5 to 10 days. If you don't have a container with an airlock, use a canning jar and release the pressure by opening the lid a couple times a day. At this point, the juice will have become soft cider.

Pour the cider into a medium heavy-bottomed saucepan and simmer over very low heat, stirring occasionally, until reduced to 2 cups/480 ml, about 4 hours. As it nears the point where it has sufficiently reduced, the bubbles will get very small. Watch closely, particularly as the reduction nears the finishing point, as it can burn quickly. The syrup is ready when it coats the back of a spoon.

Let cool completely, transfer to a nonreactive airtight container, and store at room temperature for up to 1 year.

Tomato Reduction

The idea for this condiment came to us when we tasted the drippings on the bottom of the dehydrator tray after drying a batch of tomatoes. This can be used for almost anything, sweet or savory.

Makes ½ to ¾ cup/120 to 180 ml

8 lb/3.6 kg tomatoes, cored and quartered
1 tbsp kosher salt

Line a large fine-mesh sieve or a colander with cheesecloth and place over a large bowl. Working in batches if necessary, combine the tomatoes and salt in a blender and pulse until the tomatoes are crushed. Do not homogenize them. Transfer to the prepared sieve and refrigerate overnight. The next day there should be about 2 qt/1.8 L tomato water. Discard the solids.

Transfer the tomato water to a medium heavy-bottomed saucepan over very low heat and simmer, stirring occasionally, until reduced to ½ to ¾ cup/120 to 180 ml, about 5 hours. As it nears the point where it has sufficiently reduced, the bubbles will get very small. Watch closely, particularly as the reduction nears the finishing point, as it can burn quickly. The syrup is ready when it coats the back of a spoon.

Let cool completely, transfer to a nonreactive airtight container, and store at room temperature for up to 1 year.

Mushroom Reduction

Similar in flavor to soy sauce, this syrup has a sweet, earthy taste but a less assertive aroma than the more famous Asian condiment.

Makes ½ cup/120 ml

6 cups/1.4 L mushroom broth → 139

Pour the broth into a large heavy-bottomed saucepan over very low heat and cook, stirring occasionally, until reduced to ½ cup/120 ml, about 2 hours. As it nears the point where it has sufficiently reduced, the bubbles will get small. Watch closely, particularly as the reduction nears the finishing point, as it can burn quickly. The syrup is ready when it coats the back of a spoon.

Let cool completely, transfer to a nonreactive airtight container, and store in the refrigerator for up to 1 year.

Beverages

Water kefir and lacto-fermented sodas are a delicious alternative to store-bought beverages. They are loaded with probiotics and are easy to make at home. Cortney has made both types for years, long before they became staples on the menu at Bar Tartine. She is adept at working with these very active, naturally carbonated beverages. If the bottles are shaken or get too warm, they can make a big mess when you open them. To avoid a gusher, open the bottles over a sink with a towel held over the top of the bottle.

Lacto Soda Starter

Also known as ginger bug, this soda starter works in much the same way a sourdough starter does: it captures wild yeasts and beneficial bacteria that eat the sugar and produce carbon dioxide, which starts a lactic fermentation. The quantity of ginger is so small that it imparts little flavor to the starter. The ginger aids in getting the fermentation started.

Makes 1 qt/960 ml

4 cups/960 ml filtered water
5 tsp peeled and finely
    grated ginger
5 tsp sugar

In a 1-qt/960-ml canning or similar jar, combine the water and 1 tsp each of the ginger and sugar. Cover the mouth of the jar with cheesecloth, secure with a rubber band, and let stand out of direct sunlight at room temperature. For 4 days, add 1 tsp each sugar and ginger each day to continue feeding the starter, at which point the starter should have begun to bubble and foam. The starter is now ready to use.

If you are not using the starter right away, cover and refrigerate it and then feed it once a week with 1 tsp each ginger and sugar. When you are ready to make soda, bring the starter to room temperature and feed it daily with 1 tsp each ginger and sugar until it is bubbly again, about 3 days.

Concord Grape Soda

Nearly any seasonal fruit juice can be inoculated with a starter and fermented to make soda. This one mimics the canned grape soda that we loved growing up. Our favorite version is made with the Concord grapes that come into season each fall. We sometimes make it with wine grapes during harvest season, when our winemaker friends have extra juice to share. Table grapes work well, too. Whichever variety you use, be sure it has some acidity.

Makes 1 qt/960 ml

4 lb/1.8 kg Concord grapes,
    juiced (see Juicing → 129), or
    1 qt/960 ml grape juice
½ cup/120 ml strained lacto
    soda starter → 132

In a nonreactive container large enough to hold the juice with some head space, combine the grape juice and starter. Cover the container with cheesecloth and secure with a rubber band. Let stand out of direct sunlight at room temperature, ideally between 65°F and 72°F/18°C and 22°C, until the mixture is slightly foamy and releases bubbles when stirred, 3 to 4 days. If mold forms on the surface during this time, carefully skim it off.

Transfer the liquid to one or more flip-top bottles or canning jars with tight-fitting lids, leaving at least 1 in/2.5 cm of head space to allow the carbon dioxide to expand. Let stand at room temperature until pressure builds in the container(s), about 24 hours. Refrigerate for up to 1 month. Serve cold straight out of the bottle or over ice.

CONCORD GRAPE SODA

Ginger Burns Water Kefir

This is the most popular soda at the restaurant. We call it Ginger Burns in honor of Cortney's spicy personality. It is almost always available on tap alongside whichever seasonal lacto soda we are serving. It is always refreshing. We serve it over ice, mixed with iced tea, with sherry like a *rebujito*, and with pilsner for a shandy.

Makes 3 cups/720 ml

3 cups/720 ml filtered water
¼ cup/50 g sugar
½ tsp molasses, preferably blackstrap
Pinch of Himalayan salt or Celtic-style sea salt with high mineral content
½ lemon, halved, plus 6 tbsp/ 90 ml fresh lemon juice
2 dried apricots → 56

1-in/2.5-cm piece fresh ginger, sliced
¼ cup/45 g water kefir grains
2 tbsp fresh ginger juice

In a 2-qt/2-L nonreactive container, mix the water and sugar and stir to dissolve. Stir in the molasses and add the salt, lemon halves, apricots, ginger, and kefir grains. Seal the container closed, using a lid with an airlock, if you have one; otherwise, release carbon dioxide buildup every 8 hours or so by opening the container. Let stand in a place with an ambient temperature of 68° to 72°F/18° to 22°C for 48 hours (72 hours if the room is cooler than 68°F/20°C). It should be gently fizzy.

Remove and discard the apricots (you can eat them) and lemon pieces. Strain the liquid through a nylon-mesh sieve placed over a pitcher or bowl, capturing the kefir grains in the sieve. (Be sure to use a nylon sieve, as kefir grains can be sensitive to metal.) Stir the lemon juice and ginger juice into the liquid, using more or less depending on how strongly flavored you'd like it to taste.

Transfer the liquid to one or more flip-top bottles or canning jars with tight-fitting lids, leaving at least 1 in/2.5 cm of head space to allow the carbon dioxide to expand. Let stand at room temperature until pressure builds in the container(s), about 24 hours. Refrigerate for up to 1 month. Serve cold straight out of the bottle or over ice.

From this point, you can start a new batch of kefir or pause the kefiring process by storing the grains in a sugar-water mixture and refrigerating. Store water kefir grains in a sugar-water mixture of ¼ cup/ 50 g sugar to 1 qt/960 ml water, depending on the amount of grains in use. Refrigerate in an airtight container for up to 4 weeks. Drain and add fresh sugar-water every 7 days. For more about making kefir, see → 74.

Beet Kvass

This fermented beverage does not get the respect it deserves. The classic is made with whey and bread. Some recipes are sweet, some are saline and acidic. This one contains beets but many versions are instead flavored with herbs, fruit, or vegetables—just about anything can work. We like to drink this before and after meals, in a light beer, or as a pickle back with whiskey. We sometimes add grated serrano or horseradish for an extra bite. The lightly fermented beets left over from this recipe can be added to soups or salads, served as pickles, or juiced for Beet, Carrot, and Apple Kvass → 134.

Makes 7 cups/1.7 L

5 cups /1.2 L water
2 cups/480 ml sour whey → 67 or beet juice, or 2 cups additional water plus 1 tbsp kosher salt
1 tbsp kosher salt, if using water
2 lb/910 g beets, peeled and chopped
2 rye bread ends

Pour the water, whey or juice, and salt into a large nonreactive container. Stir to dissolve. Add the beets and rye bread and top with a weight to keep the beets and bread submerged in the brine. Seal the container, using a lid with an airlock, if you have one. If you have sealed it without an airlock, open the container every few days or so to release carbon dioxide buildup, and check for mold. Place in a clean, well-protected, low-light area with an ambient temperature of 60° to 68°F/16° to 20°C until the beets develop a mild sour flavor, 7 to 10 days.

Strain the liquid, reserving the beets and liquid separately. Transfer the liquid to one or more fliptop bottles or canning jars with tight-fitting lids and refrigerate for up to 2 months. Pack the beets into one or more airtight containers and refrigerate for up to 4 days, or juice and drink.

Beet, Carrot, and Apple Kvass

This is a great way to instantly use the solids from the Beet Kvass base so they aren't hanging around your refrigerator (pictured on page 128). To serve, drink it cold, straight up or on the rocks.

GINGER BUG

Makes 1 qt/1 L

2 lb/910 g beets from beet kvass, juiced (see Juicing → **129**)

1 lb/455 g apples, juiced (see Juicing → **129**)

1 lb/455 g carrots, juiced (see Juicing → **129**)

3 large limes, juiced

In a 2-qt/2-L container or bowl, combine the beet juice, apple juice, carrot juice, and lime juice. Transfer the liquid to one or more flip-top bottles or canning jars with tight-fitting lids, leaving at least 1 in/2.5 cm of head space to allow the carbon dioxide to expand. Let stand at room temperature until pressure builds in the container(s), about 24 hours. Refrigerate for up to 1 month. Serve cold straight out of the bottle or over ice.

STOCKS

Dashi is the base of much of our cooking. Although it is unlikely that many Hungarians ever used dashi in sour cherry soup, we find it to be the perfect choice. Kombu seaweed is the reason. High in glutamic acid, it is packed with flavor.

Kombu is harvested in many parts of the world. We source ours from California and Maine. But for dashi, we prefer the subtle aroma of kombu from northern Japan.

Kombu Dashi

This is the most basic form of dashi. It contains only kombu and water. In many savory recipes, kombu dashi can be substituted for the water. It's the seaweed version of bouillon cubes.

Makes 3.5 qt/3 L

4 sheets dried kombu, each 3 by 6 in/7.5 by 15 cm
4 qt/3.8 L soft or filtered water

Trim small slits into the kombu with a pair of scissors to help it release its flavor. In a large pot, combine the kombu and water and let soak until the kombu starts to soften, about 2 hours.

Place the pot over medium heat and bring to a gentle simmer (ideally 140° to 160°F/60° to 71°C), making sure that the water never boils. (Boiling the kombu will give the dashi an intense oceanic flavor and turn the broth cloudy. Cooking the kombu at a lower temperature yields a clearer broth.) Cook gently until the broth develops a mild sealike aroma and a noticeable but delicate salinity and flavor, about 1 hour. At this point, the kombu should be tender enough to pierce easily with a chopstick.

Strain the dashi through a fine-mesh sieve, discarding solids. If not using immediately, let the dashi cool at room temperature until lukewarm, about 30 minutes. Cover and refrigerate for up to 2 days, or freeze for up to 3 months.

Katsuo Dashi

Adding smoked bonito flakes (*katsuobushi*) to kombu dashi makes katsuo dashi, the base of miso soup.

Makes 3 qt/2.8 L

3½ qt/3.3 L kombu dashi → 137
2 cups/50 g packed katsuobushi flakes

In a large pot over medium-low heat, warm the kombu dashi until steam rises from the surface of the liquid (about 185°F/85°C). Add the katsuobushi flakes and push it down gently with a spoon but do not stir. Turn off the heat and let the katsuobushi steep in the hot broth for 5 minutes, until the dashi tastes of gentle smoke.

Strain the dashi through a fine-mesh sieve, taking care not to squeeze or press the flakes. Discard the flakes. If not using immediately, let the dashi cool at room temperature until lukewarm, about 30 minutes. Cover and refrigerate for up to 2 days.

to maintain a simmer, until the liquid is reduced by half, about 3 hours.

Trim small slits into the kombu with a pair of scissors to help release its flavor. Add the kombu and continue to simmer until the kombu begins to fall apart, about 1½ hours longer.

Strain the broth through a fine-mesh sieve into a storage container. Discard all solids. Let the broth cool to room temperature, then cover and refrigerate for up to 4 days, or freeze for up to 3 months. Skim off the fat that has solidified on the surface before using, and save for another use, such as schmaltz → 93.

Beef Broth

Makes 6 cups/1.4 L

2 lb/910 g beef shoulder bones
2 lb/910 g beef trimmings
  or chuck
6 qt/5.7 L cold water
3 sheets dried kombu, each
  3 by 6 in/7.5 by 15 cm

In a stockpot or large soup pot over medium heat, combine the beef bones, trimmings, and water and bring to a simmer, skimming off any foam that forms on the surface. Simmer, covered, skimming every 30 minutes or so and adjusting the heat as needed

to maintain a simmer, until the liquid is fragrant, about 4 hours.

Trim small slits into the kombu with a pair of scissors to help release its flavor. Add the kombu and reduce the heat so that the temperature of the liquid drops to 140°F/60°C. Simmer until the kombu can be easily pierced with a chopstick, about 1 hour longer.

Strain the broth through a fine-mesh sieve into a storage container. Discard all solids. Let the broth cool to room temperature, then cover and refrigerate for up to 4 days, or freeze for up to 3 months. Skim off the fat that has solidified on the surface before using, and save for another use, such as tallow → 94.

Fish Stock

Emulsified with the fat and bones of the freshwater fish used to make it, this fish stock is loaded with flavor. It is good for most recipes that call for fish stock, as long as the stock does not need to be clear. It's perfect for starting the fisherman's stews → 176 or → 178.

Makes 2 qt/2 L

3 sheets dried kombu, each
  3 by 6 in/7.5 by 15 cm
3 qt/2.8 L water

2 lb/910 g carp, sturgeon, or
  catfish trimmings and bones,
  rinsed and any scales removed
2 large sweet white onions,
  quartered
1 fennel bulb, cored and
  thinly sliced
2 tbsp chopped garlic

Trim small slits into the kombu with a pair of scissors to help it release its flavor. In a large pot, combine the kombu and water and let soak until it starts to soften, about 2 hours.

Add the fish trimmings and bones, onions, fennel, and garlic to the pot with the kombu, cover, and bring to a simmer (ideally 140° to 160°F/60° to 71°C). Adjust the heat to maintain a gentle simmer and cook until the bones fall apart, about 1 hour. Remove the kombu and discard.

Remove the pot from the heat and pass its contents through a heavy-duty food mill. Not everything will pass through the mill; discard any bones that get stuck. Alternatively, smash the solids with a large spoon while in the pot and press against them to extract as much flavor as possible. Pass the stock through a fine-mesh sieve to remove any remaining small particles. If not using immediately, let cool at room temperature until lukewarm, about 30 minutes. Cover and refrigerate for up to 3 days.

CATFISH KAMABOKO WITH MATSUTAKE MUSHROOMS AND STRONG DASHI

PART TWO

RECIPES

SOUPS

So many of the things we love about cooking are found
in a bowl of soup—abundance, hospitality, and comfort.
Soup is where the scraps go—the bones and vegetable
peels, the leftover glass of wine. Flavorful pieces that would
otherwise get tossed are redeemed by a little broth.
Soups lend themselves to improvisation—more of this,
less of that. They are greater than the sum of their parts
and our favorite kind of kitchen alchemy.

CHILLED SOUR CHERRY SOUP

This chilled soup is arguably Hungary's most iconic summertime dish. The harvest season for sour cherries is short, and during those weeks, this soup is found on almost every restaurant menu and in nearly every home, where grandchildren are often given the task of pitting the cherries.

Michigan produces 80 percent of the sour cherry crop in the United States, where the fruits are best known as the flavor of cherry soda or as a garnish for old-timey cocktails and ice cream sundaes. Having grown up in the Midwest, we developed a taste for them when we were young. During the few short weeks when we can get them fresh, we try to process as many as we can for this soup and for our sour cherry syrup → 129.

Serves 4 to 6

½ cup/120 ml filtered grapeseed oil

1 medium sweet white onion, chopped

1 fennel bulb, cored and chopped

2 cups/480 ml Tokaji aszú or other sweet white wine

2 cups/480 ml kombu dashi → 137

2½ lb/1.2 kg fresh sour cherries, pitted, or 1¾ lb/795 g frozen sour cherries, pitted; 20 reserved for garnish

1½ tbsp kosher salt

Sour cream → 71 for garnish

Freshly ground black pepper

Chopped fresh dill for garnish

Chopped fresh flat-leaf parsley for garnish

Toasted sunflower seeds for garnish

Unfiltered grapeseed oil for garnish

Heat a medium saucepan over medium heat until a drop of water flicked on the surface sizzles gently on contact. Add the filtered grapeseed oil, then immediately add the onion and fennel and cook, stirring occasionally, until the vegetables are slightly softened but not browned, about 5 minutes. Add the wine and dashi and bring to a simmer. Cook until the liquid is reduced by one-third, about 20 minutes.

Add the cherries, return the liquid to a simmer, and cook just until the fruit starts to break down and release their juices, about 10 minutes. Stir in the salt, remove from the heat, and let cool slightly.

Transfer the mixture to a blender, working in batches if necessary (the machine should be no more than half full), and purée until smooth. Pass the mixture through a fine-mesh sieve into a container and refrigerate uncovered until well chilled, about 4 hours.

Chill individual bowls in the refrigerator for at least 15 minutes. Ladle the soup into the bowls and top each serving with a scoop of sour cream. Garnish with the reserved cherries, pepper, dill, parsley, sunflower seeds, and unfiltered grapeseed oil. Leftover soup will keep in an airtight container in the refrigerator for up to 4 days.

CHILLED APRICOT SOUP WITH FENNEL & NOYAUX

During the final weeks of spring, the local apricot season explodes. For a few frenetic days, we stay busy processing as many of these fruits as we can (1,800 lb/816 kg is the current record). We dry apricots to use as a sweetener, turn them into jams, ferment them for sodas, and make syrups to use in our desserts; but to our minds, the best showcase for local apricots is this chilled soup. Fennel is an aromatic counterpart to apricots, and we use every bit of the plant here, including the bulb, the leafy fronds, the flowers, the seeds, and even a fennel-infused oil, to layer its flavor into the soup.

Serves 4 to 6

2 lb/910 g fresh apricots or 1½ lb/680 g frozen apricots

2 fennel bulbs, plus fresh fennel flowers and picked fronds for garnish

½ cup/120 ml filtered grapeseed oil

1 small sweet white onion, chopped

One 750-ml bottle dry, non-oaked white wine, such as Sylvaner or Pinot Grigio

2 cups/480 ml kombu dashi → 137

12 dried apricots → 56

2 to 3 tbsp fermented honey → 121, or honey (use more for tart apricots)

1½ tsp fennel seeds, toasted and ground → 31

Kosher salt

Juice of ½ lemon

Drained yogurt → 74 for garnish

Fennel flowers → 33 for garnish

Fennel oil → 90 for garnish

Freshly ground black pepper

Toasted and lightly crushed noyaux → 84 or almonds for garnish

With a paring knife, cut the apricots in half and remove and reserve the pits for noyaux. Set the halved apricots aside.

Halve and core both fennel bulbs, then chop 1 bulb for the soup base. Slice each half of the remaining bulb crosswise into thin half-moons using a mandoline or a sharp knife. Reserve the sliced fennel for garnish.

Heat a medium saucepan over medium heat until a drop of water flicked on the surface sizzles gently on contact. Add the grapeseed oil and then immediately add the onion and chopped fennel and cook, stirring occasionally, until the vegetables are slightly softened but not browned, about 5 minutes. Add the wine and dashi and bring to a simmer. Add the dried apricots and simmer until tender, 5 to 7 minutes. Remove the dried apricots from the liquid and reserve for garnish. Continue to simmer the liquid until it is reduced by half, about 30 minutes. Add the halved apricots, bring the liquid back to a simmer, and

cook for 10 minutes. Remove from the heat and let cool slightly.

Transfer the mixture to a blender, working in batches if necessary (the machine should be no more than half full), and add the honey, ground fennel seeds, and 1½ tbsp salt and purée until smooth. Pass the mixture through a fine-mesh sieve into a container and refrigerate uncovered until well chilled, about 4 hours.

Chill individual bowls in the refrigerator for at least 15 minutes. In a small bowl, combine the reserved sliced fennel, lemon juice, and a pinch of salt and toss to mix. Ladle the soup into the bowls and top each serving with a scoop of yogurt. Garnish with fresh fennel flowers and fronds, powdered fennel flowers, sliced fennel, fennel oil, reserved apricots, pepper, and noyaux. Leftover soup will keep in an airtight container in the refrigerator for up to 4 days.

CHILLED HERB SOUP WITH TOMATOES & SOURDOUGH

Herbs are often relegated to the role of garnish. But in this soup, fresh herbs are key ingredients. Although many people stop cooking with herbs once the plants start to bolt, we find that's when they have the most to offer—leaves, flowers, seeds. We use all of the parts in this soup. Consider this recipe a template, and vary the amounts and types of herbs you use depending on what's in the market or what's gone to seed.

Serves 4 to 6

8 oz/225 g russet potato

Leaves from 2 bunches each fresh dill, cilantro, parsley, marjoram, tarragon, and basil

1 qt/800 ml kombu dashi → 137, well chilled

½ bunch fresh chives, chopped

1 serrano chile, stemmed and seeded if you want less heat

Kosher salt

1 lb/455 g crusty sourdough bread, torn into 1-in/2.5-cm pieces

¾ cup/180 ml filtered grapeseed, sunflower, or hazelnut oil

2 garlic cloves

2 tomatoes, cored and cut into 1-in/2.5-cm chunks

Finishing salt

1 to 2 tbsp apple cider vinegar

Mixed torn fresh herbs for garnish

Basil flowers and leaves for garnish

Fresh seeds from bolted plants for garnish

Freshly ground black pepper

Preheat the oven to 350°F/180°C. Put the potato directly on the oven rack and roast until tender enough to be easily pierced with a skewer, about 40 minutes. Let it cool just until it can be handled, then peel. The potato can be cooked a day in advance and stored, refrigerated.

Prepare an ice bath. Bring a large saucepan of salted water to a boil. Add the dill, cilantro, parsley, marjoram, tarragon, and basil and cook until they are bright green and tender, about 45 seconds. With a slotted spoon, immediately transfer the herbs to the ice bath. When cool, remove them, squeeze out any extra water, pat dry, and coarsely chop. Refrigerate the herbs until ready to use.

Chill a blender beaker in the freezer for at least 15 minutes. Combine the chopped herbs, dashi, chives, chile, and 1 tbsp kosher salt in the cold blender, working in batches if necessary (the machine should be no more than half full), and purée until very smooth. Add the potato and purée completely into the soup. Do not over-blend or the mixture will heat up, which can spoil

the flavor of the herbs. Push the soup through a fine-mesh sieve directly into an airtight container, cover, and refrigerate until ready to use. This tastes best if eaten the same day it is made.

In a medium bowl, toss the bread with the grapeseed oil and a pinch of kosher salt, coating evenly. Let stand until the bread has absorbed most of the oil, about 5 minutes. Spread the bread in a large cast-iron skillet over medium heat. The pieces can be touching but should not be pressed together or stacked. (You may need to do this in two or three batches, depending on the size of your pan.) Set a heavy pan on top of the bread and cook until the bread starts to smoke,

about 2 minutes. Do not let the bread burn; golden brown is the goal. With a spatula, turn the bread pieces over, set the heavy pan back on top, and repeat. Rub the croutons with the garlic cloves. Set aside until ready to use, within 3 hours.

Chill individual bowls in the refrigerator for at least 15 minutes. Ladle the soup into the bowls and top each serving with croutons and tomatoes. Season with finishing salt and pour the vinegar over everything. Garnish with torn herbs, basil flowers and leaves, seeds, and pepper. Leftover soup will keep in an airtight container in the refrigerator for up to 2 days.

CHILLED BUTTERMILK & CUCUMBER SOUP

Buttermilk gets far too little respect. Its acidity and creamy texture make it useful well beyond its traditional role in biscuits and salad dressings. Here, we combine it with cucumbers and fresh fennel to make a particularly refreshing soup. The ingredients are inexpensive and easy to source and you can make it without ever turning on your stove—in short, it's the perfect food for a hot summer day. We like it with a chunk of black bread on the side.

Serves 4 to 6

2 qt/1.8 L kefir buttermilk → 76

1 cup/240 ml sour cream → 71

¼ cup/60 ml apple cider vinegar → 95

2 tbsp kosher salt

1 sweet white onion, cut into thin half-moons

1 lb/455 g Persian or Japanese cucumbers, cut on a bias into thin half-moons (seeds and skin are fine if not tough)

½ fennel bulb, halved lengthwise, cored, and cut crosswise into thin half-moons

Fenugreek sprouts → 79 for garnish

Fennel oil → 90 or extra-virgin olive oil for garnish

Cucumber flowers, dill leaves, sliced green onions, and halved mouse melons for garnish

In a large bowl, whisk together the buttermilk, sour cream, vinegar, and salt. Fold in the onion, cucumber, and fennel, mixing thoroughly to ensure all of the vegetables are evenly distributed. Cover and refrigerate for at least 1 hour to marinate the vegetables and allow them to soften.

Chill individual bowls in the refrigerator for at least 15 minutes. Ladle the soup into the bowls and top each serving with fenugreek sprouts and fennel oil. Garnish with cucumber flowers, dill, green onions, and mouse melons. Leftover soup will keep in an airtight container in the refrigerator for up to 4 days.

CHILLED BEET SOUP WITH CORIANDER & YOGURT

We both grew up with grandmothers who loved to cook. The smell of beets cooking on the stove takes us straight back to their kitchens. There is little that is more comforting than this soup. At Bar Tartine, borscht shows up in a number of variations—both hot and cold—all year long. This chilled version filled with fermented ingredients is one of our favorites.

It is important to add the sauerkraut and kvass to the soup after the beets and potato are cooked. Keeping these probiotic-packed ingredients away from heat ensures that they are alive and active and that the sauerkraut will remain crunchy.

Serves 4 to 6

SOUP

2 lb/910 g red beets (without greens), trimmed

½ cup/120 ml water

2 cups/480 ml kombu dashi → 137

1 sweet white onion, diced

1 medium russet potato, peeled and diced

6 garlic cloves, minced

1 serrano chile, stemmed and minced

2 tbsp fermented honey → 121, or honey

1 tsp caraway seeds, toasted and ground → 30

1 tsp fennel seeds, toasted and ground → 30

1 tsp freshly ground black pepper

3 cups/555 g sauerkraut with brine → 111, chopped

3 cups/720 ml beet kvass → 134, or 3 cups kombu dashi → 137 plus 1 tsp kosher salt

2 tbsp unfiltered grapeseed or sunflower oil

1 tbsp kosher salt

CORIANDER SAUCE

Leaves from 1 bunch fresh flat-leaf parsley

Leaves from 1 bunch fresh cilantro

3 tbsp kombu dashi → 137 or water, chilled

1 tsp coriander seeds, toasted and ground → 30

½ tsp kosher salt

Drained yogurt → 74 for garnish

Chopped fresh dill for garnish

Freshly ground black pepper

Arugula flowers for garnish

TO MAKE THE SOUP: Preheat the oven to 350°F/180°C. Spread the beets in a single layer in a shallow roasting pan. Add the water to the pan and cover tightly. Bake until tender enough to be easily pierced with a skewer, about 1 hour. Let the beets cool to room temperature, then peel them and, using a sharp knife, square off the sides of each beet, reserving the trimmings. Cut the squared beets into ¼-in/6-mm dice until you have 2 cups/315 g diced. Reserve the scraps.

In a large saucepan over medium heat, combine the dashi, onion, and potato and bring to a simmer. Cook until the potato is tender, about 30 minutes. Add the diced beets, garlic, chile, honey, caraway seeds, fennel seeds, and pepper and immediately remove from the heat. Let cool to room temperature and transfer to a large container. Stir in the sauerkraut and its brine.

In a blender, combine the beet scraps, kvass, and grapeseed oil and purée until smooth. Add to the cooled vegetables, stir in the salt, and refrigerate until well chilled, at least 2 hours.

TO MAKE THE CORIANDER SAUCE: Chill a blender beaker in the freezer for at least 15 minutes. Prepare an ice bath. Bring a large pot of water to a boil. Add the parsley and cilantro and boil until they are bright green and tender, about

15 seconds. With a slotted spoon, immediately transfer the herbs to the ice bath. When cool, remove them, squeeze out any excess water, pat dry, and coarsely chop.

In the cold blender, combine the herbs and dashi and blend on high speed until smooth. Do not overblend or the mixture will heat up, which can spoil the flavor of the herbs. Transfer to a bowl and stir in the coriander seeds and salt. Immediately cover and refrigerate until ready to use. This sauce tastes best if eaten the same day it is made.

To serve, chill individual bowls in the refrigerator for at least 15 minutes. Ladle the soup into the bowls and garnish each serving with coriander sauce, yogurt, dill, black pepper, and argula flowers. Leftover soup will keep in an airtight container in the refrigerator for up to 1 week.

WARM BEET SOUP WITH SMOKED BRISKET & BRUSSELS KRAUT

This soup is a bit of a project. It calls for a long-smoked brisket, which takes 3 days to make, and Brussels kraut, which takes months to ferment. Plan the summer holiday party early. Start the Brussels sprout pickle in December when they are sweet, forget about them until August, and serve with brisket that is smoked on the grill. Or substitute store-bought sauerkraut.

Serves 4 to 6

SMOKED BRISKET

1½ lb/680 g beef brisket, cut from the thicker section if possible

4 qt/3.8 L onion brine → 115

BEET SOUP

1 lb/455 g red beets (without greens)

½ cup/120 ml water

½ cup/120 ml tallow → 94

2 sweet white onions, cut into ½-in/12-mm dice

10 garlic cloves, thinly sliced

8 dried árbol chiles, toasted and crushed, or 1 tbsp red pepper flakes → 42

2 tbsp hot paprika → 42

2 qt/2 L beef broth → 142

3 cups/550 g Brussels kraut → 112, sprouts halved

2 cups/480 ml Brussels kraut brine → 112

6 fully dried tomatoes → 40, minced

Reserved cubed smoked brisket

1 tbsp plus 1 tsp kosher salt

1 tsp freshly ground black pepper

Sour cream → 71 for garnish

Freshly ground black pepper

Chopped fresh dill for garnish

Chopped green onions (white and tender green parts, cut on a bias) for garnish

Chopped fresh flat-leaf parsley leaves for garnish

TO MAKE THE SMOKED BRISKET: In a large container, combine the brisket and brine, cover, and refrigerate for 48 hours. Remove the brisket from the brine and pat dry with a towel.

Soak six generous handfuls of hardwood chips in water to cover for at least 1 hour.

If using a smoker: Following the manufacturer's instructions, set up and smoke the brisket at 180°F/82°C until the meat is very tender but not falling apart, 10 to 12 hours.

CONTINUED

BAR TARTINE

If using a gas grill: Light one burner to medium. Put a smoker box over the lit burner, add a handful of soaked wood chips to the box, and close the grill. Adjust the heat as needed to keep the temperature at 180°F/82°C. The wood chips should begin to smolder and release a steady stream of smoke. Put the brisket, fat-side up, on the grate opposite the lit burner. Cover the grill and smoke the meat, adjusting the heat as needed to keep the temperature at 180°F/82°C. Check the wood chips every 45 minutes or so and add more soaked chips as necessary to keep the smoke level constant. Rotate the brisket every 3 hours, flipping as needed if one side is coloring faster than the other, until the meat is very tender but not falling apart, 10 to 12 hours.

If using a charcoal grill: Fill a chimney starter with charcoal; light it and let burn until the coals are covered with a thin layer of ash. Pour the hot coals on one side of the grill. Add a handful of soaked wood chips next to the hot coals, put the grate on the grill, and cover the grill, positioning the vent on the lid on the side opposite the fire. Stick a thermometer through the vent and heat the grill to 180°F/82°C, adjusting the vents on the top and bottom of the grill as necessary to maintain the temperature. Put the brisket, fat-side up, on the grate opposite the coals. Cover the grill and smoke the meat, adjusting the vents as needed to keep the temperature at 180°F/82°C. Check the fire every 45 minutes or so and add more hot coals and soaked chips as necessary to keep the smoke level constant. Rotate the brisket every 3 hours, flipping as needed if one side is coloring faster than the other, until the meat is very tender but not falling apart, 10 to 12 hours.

When the brisket is ready, remove from the heat. Transfer to a cutting board or tray. Let the meat rest until it is cool enough to handle, about 20 minutes. (We keep the fat cap because the fat adds good flavor to the finished dish, but you can trim off some of it if you like.) Cut the meat into ½-in/12-mm cubes and reserve.

TO MAKE THE BEET SOUP: Preheat the oven to 350°F/180°C. Spread the beets in a single layer in a shallow roasting pan. Add the water to the pan and cover tightly. Bake until tender enough to be easily pierced with a skewer, about 1 hour. Let the beets cool to room temperature, then peel them and cut into ½-in/12-mm cubes. Set aside. The beets can be cooked up to 3 days ahead.

Heat a large saucepan over medium heat until a drop of water flicked on the surface sizzles gently on contact. Add the tallow, onions, garlic, and chiles and cook, stirring occasionally, until the vegetables are slightly softened but not browned, about 10 minutes. Add the paprika and stir until fragrant, about 1 minute. Add the broth, Brussels kraut with its brine, and tomatoes. Turn the heat to low and simmer until the Brussels kraut is tender, about 1 hour.

Add the reserved brisket and the beets, salt, and pepper. Mix well and turn down the heat to the very lowest setting. Cook until all of the ingredients are warmed through and flavorful, about 30 minutes longer.

To serve, ladle the soup into individual bowls and garnish each serving with sour cream, black pepper, dill, green onions, and parsley. Leftover soup will keep in an airtight container in the refrigerator for up to 5 days.

POTATO & GREEN BEAN SOUP

This is a soup to make in late summer, when the days get shorter and the green beans grow big and tough. It is ideal for those end-of-season beans, which are much better cooked well past the bright green and crisp stage that culinary professionals prize. In this soup, the beans are cooked grandmother-style, until they are quite tender and develop a deep, earthy flavor.

The butter that floats on the surface of this soup is essential to the soup's texture and flavor. We recommend you use cultured butter, which has a subtle tang. You can make it yourself or purchase it.

Serves 4 to 6

1 tbsp filtered grapeseed oil

1 sweet white onion, cut into ¼-in/6-mm dice

4 garlic cloves, minced

3 cups/720 ml strong dashi → 138

12 oz/335 g russet potatoes, peeled and cut into ¼-in/6-mm dice

1 lb/455 g green beans, trimmed and cut into ¾-in/2-cm pieces

3 cups/720 ml kefir buttermilk → 76

1 tbsp plus 2 tsp kosher salt

Freshly ground black pepper

1 cup/240 ml sour cream → 71

3 tbsp apple cider vinegar → 95

2 tbsp kefir butter → 76, melted

Chopped fresh flat-leaf parsley for garnish

Chopped fresh dill for garnish

Chopped fresh chives for garnish

Heat a medium saucepan over medium heat until a drop of water flicked on the surface sizzles gently on contact. Add the grapeseed oil, then immediately add the onion and garlic and cook, stirring occasionally, until the vegetables are slightly softened but not browned, about 10 minutes. Add the dashi, potatoes, and green beans and simmer until the potatoes are tender enough to be easily pierced with a skewer, about 25 minutes. Remove from the heat.

In a blender, combine 2 cups/475 ml of the broth and vegetables and the buttermilk and purée until smooth. Add the purée back to the saucepan, add the salt and ½ tsp pepper, and place over medium heat. Bring to a simmer and cook gently until heated through, about 5 minutes. Remove from the heat and stir in ¾ cup/180 ml of the sour cream and the vinegar.

Ladle the soup into individual bowls and garnish with melted butter, the remaining ¼ cup/60 ml sour cream, the parsley, dill, and chives, and plenty of pepper. Leftover soup will keep in an airtight container in the refrigerator for up to 4 days.

BLACK GARLIC & LENTIL SOUP

Lentil soup, or *lencseleves*, is a favorite in Hungary. There are many variations, but most include onion and some type of smoked pork product. We use sprouted lentils here, but unsprouted lentils work well, too. They cook differently, so if you opt for unsprouted, use half the amount of lentils to prevent the broth from becoming too thick.

Serves 4 to 6

1 tbsp lard → 93 or filtered grapeseed oil

1 sweet white onion, cut into half-moons ¼ in/ 6 mm thick

2 green bell peppers, stemmed, seeded, and cut into ½-in/12-mm dice

1 green serrano chile, stemmed, halved lengthwise, and cut into thin half-moons

6 cups/1.4 L chicken broth → 139

25 peeled black garlic cloves → 39 or roasted garlic cloves

8 dried árbol chiles, stemmed, charred, and crushed, or 1 tbsp red pepper flakes → 42

3 tomatoes, cored and roughly chopped

2 cups/380 g black lentils → 79, sprouted

12 oz/340 g dry paprika sausage, dry chorizo, Hungarian gyulai, or pepperoni, sliced

12 garlic cloves, finely chopped

12 oz/340 g button mushrooms, sliced thin

2 bay leaves

2 tbsp hot paprika → 42

2 tbsp apple cider vinegar → 95

2 tsp kosher salt

Freshly ground black pepper

Sour cream → 71 for garnish

Chopped green onions, white and tender green parts, for garnish

Chopped fresh cilantro, for garnish

Heat a large cast-iron skillet over medium-high heat until a drop of water flicked on the surface sizzles gently on contact. Add the lard to the pan and, once it has melted, add the onion, bell peppers, and serrano. Cook, stirring occasionally, until the vegetables are well charred but not blackened, about 15 minutes. Remove from the heat and let cool.

In a blender, combine 2 cups/480 ml of the broth, the black garlic, and the árbol chiles. Purée until smooth.

In a large pot, combine the purée, the remaining broth, and the tomatoes, lentils, sausage, garlic, mushrooms, and bay leaves and bring to a simmer over medium-low heat. Cook until the lentils just begin to soften, about 25 minutes. Add the paprika and charred vegetables and simmer gently until the lentils begin to fall apart and thicken the soup, about 20 minutes longer. Remove and discard the bay leaves. Add the vinegar and salt, and season with pepper.

Ladle the soup into individual bowls and garnish each serving with sour cream, green onions, and cilantro. Leftover soup will keep in an airtight container in the refrigerator for up to 4 days.

SAUERKRAUT SOUP

Nick's father first made this soup when he was living in Slovakia. It's a traditional part of the Christmas Eve meal there and is only slightly less popular every other day of the year. It's still the first—or maybe the second—dish Nick requests when his dad is cooking. It's the very essence of agrodolce— the marriage of sweet and sour. There's umami here, too, as well as spice and smoke. Ultimately, it's the flavor of comfort.

Nick's dad likes to put a scoop of mashed potatoes into each bowl before he ladles in the soup. If you go this route, don't use potatoes in the recipe.

Serves 4 to 8

2 qt/2 L chicken broth → 139

3 cups/415 g drained sauerkraut → 111

1 cup/240 ml sauerkraut brine → 111

1 lb/455 g dry paprika sausage, dry chorizo, Hungarian gyulai, or pepperoni sliced into ¼-in/6-mm half-moons

4 oz/115 g slab bacon, cut into small dice

8 oz/230 g button mushrooms, stemmed and halved

4 green serrano chiles, stemmed and thinly sliced

2 green bell peppers, stemmed, seeded, and cut into ½-in/12-mm dice

2 sweet white onions, cut into large dice

2 oz/60 g apple wedges, pitted prunes, dried apricots → 56, or dried sour cherries → 58, cut into bite-size pieces

8 oz/225 g russet potato, peeled and cut into ½-in/12-mm dice

2 large tomatoes, cored and cut into ½-in/12-mm dice, with their juice

12 garlic cloves, chopped

5 tbsp hot paprika → 42

10 dried chipotle chiles → 42 or árbol chiles (optional, for a spicy soup)

1 tbsp caraway seeds, toasted → 30

2 bay leaves

2 tbsp kosher salt

Sour cream → 71 for garnish

Freshly ground black pepper

In a large saucepan over medium-high heat, combine the broth, sauerkraut and brine, sausage, bacon, mushrooms, serranos, bell peppers, onions, fruit, and potato and bring to a simmer. Cover and turn the heat to medium-low. Maintain a gentle simmer and cook gently until the potatoes are tender but firm, about 30 minutes.

Add the tomatoes, garlic, paprika, chipotles (if using), caraway seeds, bay leaves, and salt and continue to simmer, uncovered, until the potatoes are just about to fall apart, about 20 minutes longer. Remove and discard the bay leaves.

Ladle the soup into individual bowls and garnish each serving with sour cream and pepper. Leftover soup will keep in an airtight container in the refrigerator for up to 1 week.

BEEF GULYAS WITH MARROW TOAST

Gulyas, Hungary's best-known dish, is traditionally cooked in an iron kettle (*bogrács*) over an open fire. Many versions exist, but the most recognized one is based on a meat broth, usually beef, with onion, potato, fresh green pepper, paprika, and caraway. It is sometimes served with egg noodles and even sauerkraut. In the Czech Republic, bread dumplings often show up in the soup, and the broth is sometimes thickened like gravy. In the United States, someone decided that elbow macaroni with ground beef and tomatoes could also be called gulyas (although the innovator changed the spelling to goulash). We love them all, but this is our favorite.

Bone marrow on toast was Nick's grandfather Bill's favorite snack. It's also the perfect accompaniment to gulyas.

Serves 4 to 8

ROASTED MARROWBONES

6 tbsp/60 g kosher salt

8 cups/1.8 L water

8 beef marrowbones, cut into 2-in/5-cm lengths

Finishing salt

GULYAS

One 750-ml bottle dry red wine

1 lb/455 g boneless beef chuck, cut into ½-in/12-mm chunks

Kosher salt

Freshly ground black pepper

1 tbsp lard → 93 or unfiltered grapeseed oil

4 oz/115 g slab bacon, cut into ¼-in/6-mm dice

2 sweet white onions, cut into ¼-in/6-mm dice

2 tbsp sweet paprika → 42

2 tbsp hot paprika → 42

8 cups/1.9 L beef broth → 142

2 medium russet potatoes, peeled and cut into ½-in/12-mm dice

3 green bell peppers, seeded and cut into ½-in/12-mm dice

2 green serrano chiles, stemmed and minced

20 garlic cloves, chopped

2 tsp caraway seeds, toasted and ground → 30

Fresh marjoram leaves for garnish

6 to 8 slices country-style bread, toasted

TO PREPARE THE ROASTED MARROWBONES: In a large nonreactive container, dissolve the kosher salt in the water. Add the marrowbones and refrigerate for 12 hours.

TO MAKE THE GULYAS: Pour the wine into a small saucepan, place over low heat, and simmer until reduced to 2 cups/480 ml, about 1 hour. Remove from the heat. Season the beef with 2 tsp of the kosher salt and let stand for about 15 minutes.

CONTINUED

Heat a heavy-bottomed Dutch oven over high heat until a drop of water flicked on the surface sizzles gently on contact. Add the lard and, once it has melted, add the seasoned beef and cook, turning as needed, until well browned on all sides, about 10 minutes. Turn the heat to medium, add the bacon and onions, and cook until the onions begin to brown, about 10 minutes. Add the sweet and hot paprikas and stir until fragrant, about 1 minute. Add the reduced wine, the broth, 2 tsp kosher salt, and 1 tsp black pepper, turn the heat to low, cover, and cook, stirring occasionally, until the meat is almost tender, about 1½ hours.

Add the potatoes, bell peppers, serranos, garlic, and caraway seeds to the Dutch oven and cook until the potatoes are tender enough to be easily pierced with a skewer, about 15 minutes. Cover the soup to keep hot.

After adding the vegetables to the gulyas, preheat the oven to 350°F/180°C. Remove the marrowbones from the soaking water and pat dry. Arrange the bones in a single layer in a roasting pan.

Roast the bones until the marrow is hot and beginning to render into the pan, about 20 minutes. Poke through the marrow with a metal skewer and then touch the skewer to ensure the marrow is hot throughout. Transfer the hot bones to a serving plate and season with finishing salt.

Ladle the hot soup into individual bowls, garnish with marjoram leaves and pepper, and serve with the marrowbones and toasted bread. Leftover soup will keep in an airtight container in the refrigerator for up to 4 days.

BAR TARTINE

FISHERMAN'S STEW WITH GREEN CHILE & COLLARDS

This Southwestern riff on Hungarian fish stew was born by accident one winter when we ran out of red paprika and moved into our stash of dried green Hatch chiles. These peppers from New Mexico have a grassy aroma that stands out in a wonderful way next to the earthy flavor of freshwater fish.

If you can find a whole fish and you are comfortable using a fillet knife, a 3½ to 4 lb/ 1.6 to 1.8 kg fish will yield plenty of meat for the stew and enough scraps to make the stock. Don't use the gills, guts, or scales in the stock, but if you have the liver, it will add richness. If you prefer, have the fish filleted for you and ask your fishmonger for the scraps.

Serves 4 to 6

2 cups/55 g packed fresh flat-leaf parsley leaves

8 cups/2 L fish stock → 142

2 tsp filtered sunflower oil

2 small sweet white onions, thinly sliced

8 garlic cloves, thinly sliced

4 oz/115 g hen-of-the-woods or oyster mushrooms, stemmed

One 8-oz/225-g fennel bulb, halved, cored, and thinly sliced

1 tbsp kosher salt

3 tbsp Hatch or other green chile powder → 45

1 lb/455 g skinless sturgeon, carp, or catfish fillets, cut into ½-in/12-mm pieces

4 oz/115 g young collard greens, stemmed and torn into 1-in/2.5-cm pieces

¼ cup/60 ml fish sauce

12 oil-packed anchovy fillets, minced

1 lemon, halved

Green onions, white and tender green parts, thinly sliced, for garnish

Fresh flat-leaf parsley for garnish

Freshly ground black pepper

In a blender or food processor, combine 1½ cups/ 40 g of the parsley leaves and 2 cups/480 ml of the stock and purée until smooth. Set aside.

In a large saucepan over medium-high heat, bring the remaining stock to a simmer. Heat a medium sauté pan over medium heat until a drop of water flicked on the surface sizzles gently on contact. Add the sunflower oil to the sauté pan and then immediately add the onions, garlic, mushrooms, fennel, and 1 tsp of the salt. Cook, stirring occasionally, until the vegetables begin to soften, about 10 minutes. Add the chile powder and stir until fragrant, about 1 minute. Transfer the cooked vegetables to the simmering stock along with the fish pieces, collard greens, fish sauce, anchovies, and remaining 2 tsp salt. Simmer until the fish is cooked and the collards are tender, about 5 minutes. Note that carp and catfish are more delicate than sturgeon. They will fall apart if cooked for more than 5 minutes or

stirred too vigorously. Stir in the puréed parsley mixture and remove from the heat.

Ladle the stew into individual bowls. Tear the remaining parsley leaves directly into each serving. Add a squeeze of lemon juice to each bowl and garnish with green onions, parsley, and pepper. Leftover stew will keep in an airtight container in the refrigerator for up to 4 days.

FISHERMAN'S STEW WITH PAPRIKA & EGG NOODLES

The Hungarian town of Baja is famous for its fish stew, and its citizens are locked in an unending argument with the nearby town of Szeged (and every other town in the country) as to whose fish stew is best. In Baja, the bright-red broth is usually poured over spiral egg noodles and the fish is served on the side. We've included a recipe for a simple noodle dough, but dried spaghetti broken into random-sized pieces makes a good substitute.

Serves 4 to 6

NOODLES

½ cup/60 g "oo" flour

½ cup/60 g all-purpose flour

8 egg yolks, beaten

Two 1-lb/455-g carp or catfish, cleaned and cut crosswise into steaks 1 in/2.5 cm thick

2 tsp kosher salt

PAPRIKA BROTH

2 tbsp lard → 93

2 green bell peppers, diced

4 sweet white onions, diced

12 garlic cloves, thinly sliced

½ cup/55 g hot paprika → 42, chile powder, or a mixture of hot and sweet paprikas

2 cups/480 ml dry red wine

6 cups/1.4 L fish stock → 142

Kosher salt

Chopped fresh chives for garnish

Fresh curly parsley leaves for garnish

Sour cream → 71 for garnish

TO MAKE THE NOODLES: Set a large mixing bowl on a wet towel. Sift the "oo" and all-purpose flours into the bowl. Make a well in the flour and pour the egg yolks into it. Starting from the yolks and working out to the edges of the bowl, swirl the mixture with your hands or a spoon, slowly and gradually pulling the flour into the yolks until a cohesive dough forms; add a bit more water if the dough is dry.

Remove the dough from the bowl and place it on a dry, clean work surface. Knead the dough until it is silky and taut, about 5 minutes. Flatten into a disk and wrap with plastic wrap. Rest at room temperature for at least 1 hour or up to 6 hours, to relax the glutens.

Unwrap the dough and gently flatten it as much as possible with the heel of your hand. If rolling by hand, lightly flour the work surface and roll the dough to ⅛ in/3 mm thick. If using a pasta machine, set it to its widest setting. Lightly flour the dough and run it through the rollers, folding the dough in half and then rolling again. Continue folding and rolling until the dough is silky smooth, six to eight passes. Continue rolling, setting the machine one setting lower each time to produce a dough that is ⅛ in/3 mm thick.

Have a small bowl of water at hand. By hand or using a cutting attachment, cut the noodles into strips about ⅛ in/3mm thick. Now cut the long ribbons into 2-in/5-cm pieces. Cover the extra dough with a damp cloth while you work. Take two pieces in your hand and pinch them together at the top, using a bit of water to adhere them. Twist until the other ends meet, and secure them with a bit of water and a good pinch. Set aside and continue twisting until you have formed all of the noodles. Use immediately, or leave to dry, uncovered.

Season the fish steaks on both sides with the salt and refrigerate for 1 hour.

TO MAKE THE PAPRIKA BROTH: In a heavy-bottomed Dutch oven over medium-low heat, melt the lard and then add the bell peppers, onions, and garlic. Cook, stirring occasionally, until the onions are soft but not browned, about 20 minutes. Add the paprika and stir constantly until fragrant, about 1 minute. Add the wine and simmer until much of the alcohol aroma has dissipated, about 10 minutes. Add the stock and simmer for another 40 minutes. At this point, the onions should be tender and the broth flavorful. Add 4 tsp salt, then taste and adjust the seasoning if needed. If not using right away, let cool, transfer to an airtight container, and refrigerate for up to 1 week. Pour the broth into a Dutch oven and bring to a simmer over medium heat when ready to finish.

Bring a large pot of salted water to a boil over high heat. Add the noodles and cook until just tender, about 4 minutes for fresh, 8 minutes for dried, then drain. When the broth is simmering gently with no bubbles visible, lower the fish steaks into it and cook just until the fish flakes easily, about 5 minutes.

Using a slotted spoon, carefully transfer the fish steaks to a serving platter. Ladle the broth into a large serving bowl and add the cooked noodles. Garnish the broth and noodles with chives, parsley, and sour cream. Serve the fish alongside the noodles and broth.

SALADS

To us, a salad is a meal and, like most things we eat,
we like salads generous and bold.

We have nothing against lettuce, but many of our favorite
salads have no greens at all. Instead, they combine cut-up
vegetables like cauliflower and cucumbers that marinate
until their juices collect in the bottom of the bowl. Those
juices are the best part of the salad, and they beg to
be sopped up with a hunk of bread. At the restaurant,
we call these "spoon salads" because you can never
get to all those delicious juices with a fork.

There are a variety of salads in this chapter. Try some
of them *as* dinner instead of *with* dinner, or have them
with one of the soups from this book. Your notion of
what an entrée is may change.

CHICORY SALAD WITH ANCHOVY DRESSING

This is one of our favorite salads to make at home, and we consider it a meal in itself. Since neither of us is very good at cooking for two, the first time we made it at home, we made enough for ten and ate it out of an 18-qt/17-L Dutch oven, as that was the only container on hand big enough for mixing the greens. Chicories are bitter, hardy, and stand up well to a strong dressing, but underneath their bite is a sweetness that begs for layers of acid, salt, and spice.

Serves 4 to 6

ANCHOVY DRESSING

7 tbsp/100 ml fresh lemon juice

1 tsp fish sauce

1 tbsp red wine vinegar → 95

2 tbsp fermented honey → 121, or honey

18 oil-packed anchovy fillets, minced

6 garlic cloves, minced

1 cup plus 2 tbsp/115 g freshly grated hard cheese such as Parmesan or Piave Vecchio cheese

¾ cup/180 ml unfiltered sunflower oil

2 tsp kosher salt

1 tsp freshly ground black pepper

⅛ tsp Hatch chile powder or spicy red paprika powder → 42

1 tbsp freshly grated horseradish

SALAD

1 lb/455 g mixed chicories, such as Treviso, puntarelle, radicchio, escarole, and endive, trimmed and roughly torn into 1-in/2.5-cm pieces

1 fennel bulb, halved, cored and thinly sliced

1 bunch radishes, trimmed and thinly sliced

2 kohlrabies or small daikon radishes, peeled and cut into thin half-moons

1 bunch green onions, white and tender green parts, thinly sliced ¼ in/6 mm thick

½ bunch fresh dill, chopped

½ bunch fresh flat-leaf parsley, chopped

Fresh horseradish for garnish

TO MAKE THE ANCHOVY DRESSING: In a small bowl, whisk together the lemon juice, fish sauce, vinegar, honey, anchovies, garlic, Parmesan, sunflower oil, salt, pepper, chile powder, and horseradish. Cover and refrigerate until ready to use. The dressing can be stored in an airtight container and refrigerated for up to 5 days. Shake well before using.

TO MAKE THE SALAD: In a large bowl, combine the chicories, fennel, radishes, kohlrabies, green onions, dill, and parsley. Add the dressing and toss to coat evenly. Finely grate the horseradish over the salad and serve.

WEDGE SALAD WITH BUTTERMILK, BARLEY & SPROUTS

We love iceberg lettuce. It is delicious, crunchy, and moist, and the perfect vehicle for this ranch-style dressing. An American classic, ranch dressing is a favorite from our childhoods, when we smothered everything from pizza to broccoli in it. Here, we try to create a dressing as satisfying as the one we remember from our youth, using our own cultured dairy products and house-made spices.

Serves 4 to 6

BUTTERMILK DRESSING

⅓ cup/75 ml sour cream → 71

⅓ cup/75 ml kefir buttermilk → 76

⅓ cup/75 ml mayonnaise (see Ramp Mayonnaise → 226; omit ramps)

2 tsp sweet onion powder → 34

½ tsp garlic powder → 37

½ tsp dill powder → 31

½ green serrano chile, minced

2 garlic cloves, minced

½ bunch fresh chives, minced

1 tsp minced fresh dill

1 tsp minced fresh flat-leaf parsley

½ tsp minced fresh thyme

½ tsp minced fresh marjoram

2 tsp fresh lemon juice

2 tsp kosher salt

1 tsp freshly ground black pepper

SALAD

1 cup/225 g pearl barley

3 cups/720 ml kombu dashi → 137

Kosher salt

¼ cup/60 ml fresh lemon juice

6 tbsp/90 ml marjoram oil or parsley oil → 87, plus more for garnish

1 bunch radishes, trimmed and thinly sliced

1 kohlrabi or daikon radish, peeled and cut into thin half-moons

2 Tokyo turnips, peeled and thinly sliced

1 fennel bulb, cored and thinly sliced

½ cup/75 g mung bean sprouts or other bean sprouts → 79

½ cup/80 g lentil sprouts or other sprouts → 79

1 head iceberg lettuce, cut into 4 to 6 wedges through the core

Leaves from ¼ bunch each fresh dill, chervil, and flat-leaf parsley

Freshly ground black pepper

Finishing salt

TO MAKE THE SALAD: In a medium saucepan over medium-high heat, combine the barley, dashi, and a pinch of salt and bring to a boil. Turn the heat to low, cover, and simmer, stirring occasionally, until all of the liquid has been absorbed and the barley is tender, 30 to 40 minutes. Turn the barley out onto a flat plate or a small sheet pan and spread in an even layer to cool. The cooled barley will keep in an airtight container in the refrigerator for up to 4 days.

In a small bowl, whisk together the lemon juice and marjoram oil with 2 tsp salt. In a large bowl, combine the cooled barley with the radishes, kohlrabi, turnips, fennel, mung bean sprouts, and lentil sprouts. Add ⅓ cup/75 ml of the lemon juice mixture to the bowl and toss to coat evenly. Put the lettuce wedges in a separate large bowl and moisten them with the remaining lemon juice mixture, making sure the dressing seeps into the crevices of each wedge. Season the wedges with salt.

Arrange the iceberg wedges on individual salad plates or on a serving platter. Pour the buttermilk dressing over the wedges, then distribute the dressed vegetables and barley evenly over the wedges, allowing them to fall naturally over the top and onto the plate. Garnish with the dill, chervil, parsley, and more marjoram oil. Season with salt and pepper and serve. This salad tastes best if eaten immediately.

TO MAKE THE BUTTERMILK DRESSING: In a medium bowl, combine the sour cream, buttermilk, mayonnaise, onion powder, garlic powder, dill powder, serrano, garlic, chives, dill, parsley, thyme, marjoram, lemon juice, salt, and pepper and mix well. Transfer to an airtight container and refrigerate for up to 1 week.

KALE SALAD WITH RYE BREAD, SEEDS & YOGURT

Bread salads, such as *panzanella* and *fattoush*, are most often associated with Mediterranean cooking, but this one made with rye bread draws from northern Europe with a nod to the Middle East. It came together when our friends at Little City Gardens, an urban garden located not far from the restaurant, brought us an especially large harvest of kale. We decided to try a salad with sunflower tahini we had been using on another dish and extra rye bread. It turned into one of the dishes that is a constant on our menu. Some of our favorite dishes have been fated into existence when we were faced with a glut of ingredients that we would never have thought of pairing and yet turn out to be delicious when combined.

Serves 4 to 6

SUNFLOWER TAHINI

6 garlic cloves

¼ cup/60 ml unfiltered grapeseed oil

1 cup/115 g sunflower seeds, toasted

1 tbsp chutney spice → 53

¼ green serrano chile

½ cup/120 ml kombu dashi → 137 or water

1½ tbsp fresh lemon juice

1 tsp fermented honey → 121, or honey

Kosher salt

1 cup/240 ml drained yogurt → 74

¾ tsp fermented honey → 121, or honey

2 tbsp unfiltered grapeseed oil

1 lb/455 g lacinato or other kale, stems removed and leaves torn into 1- to 2-in/ 2.5- to 5-cm pieces

2 tbsp water

8 oz/225 g Danish-style rye bread, crust removed and torn into bite-size pieces

Sunflower seeds, toasted, for garnish

Sesame seeds, toasted, for garnish

Shelled pumpkin seeds, toasted, for garnish

Golden flaxseeds for garnish

Yogurt powder → 48 for garnish

Garlic oil → 91 or unfiltered grapeseed oil for garnish

Freshly ground black pepper

Finishing salt

TO MAKE THE SUNFLOWER TAHINI: In a small saucepan over very low heat, combine the garlic and grapeseed oil and cook until the garlic is soft, about 30 minutes. Let cool to room temperature.

In a blender, combine the cooled garlic and oil, the sunflower seeds, chutney spice, serrano, dashi, lemon juice, honey, and 1 tsp salt and pulse on high speed at intervals of 15 seconds, stopping occasionally to scrape down the sides of the blender, until the tahini is slightly thinner than peanut butter. The tahini can be made up to 2 weeks in advance and stored in an airtight container in the refrigerator; bring to room temperature before using.

In a small bowl, combine the yogurt, honey, and 1 tsp salt and stir to mix.

Heat a large sauce pan over medium heat until a drop of water flicked on the surface sizzles gently on contact. Add the grapeseed oil and kale, season with salt, and cook, stirring constantly, until the kale begins to wilt, about 1 minute. Add the water and rye bread and toss to warm the bread, about 15 seconds.

Spread the tahini in a large circle on a large platter. Spread the yogurt mixture on top of the tahini. Distribute the kale mixture over the yogurt and tahini and garnish with all of the seeds and the yogurt powder. Pour the garlic oil evenly over the salad, season generously with pepper and finishing salt, and serve. This salad tastes best if eaten immediately.

TOMATO & PICKLED GREEN BEAN SALAD WITH WHIPPED FETA

In Michigan, Nick's mother grows the best tomatoes in the world. In the mid and late summer, they are the center of every meal. The combination of tomatoes, cucumbers, and green onions is classic. For this recipe, we add brined green beans and a whipped feta-like cheese. It reminds us of Greek salad.

Serves 4 to 6

WHIPPED FETA

12 oz/340 g cheese in the style of feta → 70, crumbled

½ cup/120 ml sour cream → 71

1 tbsp fresh lemon juice

1 tbsp fermented honey → 121, or honey

1 tbsp sweet onion powder → 34

1 tsp kosher salt

1 tsp freshly ground black pepper

1 qt/750 g cherry tomatoes, halved

4 Persian or Japanese cucumbers, halved lengthwise and cut into thin half-moons

¼ cup/50 g brined green beans → 110

2 bunches green onions, cut into ¼-in/6-mm rounds

3 garlic cloves, minced

¼ cup/60 ml unfiltered sunflower oil

3 tbsp red wine vinegar → 95

1½ tsp minced fresh marjoram

1½ tsp kosher salt

Freshly ground black pepper

2 tbsp marjoram oil → 87 or extra-virgin olive oil

Finishing salt

Fresh marjoram, chervil, or flat-leaf parsley for garnish

TO MAKE THE WHIPPED FETA: In a food processor, combine the feta, sour cream, lemon juice, honey, onion powder, salt, and pepper and purée until the texture resembles softened cream cheese. The whipped feta can be made in advance and stored in an airtight container in the refrigerator for up to 1 week.

In a large bowl, combine the tomatoes, cucumbers, green beans, green onions, garlic, sunflower oil, vinegar, marjoram, and salt. Season with pepper and stir gently to coat evenly. Let marinate until the vegetables begin to give off some of their juice, about 30 minutes.

Transfer the marinated vegetables to a large serving platter. With a large spoon, place a scoop of the whipped feta in the middle of the salad. Garnish the entire salad with the marjoram oil, finishing salt, and pepper. Leftover salad can be stored in an airtight container in the refrigerator for up to 3 days.

BEET & BLUE CHEESE SALAD

Food with strong flavors, such as olives, aged meat, stinky cheese, and anchovies, are staple ingredients in the foods we crave. This salad features two bold tastes and, although the combination is uncommon, has found fans among diners who swear they don't like either ingredient. Nick never liked blue cheese until his dad made this salad for him as a kid. The first time he tried it, he changed his mind.

Serves 4 to 6

2 lb/910 g red beets (without greens)

½ cup/120 ml water

2 garlic cloves, minced

½ cup/120 ml unfiltered grapeseed oil

3 tbsp red wine vinegar → 95

2 tbsp fresh lemon juice

2 tsp kosher salt

1 tsp freshly ground black pepper

8 oz/225 g firm blue cheese, crumbled

1 bunch green onions, white and tender green parts, cut into ¼-in/6-mm rounds

½ bunch fresh dill, chopped

4 tbsp dill sprouts → 79

Preheat the oven to 350°F/180°C. Spread the beets in a single layer in a shallow roasting pan. Add the water to the pan and cover tightly. Bake until tender and easily pierced with a skewer, about 1 hour. Let the beets cool to room temperature, then peel the beets and cut into ½-in/12-mm dice. Refrigerate to cool completely.

In a large bowl, whisk together the garlic, grapeseed oil, vinegar, lemon juice, salt, and pepper. Add the beets, blue cheese, green onions, dill, and dill sprouts and toss to combine. Let stand for at least 15 minutes to allow the beets to marinate.

Scoop the salad into large bowls and serve. This salad tastes best if eaten the same day it is made. Leftovers will keep in an airtight container in the refrigerator for up to 2 days.

BEET AND BLUE CHEESE SALAD WITH BEET THINNINGS AND DILL SAUCE

CAULIFLOWER SALAD WITH YOGURT & CHICKPEAS

In early autumn, when the first cauliflowers arrive at the market and summer cucumbers are still abundant, we put this salad on the menu. Those few weeks when one season straddles another are a time of movement and change, and our minds itch as we're pulled in different directions. This is a salad based on textures—the dense cauliflower, the crunchy sprouted chickpeas—so whichever way we choose to go, we still hold on to that as the core of this dish.

Serves 4 to 6

YOGURT DRESSING

1 cup/240 ml drained yogurt → 74

5 tbsp/75 ml unfiltered sunflower oil

2 garlic cloves, minced

2 tbsp fresh lemon juice

1 tbsp red wine vinegar → 95

1 tbsp fermented honey → 121, or honey

2 tsp kosher salt

Freshly ground pepper

2 Persian or Japanese cucumbers, cut into ½-in/12-mm dice

One 12-oz/340-g head cauliflower, cut into florets

1 bunch green onions, white and tender green parts, cut into ¼-in/6-mm rounds

1 cup/200 g chickpeas, sprouted → 79, or 1 cup/625 g drained cooked chickpeas

8 oz/225 g button mushrooms, stems trimmed and quartered

1 bunch radishes, trimmed and thinly sliced

1 or 2 green serrano chiles, stemmed and thinly sliced

¼ cup/35 g sunflower seeds, lightly toasted

Leaves from ½ bunch each fresh dill, flat-leaf parsley, and tarragon, chopped

Sweet paprika → 42 for garnish

TO MAKE THE YOGURT DRESSING: In a large bowl, whisk together the yogurt, sunflower oil, garlic, lemon juice, vinegar, honey, salt, and pepper to taste. The dressing can be made up to 1 week in advance and stored in an airtight container in the refrigerator.

Add the cucumbers to the bowl with the dressing along with the cauliflower, green onions, chickpeas, mushrooms, radishes, serrano(s), sunflower seeds, dill, parsley, and tarragon and let stand for 15 minutes. Toss all of the ingredients with the dressing and let stand until the vegetables begin to give off some of their liquid and the cauliflower begins to take on a silky texture, about 15 minutes longer. The salad should be slightly soupy.

Transfer the salad to a serving platter, garnish with the paprika, and serve. Leftover salad will keep in an airtight container in the refrigerator for up to 2 days.

CHOPPED SUMMER VEGETABLE SALAD WITH CHEESE & SALAMI

Anyone who has ever eaten a classic East Coast deli sandwich made with several kinds of cold cuts, sweet and spicy peppers, and onions, all drenched in vinaigrette, will immediately recognize the flavors in this salad. We like it best from late June through late September, when locally grown tomatoes and peppers fill our markets. It is among our favorite dishes to eat at home. Nick's dad makes many versions of this salad; it is a part of every feast, holiday, party, or event.

Serves 4 to 6

¾ lb/350 g dry paprika sausage, dry chorizo, Hungarian gyulai, or pepperoni, cut into ½-in/12-mm dice

½ lb/225 g Gouda, pepper Jack, or Havarti cheese, cut into ½-in/12-mm dice

8 oz/225 g button mushrooms, stems trimmed and cut into quarters or sixths

1 small sweet white onion, cut into ½-inch/12-mm dice

3 yellow or green Hungarian wax peppers, stemmed, seeded, and cut into ½-in/12-mm dice

1 or 2 green serrano or jalapeño chiles, chopped

4 tomatoes, cored and chopped into ½-in/12-mm dice

4 garlic cloves, minced

⅔ cup/160 ml unfiltered grapeseed oil or sunchoke oil → 90

¼ cup plus 1 tbsp/75 ml red wine vinegar → 95

1 tbsp chopped fresh marjoram

2 tbsp sweet or hot paprika → 42

2 tsp kosher salt

1 tsp freshly ground black pepper

Add all of the ingredients to a large bowl and let stand, mixing occasionally, for 30 minutes, until the vegetables begin to give off some of their liquid. The salad should be slightly soupy.

Transfer the salad to individual bowls and serve. This salad tastes best if eaten the same day it is made. Leftover salad can be stored in an airtight container in the refrigerator for up to 2 days.

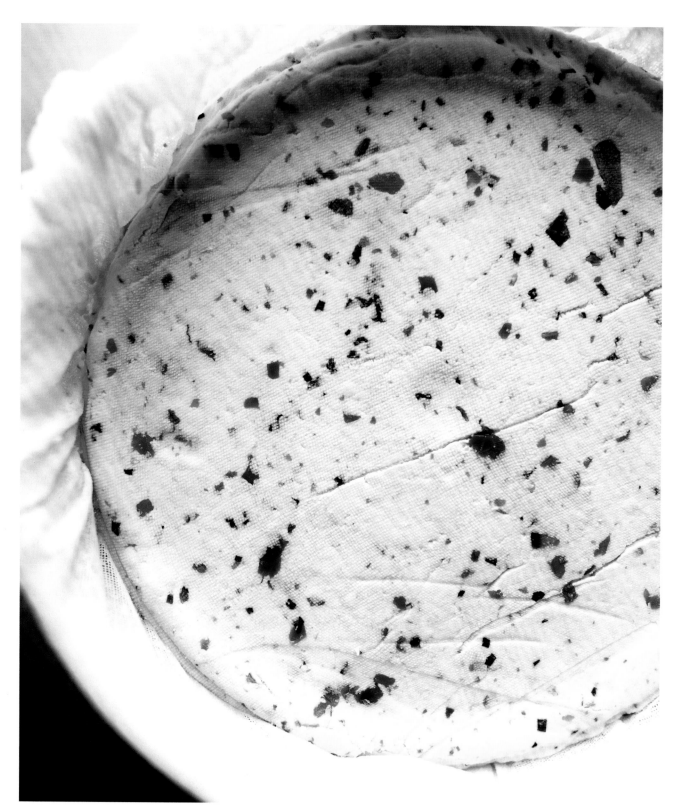

PEPPER JACK

BAR TARTINE

GRILLED POTATO SALAD WITH BACON

This salad takes us back to being kids, Nick in Michigan, Cortney in Chicago. It's summer and there are fireflies, humidity that you can cut with a knife, and sparklers. Someone's dad has the grill going, there's leftover bacon from breakfast, and a potato salad is born. A lot of our inspiration comes from a desire to re-create flavors from a more innocent time. Sure, we improvise—make everything spicier, deeper, stronger—but the base is the same. We're looking to capture the past to tell a story of where we came from and where we are now.

Serves 6 to 8

2 lb/910 g Yukon gold potatoes

1 tbsp lard → 93 or filtered grapeseed oil

12 oz/340 g bacon, cut into ¼- to ½-in/ 6- to 12-mm dice

1 sweet white onion, sliced paper-thin

2 yellow Hungarian wax peppers or 1 green bell pepper, stemmed, seeded, and cut into ½-in/12-mm dice

6 garlic cloves, minced

1 tbsp sweet paprika → 42

¼ cup/60 ml apple cider vinegar → 95

3 tbsp chopped fresh flat-leaf parsley

2 tbsp chopped fresh marjoram

1 tbsp chopped fresh dill

½ tsp light brown sugar

1 tbsp plus 1 tsp kosher salt

Freshly ground black pepper

¼ cup/55 g capers, elderberry capers, or fennel capers → 115

Prepare a medium-low fire for direct-heat cooking in a charcoal or gas grill. Put the potatoes on the grate directly over the fire, cover the grill, and cook the potatoes until almost tender (a skewer inserted into a potato will meet some resistance), about 1 hour, turning halfway through. Remove the potatoes from the grill and stoke the fire if needed to maintain the heat.

Place a large sauté pan on the grate directly over the fire and heat until a drop of water flicked on the pan sizzles on contact. Add the lard and bacon and cook until the bacon begins to render its fat, about 5 minutes. Add the onion and wax peppers and cook, stirring, until the vegetables begin to brown, about 5 minutes. Add the garlic and cook, stirring, until fragrant, about 1 minute. Add the paprika and cook, stirring, until fragrant, about 1 minute longer. Remove from the heat and add the vinegar, 2 tbsp of the parsley, 1 tbsp of the marjoram, 1 tsp of the dill, the brown sugar, and the salt to the pan. Season with pepper and stir to dissolve the brown sugar.

Transfer the bacon mixture to a serving bowl. Cut the still-warm potatoes into quarters, add to the bowl, add capers, and toss to mix everything evenly. Garnish with the remaining parsley, marjoram, and dill and serve warm. Leftover salad will keep in an airtight container in the refrigerator for up to 5 days.

PERSIMMON SALAD WITH HONEY & BLACK WALNUTS

In this salad we call for two varieties of persimmon: the tomato-shaped Fuyu, ideal for eating raw, and the ultra-tannic Hachiya, which we dry to make hoshigaki. If you aren't making your own hoshigaki, you can purchase them at some fruit stands and Asian markets and online. It may take a bit of hunting to find black walnuts, but the flavor is worth the effort. Their robust taste lies somewhere between chicory root and Candy Cap mushrooms.

Serves 4 to 6

DRESSING

- ½ cup/100 ml unfiltered sunflower oil, or a mixture of sunflower and walnut oils
- 5 tbsp/75 ml fresh lemon juice
- 2 tbsp fermented honey → 121 or honey
- 1½ tbsp rice vinegar → 98
- 1½ tsp each minced fresh marjoram, thyme, and sage
- 1½ tsp kosher salt
- 1 tsp freshly ground black pepper

SALAD

- 12 oz/340 g mixed chicories, such as Treviso, puntarelle, radicchio, escarole, or endive, trimmed and roughly torn
- 2 Fuyu persimmons, peeled and halved through the stem end and cut into half-moons
- 1 fennel bulb, halved, cored, and thinly sliced
- 2 hoshigaki → 58, cut into ¼-in/6-mm dice
- 1 cup/115 g black walnut pieces or walnuts, toasted
- 4 oz/115 g Parmesan or other dry-aged cheese
- Freshly ground black pepper

TO MAKE THE DRESSING: In a small bowl, combine the sunflower oil, lemon juice, honey, vinegar, marjoram, thyme, sage, salt, and pepper and whisk to combine. The dressing can be made up to 1 week in advance and stored in an airtight container in the refrigerator. Shake well before using.

TO MAKE THE SALAD: In a large bowl, combine the chicories, Fuyu persimmons, fennel, hoshigaki, and walnuts. Add the dressing and toss to coat all of the ingredients evenly.

Transfer to a large serving platter and shave the cheese over the top. Season with lots of pepper and serve. This salad is best eaten immediately.

SWEET POTATO SALAD WITH AVOCADO, FETA & PICKLED GREEN WALNUTS

This dish was born one afternoon at home when we went to the kitchen to make lunch and came back with a bowl of baked sweet potatoes topped with avocado, sprouts, and yogurt. Although an unexpected combination, it proved a surprisingly good one that inspired us to see how we could turn this simple snack into a dish fit for the restaurant. We swapped out yogurt in favor of feta and added pickled green walnuts, which have a caper-like flavor that gives the dish a bright, acidic finish. Pickled artichokes can be substituted for the green walnuts.

Satsuma imo is a Japanese sweet potato with a more subtle flavor, a softer texture, and a lighter color than such familiar sweet potato varieties as Garnet or Jewel. It is also denser and more savory than most sweet potatoes. If you can't find satsuma imo, use white sweet potato.

Serves 4 to 6

1 lb/455 g satsuma imo or white sweet potatoes

HONEY LEMON DRESSING

¾ cup/180 ml fresh lemon juice

⅓ cup/75 ml toasted walnut or grapeseed oil

2 tbsp fermented honey → 121, or honey

¼ bunch fresh dill

1 garlic clove

2 tsp kosher salt

1 fennel bulb, halved, cored, and thinly sliced

2 or 3 avocados, halved, pitted, peeled, and cut into slices ¼ to ½ in/6 to 12 mm thick

¼ cup/40 g mixed bean sprouts, such as mung, lentil, and/or fenugreek → 79

Kosher salt

2 cups/75 g purslane or arugula

6 pickled green walnuts → 114, thinly sliced (see headnote)

Fresh dill leaves for garnish

Fresh flat-leaf parsley leaves for garnish

Freshly ground black pepper

Toasted walnut oil for garnish

4 oz/115 g cheese in the style of feta → 70

Preheat the oven to 300°F/180°C. Set a wire rack on a sheet pan, put the sweet potatoes on the rack, and bake until just tender enough to be easily pierced with a skewer, about 45 minutes. Let cool to room temperature. Peel the potatoes and cut into rounds or half-moons ¼ in/6 mm thick. Transfer to a medium bowl, cover with plastic wrap, and store at room temperature for up to 4 hours or refrigerate for up to 3 days.

TO MAKE THE HONEY LEMON DRESSING: In a blender, combine the lemon juice, walnut oil, honey, dill, garlic, and salt and purée until smooth. The dressing can be made up to 1 week in advance and stored in an airtight container in the refrigerator. Shake well before using.

Set aside 2 tbsp of the dressing. In a medium bowl, toss the fennel with the remaining dressing, coating evenly.

Arrange an even layer of potato on a large serving platter. Top with the avocado slices, then the sprouts, and season with salt. Add the purslane to the bowl with the fennel, toss to coat, and arrange on top of the avocados and sprouts. Add the walnut slices, cover with the dill and parsley, and season with pepper. Pour the reserved dressing and the walnut oil evenly over all. Grate or crumble the cheese over the top, covering the salad completely. Serve immediately.

ENSALADA RUSA

This salad is a true world traveler: born in Spain, influenced by Russia, with a detour through South America. The classic Spanish dish has a mayonnaise dressing and often includes potato, carrot, and peas. There are many versions, sometimes with beets, sometimes lots of chile and lime. What to use is really up to the cook. This recipe is great in the winter when root vegetables are abundant. Their sweet, earthy flavor is complemented by the mildly spicy and citrusy dressing. Instead of the typical mayonnaise dressing, we make a creamy sauce using parsnip, lime, honey, chiles, pumpkin seed oil, and sour cream.

Serves 4 to 6

VEGETABLES

1 lb/455 g parsnips, peeled and cut into ½-in/12-mm dice

12 oz/340 g celery root, peeled and cut into ½-in/12-mm dice

12 oz/340 g carrots, peeled and cut into ½-in/12-mm dice

12 oz/340 g beets, peeled and cut into ½-in/12-mm dice

8 oz/225 g pumpkin or winter squash, seeded, peeled, and cut into ½-in/12-mm dice

Kosher salt

DRESSING

½ cup/100 g steamed diced parsnip

¾ cup/180 ml fresh lime juice

1 tbsp fermented honey → 121, or honey

½ cup/120 ml pumpkin seed oil

4 garlic cloves

1 or 2 serrano or jalapeño chiles

1 tsp kosher salt

¾ cup/180 ml sour cream → 71

SPICED PUMPKIN SEEDS

1 tsp unsalted butter

1 tbsp fermented honey → 121, or honey

Grated zest of 2 limes

2 tsp kosher salt

8 oz/225 g pumpkin seeds

1 tsp Hatch chile powder → 42

Juice of 2 limes

1 tsp kosher salt

2 avocados, halved, pitted, peeled, and cut into ½-in/12-mm dice

Green onions, white and tender green parts, cut into ¼-in/6-mm rounds, for garnish

Fresh cilantro, dill, and curly parsley, coarsely chopped, for garnish

carrots, and pumpkin. Season the vegetables with salt after removing them from the steamer. Cover and refrigerate until cold. The vegetables can be steamed up to 1 day in advance and stored, covered, in the refrigerator.

TO MAKE THE DRESSING: In a blender, combine the reserved steamed parsnip, lime juice, honey, pumpkin seed oil, garlic, serrano(s), and salt and purée until smooth. Transfer to a small bowl and stir in the sour cream. Cover and refrigerate until ready to use. The dressing can be made up to 5 days in advance and stored in an airtight container in the refrigerator.

TO MAKE THE SPICED PUMPKIN SEEDS: Preheat the oven to 350°F/180°C. In a small saucepan over medium heat, melt the butter with the honey, lime zest, and salt. Toss the pumpkin seeds with the butter mixture in a small bowl, then spread the seeds in a single layer on a sheet pan. Bake until the seeds are lightly toasted, about 15 minutes. Remove the seeds from the oven, toss with the chile powder, and let cool. The pumpkin seeds can be toasted up to 5 days in advance and stored in an airtight container at room temperature.

To assemble, transfer the cold vegetables to a large bowl and toss gently with the lime juice and salt. Add the dressing, avocados, and half each of the green onions, cilantro, dill, and parsley and mix gently, being careful not to mash the avocado too much. Transfer to a large serving platter and top with the spiced pumpkin seeds, the remaining green onions, and the remaining herbs. Serve immediately.

TO PREPARE THE VEGETABLES: Pour water into a steamer pan, place the steamer rack above the water, and put the parsnips on the rack. Cover the steamer, bring the water to a boil over medium heat, and steam until the parsnips can be pierced with a skewer using slight force, 15 to 20 minutes. Reserve ½ cup/100 g of the cooked parsnips at room temperature for the dressing and refrigerate the remaining pieces until cold. Steam the celery root, carrots, beets, and pumpkin in the same way until they can be pierced with a skewer using slight force, 15 to 20 minutes for the beets and 10 to 15 minutes for the celery root,

SHARED
PLATES

The flavors of Bar Tartine really become apparent when you make a few of the dishes from this chapter. We want our guests to be satiated, not just full. We want the flavors of the dishes to be so deep that they imprint permanently on the eater's memory. There are no appetizers or main courses on our menu. That's just not how we eat. Instead, a meal may start with pickles and bread, followed by rainbow trout in buttermilk sauce, then maybe a plate of roasted carrots or smoked potatoes eaten alongside some pistachio dip, and end with a bowl of buckwheat dumplings and salad. The dishes in the following section don't fall into any clean-cut categories. They're not soups or salads, pasta dishes, or typical protein-heavy mains. They can start a meal or end one or fall somewhere in between. We like to fill a table with plates, inviting everyone to share.

PISTACHIO DIP WITH FLAX CRACKERS

Nuts and seeds make a great base for dips. They are nutritionally dense, carry a lot of flavor, and, when blended, take on a satisfying, creamy texture. This dip is made with pistachios, pumpkin seeds, charred green onions, and lime juice and has a texture and a flavor that recalls both hummus and mole. Serve alongside Chilled Buttermilk and Cucumber Soup → 156.

Serves 4 to 6

FLAX CRACKERS

¼ cup/60 ml mushroom reduction → 131 or soy sauce

1 small sweet white onion, cut into quarters

3 fully dried tomatoes → 40, rehydrated in 1½ cups/360 ml kombu dashi → 137 until soft enough to chop

3 garlic cloves

½ bunch fresh dill

½ bunch fresh flat-leaf parsley

2 cups/330 g brown or golden flaxseeds

2 tsp kosher salt

PISTACHIO DIP

½ bunch green onions, white and tender green parts, halved lengthwise and cut into 1-in/2.5-cm lengths

½ cup/120 ml unfiltered grapeseed oil, plus 1 tsp

16 garlic cloves

1½ cups/220 g shelled pistachios (soaking is optional → 80)

½ cup/65 g shelled pumpkin seeds (soaking is optional → 80)

Kosher salt

1 charred Hatch chile → 47 or other mildly spicy green chile, coarsely chopped

Juice of 3 lime halves

1 bunch fresh cilantro, chopped

2 oz/55 g wild nori

2 tbsp unfiltered grapeseed oil

Thinly sliced radish for garnish

½ lime

Torn cilantro leaves or flowers for garnish

Green onions, white and tender green parts, thinly sliced, for garnish

TO MAKE THE FLAX CRACKERS: In a blender, combine the mushroom reduction, onion, tomatoes and dashi, garlic, dill, and parsley and blend until smooth. Transfer to a medium bowl and stir in the flaxseeds and salt. Cover the bowl and let stand at room temperature until the flaxseeds have absorbed most of the liquid and the mixture is thick and sticky, 1 to 2 hours.

CONTINUED

Line three 12-by-12-in/30-cm-by-30-cm sheet pans with parchment paper or silicone baking mats. Spread the flaxseed mixture onto the prepared pans in a thin, even layer, 1 to 2 seeds deep. Dehydrate in a dehydrator or a 120°F/48°C oven until the cracker sheets are dry and can be easily broken with your hands, 24 to 36 hours.

Break the sheets into large pieces and store in an airtight container at room temperature for up to 1 week. If the crackers have gone a bit stale, reheat briefly in a 200°F/110°C oven to recrisp before serving.

TO MAKE THE PISTACHIO DIP: Heat a large cast-iron skillet over medium-high heat until a drop of water flicked on the surface sizzles gently on contact. Add the green onions to the hot skillet and press down on them with a weight or heavy pan. Cook until the onions begin to char, about 3 minutes. Turn the onions over, press down on them with the weight, and cook until charred on the second side, about 3 minutes. Continue until all sides are evenly charred but not completely black. Let cool to room temperature.

In a small saucepan over low heat, combine the ½ cup/120 ml grapeseed oil and the garlic and cook until the garlic is tender enough to be easily pierced with a skewer, about 30 minutes. Let cool to room temperature.

In a large skillet over medium heat, combine the pistachios and pumpkin seeds and toast, stirring occasionally, until warm and fragrant, about 3 minutes. Pour onto a plate and let cool to room temperature. Measure out ½ cup/70 g of the pistachio-pumpkin seed mixture, season it with 1 tsp salt and the remaining 1 tsp oil, and reserve for garnish.

In a blender, combine the remaining pistachio-pumpkin seed mixture, the poached garlic and oil, the roasted chile, the charred green onions, the lime juice, the chopped cilantro, and 2 tsp salt and process until smooth.

Preheat the oven to 350°F/180°C. On a sheet pan, toss the wild nori with the grapeseed oil and bake until crisp, 3 to 5 minutes. Let cool to room temperature.

To serve, transfer the dip to a serving platter or bowl. Garnish with radish slices and squeeze the ½ lime over the top. Garnish with the nori, the reserved pistachio-pumpkin seed mixture, the torn cilantro leaves, and the green onions. Serve with crackers alongside. This dip tastes best if eaten the same day it is made. Leftover dip will keep in an airtight container in the refrigerator for up to 4 days.

ENGLISH PEA & GOAT CHEESE DIP

Peas usually come into season locally in March, just about the time when we've had our fill of root vegetables. It's always exciting to have new ingredients to play with, and we often engage in some pretty serious debate about what to do with fresh English peas. This dip, which pairs them with grassy, creamy goat cheese, often wins the argument.

Serves 4 to 6

GOAT CHEESE DIP

1 cup/225 g goat cheese → 68, at room temperature

1 tbsp sour cream → 71, at room temperature

1 tsp smoked onion powder → 34 or sweet onion powder → 34

1 tsp kosher salt

1 tsp freshly ground pepper

1 tsp fermented honey → 121, or honey

PEAS AND TENDRILS

1 tbsp filtered grapeseed or sunflower oil

2 shallots, minced

1 cup/140 g shelled English peas, from about 1 lb/455 g peas in the pod

Grated zest of 1 lemon

Kosher salt

1 large handful of pea leaves and tendrils, plus a few nice leaves for garnish

Onion flowers for garnish

Anise hyssop flowers for garnish

Furikake → 54 for garnish

Fennel oil → 90 or extra-virgin olive oil for garnish

Crackers, sliced bread, or sliced raw vegetables for serving

TO MAKE THE GOAT CHEESE DIP: In a medium bowl, combine the goat cheese, sour cream, onion powder, salt, pepper, and honey and stir until all of the ingredients are well incorporated. Cover with plastic wrap and refrigerate until chilled, at least 30 minutes, or for up to 1 week.

TO PREPARE THE PEAS AND TENDRILS: Heat a small sauté pan over low heat until a drop of water flicked on the surface sizzles gently on contact. Add 1 tsp of the grapeseed oil and the shallots and cook, stirring occasionally, until the shallots are quite soft, about 20 minutes. Remove from the heat and let cool to room temperature.

Bring a large saucepan of salted water to a boil. Prepare an ice bath. Add the peas and boil for 20 seconds. With a slotted spoon, immediately transfer the peas to the ice bath. When the peas are cold, remove them from the ice bath. Using a sharp knife or a food processor, chop three-quarters of the peas thoroughly, reserving the rest whole for garnish. Transfer the chopped peas to a small bowl, add the cooked shallots, lemon zest, and 1 tsp salt and mix well.

No more than 1 hour before serving, wipe out the small sauté pan, place over low heat, and heat until a drop of water flicked on the surface sizzles gently on contact. Add the remaining 2 tsp of oil and the pea leaves and tendrils and cook, stirring, until softened, about 1 minute. Season with salt and transfer to a plate. Let cool to room temperature.

To serve, put the goat cheese dip on a large serving platter and top with the chopped pea mixture, the reserved whole peas, the raw leaves, and the cooked leaves and tendrils. Garnish with the onion flowers and anise hyssop flowers, and season with the furikake. Pour fennel oil over the top and serve, accompanied with crackers. This dip tastes best if eaten the same day it is made. Leftovers will keep in an airtight container in the refrigerator for up to 4 days.

LIPTAUER PAPRIKA CHEESE DIP

A popular snack in central Europe, this cheese spread is the perfect appetizer for entertaining. Substitute your favorite spices or vegetables. Sometimes we make this dip with goat cheese. Sometimes we make it with smoked onion powder or curry spices, cooked greens or nuts—the variations are countless. Serve this dip with the pickled mushrooms → 103.

Serves 4 to 6

1 tbsp filtered sunflower or grapeseed oil

1 sweet white onion, cut into ¼-in/6-mm dice

1 sweet red pepper, seeded and cut into
 ¼-in/6-mm dice

1 tbsp kosher salt

1 cup/325 g well-drained farmer's cheese → 67
 or well-drained ricotta, at room temperature

½ cup/120 ml sour cream → 71, at room
 temperature

1 tbsp smoked onion powder → 34

1 tsp garlic powder → 37

1 tbsp sweet paprika → 42

1 tsp freshly ground black pepper

1 tbsp each minced fresh chives and dill

Flax crackers → 216, rye bread, or sliced raw
 vegetables for serving

Heat a large sauté pan over low heat until a drop of water flicked on the surface sizzles gently on contact. Add the sunflower oil, onion, red pepper, and salt and cook slowly until the vegetables are translucent, 10 to 15 minutes. Let cool to room temperature.

In a medium bowl, combine the cooled onion mixture, cheese, sour cream, onion powder, garlic powder, paprika, pepper, chives, and dill and mix until all of the ingredients are thoroughly combined. The dip can be made up to 5 days in advance and stored in an airtight container in the refrigerator.

Spoon the dip onto a platter or into a bowl and serve with crackers alongside.

SLOW-ROASTED CARROTS WITH BURNT BREAD & ALMOND MILK

We are surrounded by so much good bread and inevitably we have scraps. This sauce is our way of making sure they don't go to waste. Using burnt bread as an ingredient may sound unusual, but when combined with blackened chiles, it yields a smoky, spicy sauce. Almond milk cools like yogurt but brings its own nutty flavor. Roasted low and slow, the carrots are cooked until they begin to shrivel, concentrating their flavor and sweetness.

Serves 4 to 6

BURNT BREAD SAUCE

8 oz/225 g country-style bread, cut into slices ¼ in/6 mm thick

6 dried árbol chiles, stemmed

1 sweet white onion, cut into slices ¼ in/6 mm thick

6 garlic cloves, peeled

½ cup/225 g soaked and toasted almonds → 83

1 tbsp fermented honey → 121, or honey

One 4-oz/115-g tomato, cored and coarsely chopped

¾ cup/180 ml toasted almond oil

½ cup/240 ml kombu dashi → 137

½ cup/85 g burnt bread powder → 48

¼ cup/30 g charred green onion powder → 36

¼ cup/65 g sweet pepper paste → 115 or harissa

Leaves from ½ bunch fresh flat-leaf parsley

5 tbsp fresh lime juice

1 tbsp plus 1 tsp kosher salt

1 tsp freshly ground black pepper

ALMOND MILK SAUCE

2 oz/55 g Yukon gold potato

1½ cups/360 ml almond milk → 83

1-in/2.5-cm piece green serrano chile

1 tbsp fresh lime juice

2 tsp fermented honey → 121, or honey

Kosher salt

CARROTS

2 tbsp kefir butter → 76

2 tbsp chutney spice → 53 or garam masala

2 tbsp fermented honey → 121, or honey

2 tsp kosher salt

3 lb/1.4 kg baby carrots

2 tbsp carrot top oil → 87

Finishing salt

¼ cup/35 g almonds, toasted

parsley, lime juice, kosher salt, and pepper and process until a smooth paste forms. Transfer to a bowl and let stand at room temperature for at least 1 hour. The sauce can be made up to 1 week in advance and stored in an airtight container in the refrigerator. Bring to room temperature before serving.

TO MAKE THE ALMOND MILK SAUCE: In a small saucepan, cover the potato with about 1 in/2.5 cm of water and bring to a simmer over medium heat. Cook until the potato is tender enough to be easily pierced with a skewer, 10 to 15 minutes. Drain well. In a blender, combine the potato, almond milk, serrano, lime juice, honey, and 1 tsp kosher salt and purée until smooth. Strain through a fine-mesh sieve into a small bowl. Taste for seasoning and adjust as needed.

TO PREPARE THE CARROTS: Preheat the oven to 250°F/120°C. In a wide-bottomed ovenproof pan, warm the butter over low heat. When it begins to bubble, add the chutney spice, honey, and kosher salt. Bloom the spices in the butter until fragrant and toasty, 3 to 5 minutes. Put the carrots in the pan, toss to coat evenly with the butter mixture, then spread the carrots in a single layer. Place in the oven and cook the carrots, stirring occasionally, until they begin to shrivel, 1 to 1½ hours. The goal is carrots with a little bit of toothy skin and custardy interiors. Remove from the oven and let cool for 30 minutes.

To serve, spread the burnt bread sauce on a large serving platter and pour the almond milk sauce over it. Arrange the carrots on top of the almond milk sauce. Garnish with the carrot top oil and finishing salt. With a fine-tooth grater, grate the almonds over the top, creating a layer of almond dust.

TO MAKE THE BURNT BREAD SAUCE: Preheat the oven to 350°F/175°C.

In a medium cast-iron skillet over medium-high heat, char the bread slices, turning once, until blackened on both sides, about 10 minutes total. Transfer to a large plate. Put the árbol chiles in the same skillet and char, turning as needed, until blackened, about 3 minutes total. Transfer to the plate with the bread. Put the onion slices and garlic cloves in the same skillet and char, turning once, until blackened on both sides, about 5 minutes total. Transfer the skillet to the oven and cook for 10 minutes. Remove onion and garlic to the plate with the bread and chiles and let everything cool to room temperature.

In a food processor, combine the almonds and the charred bread, chiles, onion, and garlic. Add the honey, tomato, almond oil, dashi, bread powder, green onion powder, pepper paste,

SMOKED POTATOES WITH RAMP MAYONNAISE

We don't have rules or a distinct approach to creating recipes. Our best discoveries are often accidents. These smoked potatoes with ramp mayonnaise, one of the most popular dishes on the menu, evolved through several iterations and arrived at its current form because we wanted to layer as many earthy flavors as possible to stand up to the smoky potatoes. Fermented ramps, black garlic, and dried mushrooms ended up being the perfect trio to pair with the potatoes.

Serves 4 to 6

SMOKED POTATOES

2 lb/910 g small Yukon gold potatoes (smaller than 1½ in/4 cm in diameter)

1 tbsp filtered grapeseed oil

1 tsp kosher salt

BLACK GARLIC VINAIGRETTE

6 dried mushrooms, such as shiitake or porcini

1 cup/240 ml rice vinegar → 98

12 black garlic cloves → 39

3 garlic cloves

2 tsp light brown sugar

1 tbsp kosher salt

2 tbsp unfiltered grapeseed oil

RAMP MAYONNAISE

2 egg yolks

1 tsp kosher salt

1 tbsp fresh lemon juice

½ cup/115 g brined ramps → 107 or brined garlic chives, drained and chopped

Freshly ground black pepper

1 cup/240 ml unfiltered grapeseed oil or other light vegetable oil

Rice bran oil for deep-frying

½ bunch fresh dill, leaves picked, half chopped and half intact

½ bunch fresh flat-leaf parsley, leaves picked, half chopped and half intact

½ bunch green onions, white and tender green parts, thinly sliced

6 ramps, thinly sliced

Freshly ground black pepper

TO MAKE THE SMOKED POTATOES: Soak three generous handfuls of alder or fruitwood chips in water to cover for at least 1 hour.

Preheat the oven to 350°F/180°C. In a large bowl, toss the potatoes with the grapeseed oil and salt. Transfer the potatoes to a sheet pan and roast until barely tender, 30 to 40 minutes.

CONTINUED

If using a smoker: Following the manufacturer's instructions, set up and smoke the potatoes at 180°F/80°C for 2 hours, using two rounds of chips.

If using a gas grill: Light one burner to medium. Put a smoker box over the lit burner, add some of the soaked wood chips to the box, and close the grill. Adjust the heat as needed to keep the temperature at about 180°F/80°C. The wood chips should begin to smolder and release a steady stream of smoke. Put the potatoes on the grate opposite the lit burner. Cover the grill and smoke the potatoes, adjusting the heat as needed to maintain the temperature, until browned from the smoke and tender to the touch, about 2 hours. Let cool to room temperature.

If using a charcoal grill: Fill a chimney starter with charcoal. Light it and let burn until the coals are covered with a thin layer of ash. Pour the hot coals on one side of the grill. Put some of the soaked wood chips on the hot coals and put the grate on the grill. Put the potatoes on the grate opposite the fire. Cover the grill, positioning the vent on the lid on the side opposite the fire. Stick a thermometer through the vent and heat the grill to about 180°F/80°C. Smoke the potatoes, adjusting the vents as needed to maintain the temperature, until browned from the smoke and tender to the touch, about 1 hour. Let cool to room temperature.

TO MAKE THE BLACK GARLIC VINAIGRETTE: In a small saucepan over high heat, combine the mushrooms and vinegar. Bring to a boil, cover, remove from the heat, and let steep for 30 minutes. Using a slotted spoon, remove the mushrooms from the vinegar. With your hands, squeeze the vinegar from the mushrooms back into the pan. Reserve the mushrooms for another use. (Slice them into a soup or salad.)

In a blender, combine the steeped vinegar, black garlic, garlic, brown sugar, salt, and grapeseed oil and purée until smooth. If not using immediately, transfer to an airtight container and refrigerate for up to 1 month. Bring to room temperature before using.

TO MAKE THE RAMP MAYONNAISE: Chill a food processor bowl and blade in the freezer for at least 15 minutes. In the chilled bowl, combine the egg yolks, salt, lemon juice, ramp greens, and plenty of pepper and process until all of the ingredients are fully incorporated, about 1 minute. With the food processor running, slowly pour in the grapeseed oil. The mixture should be quite thick. If not using immediately, transfer to an airtight container and refrigerate for up to 3 days.

To fry the potatoes, pour the rice bran oil to a depth of 6 in/15 cm in a cast-iron or other heavy-bottomed saucepan and heat to 350°F/180°C. Line a sheet pan with paper towels and set a wire rack on the pan.

Gently press each potato between your palms to smash it slightly without breaking it up. This helps to ensure crisp edges and allows the vinaigrette to soak into the potatoes. A few at a time, add the potatoes to the hot oil and fry until crisp, about 4 minutes. Transfer the fried potatoes to the wire rack and let drain for about 1 minute. Repeat until all of the potatoes are fried.

Put the hot potatoes into a large bowl, add the vinaigrette, the chopped dill and parsley, and half of the green onions and toss to combine. Transfer to a serving platter and tear the leaves of dill and parsley over the top. Add the ramps and the remaining green onions. Serve with the ramp mayonnaise and top with pepper.

PADRÓN PEPPERS WITH GOAT CHEESE SAUCE

The farmer who grows our padróns also has a goat dairy, and we make cheese with milk from animals that graze in the fields where the peppers grow. It seems fitting that the two ingredients end up on the same plate. The cheese helps tame the peppers' heat. The combination of the two has the same satisfying effect as jalapeño poppers. Padróns are best early in the season when they're flavorful and sweet, before they get too spicy.

Serves 4 to 6

GOAT CHEESE SAUCE

½ cup/115 g goat's milk butter or kefir butter → 76

1 sweet white onion, cut into rings ¼ in/6 mm thick

1 Yukon gold potato, cut into chunks

1 tbsp kosher salt

½ cup/120 ml kombu dashi → 137 or goat cheese whey → 68

1½ cups/330 g goat cheese → 68

PADRÓN PEPPERS AND ONIONS

1 lb/455 g young padrón or shishito peppers

1 tsp kosher salt

1 tsp filtered grapeseed oil

1 sweet white onion, cut into rings ¼ in/6 mm thick

¼ cup/55 g goat cheese → 68

Chopped fresh marjoram for garnish

Minced fresh chives for garnish

Charred eggplant spice → 51 for garnish

Finishing salt

Freshly ground black pepper

TO MAKE THE GOAT CHEESE SAUCE: Heat a large sauté pan over medium-low heat until a drop of water flicked on the surface sizzles gently on contact. Add the butter. Once it has melted, add the onion, potato, and salt. Cook, stirring occasionally, until the onion is translucent, about 10 minutes. Add the dashi and simmer until the potato is tender enough to smash with a fork, about 10 minutes. Add the goat cheese and stir until melted, about 5 minutes.

Transfer the cheese mixture to a blender and purée until very smooth. Cover to keep warm until ready to serve. The sauce can be made up to 4 days in advance and stored in an air-tight container in the refrigerator. Just before serving, warm the sauce in a small saucepan over low heat.

TO CHAR THE PEPPERS AND ONIONS: Heat a large cast-iron skillet over high heat until a drop of water flicked on the surface sizzles on contact. Char the peppers in the hot skillet, pressing down on them with a spatula and turning them

frequently to keep them from burning, until well charred on all sides, 1 to 2 minutes. Toss the charred peppers with ½ tsp of the salt and ½ tsp of the grapeseed oil. In the same skillet over high heat, char the onion rings until they start to blacken, about 1 minute on each side. Toss the charred onion with the remaining ½ tsp salt and remaining ½ tsp grapeseed oil.

To serve, spread the warm goat cheese sauce on a large serving platter and arrange the charred peppers and onions on top. Crumble the goat cheese evenly over the top. Garnish with the marjoram, chives, charred eggplant spice, finishing salt, and plenty of pepper. Serve immediately.

WARM FARMER'S CHEESE

Well suited for making at home, this cheese requires no cultures or special handling. Time is a key ingredient here, beginning with a three-day wait for the milk to acidify. The process is a largely passive one, during which we act more as witnesses to the transformation rather than as agents of it. Once the cheese begins to set, we transfer it to the oven, where the heat separates the curds and whey. Then we drain it, and that's when the magic begins. As the whey slowly drains, the curds are revealed, and the bright yellow butterfat pools to the surface. This moment, while the cheese is still warm, before all the whey has drained off, is the one we wait for. Naturally sweet, gently sour, and wildly unctuous, warm farmer's cheese is delicious spread on thick slices of freshly baked bread with pepper paste → 118 and raw baby wild onion or sweet red onion.

Serves 4 to 6

1 qt/1.28 kg warm farmer's cheese → 67

Finishing salt and freshly ground black pepper

Thick slices of crusty country-style bread

Sweet pepper paste → 118

Baby wild onion or red sweet onion, sliced

After the curds have drained from the farmer's cheese for 30 minutes, transfer the warm cheese to a warm serving bowl, making sure to scoop up the butterfat with the cheese. Season with salt and pepper. Serve with bread, pepper paste, and onion slices. Leftover cheese can be stored in an airtight container in the refrigerator for up to 1 week.

FARMER'S CHEESE DUMPLINGS WITH MUSHROOM BROTH

This dish has been in a state of constant evolution since the beginning of our time at Bar Tartine. It began with a trip to Hungary and a meal at Cafe Marvelosa near the Chain Bridge in Budapest. This small restaurant, run by a mother and daughter, has great food. On one visit, they served *turó gomboc*, a cheese dumpling with sour cream and sugar. We were inspired to make a savory version with our homemade farmer's cheese. It has a dense, creamy, tofulike texture and is very satisfying.

Serves 6

6 cups/1.4 L mushroom broth → 139

14 oz/390 g well-drained farmer's cheese → 67 or well-drained ricotta, at room temperature

⅓ cup/40 g rice powder → 48 or rice flour

2 eggs

Kosher salt

2 lb/910 g mushrooms, such as hen-of-the-woods, chanterelle, or black trumpet, stems trimmed

2 tbsp kefir butter → 76

Fresh marjoram leaves for garnish

Fresh chives, chopped into small sticks, for garnish

Onion flowers or pea tendrils for garnish

Finishing salt

In a medium saucepan over medium heat, reduce the mushroom broth by half, about 1 hour. Set aside.

In a food processor, combine the cheese, rice powder, eggs, and 2 tsp kosher salt and process until smooth. Taste the batter; if you are uneasy tasting raw egg, bake a small piece in a 300°F/ 150°C oven for about 5 minutes to heat through before tasting. Add more salt if necessary.

Have ready six 8-in/20-cm squares of plastic wrap. Divide the cheese mixture into six equal portions; each portion should weigh about 3.5 oz/95 g. Place a portion in the center of a square, then gather the edges of the sheet and twist them together until the cheese has formed a tight ball. Tie the twisted wrap into a knot to secure the cheese ball. The tighter the package, the more evenly the dumpling will steam. Repeat with the remaining cheese portions and squares of plastic wrap.

Pour water into a steamer pan and place the steamer rack above the water. Bring the water to a boil over medium-high heat. Place the dumplings, knot-side down, on the steamer rack, cover the steamer, and steam just until the batter sets, 12 to 14 minutes. After 12 minutes, check the

in the plastic wrap. Bring to room temperature before reheating.

Place the unwrapped dumplings on a heatproof plate. Pour water into the steamer pan and place the steamer rack above the water. Bring the water to a boil over medium heat, place the plate on the steamer rack, and cover the steamer. Steam the dumplings until warmed through, about 6 minutes.

Heat a large sauté pan over medium heat until a drop of water flicked on the surface sizzles gently on contact. Add the mushrooms to the pan, season with salt, and cook until any moisture they release evaporates, about 2 minutes. Then add the butter and sauté until the mushrooms are tender, 3 to 5 minutes. Keep warm.

Bring the reduced mushroom broth to a boil over high heat and taste for seasoning. Divide the broth evenly among shallow individual bowls, and place a dumpling in each bowl. Divide the sautéed mushrooms among the bowls, spooning them and any butter from the pan around the dumplings. Garnish with marjoram, chives, onion flowers, and finishing salt. Serve immediately.

dumplings. They should feel set and a skin should be starting to form under the plastic wrap. If the batter still seems loose, continue cooking the dumplings for a couple minutes longer. Ideally, they will be firm on the surface and still creamy in the middle. Every batch of cheese has a different moisture content, so the timing will vary.

Transfer the cooked dumplings from the steamer to a large plate, placing them knot-side down. Refrigerate for 20 minutes; chilling helps the dumplings form a skin that makes them easier to unwrap and reheat. Cut off the knots and remove the plastic wrap. The dumplings can be made up to 3 days in advance and refrigerated

BUCKWHEAT DUMPLINGS WITH PAPRIKÁS SAUCE

Chicken paprikás is the most recognized grandmother dish in Hungarian cooking. Even if they don't remember anything else about Hungarian cuisine, our Hungarian American guests all had a grandmother who made the best paprikás. This is also true in Hungary. Paprikás is essentially stewed chicken in paprika gravy. It is served with egg dumplings or grated egg noodles. Sour cream is mandatory and green pepper, onion, and button mushrooms are usually involved. Our version of paprikas sauce is thickened with chicken skin and potato instead of the typical wheat flour. The resulting sauce is thick but doesn't pick up the flour flavor that is typical of using roux. This recipe doesn't include pieces of meat, but it has lots of chicken flavor from the liver and schmaltz in the dumplings and from the sauce. You can also serve this over chicken in the traditional fashion, or even as a sauce for vegetables.

Serves 6 to 8

PAPRIKÁS SAUCE

4 oz/115 g sliced bacon, minced

4 oz/115 g chicken skin

1 sweet white onion, peeled and chopped

12 garlic cloves, peeled and smashed

1 serrano chile, chopped

1 green bell pepper, seeded and chopped

½ cup/145 g paprika powder → 42 (sweet or hot, as you like it)

2 qt/2 L chicken broth → 139

4 oz/115 g Yukon gold potato, peeled and chopped

4 fully dried tomatoes → 40

1 tbsp plus 1 tsp kosher salt

Freshly ground black pepper

BUCKWHEAT DUMPLINGS

1 cup/185 g buckwheat groats, soaked → 81

6 tbsp/80 g schmaltz → 93

1 tbsp kosher salt

4 oz/115 g chicken livers

1 egg

Buckwheat flour or rice flour for rolling

2 tbsp schmaltz → 93

6 oz/170 g button mushrooms, cut in half if large

½ tsp kosher salt

Sour cream → 71 for garnish

Fresh chives for garnish

Freshly ground black pepper

CONTINUED

TO MAKE THE PAPRIKÁS SAUCE: Heat a large saucepan over medium heat until a drop of water flicked on the surface sizzles gently on contact. Add the bacon and chicken skin and stir for 2 minutes to start rendering the fat. Add the onion, garlic, serrano, and bell pepper and stir until they start to soften, about 10 minutes. Add the paprika and stir for 1 minute until fragrant. Add the chicken broth, potato, and dried tomatoes; bring to a simmer; and cook until the liquid reduces by half, about 1 hour. Stir in the salt, season with pepper, and allow the sauce to cool off the heat for 20 minutes. In batches in a blender, purée the sauce until smooth and then pass through a fine-mesh sieve to remove any fibrous bits. The sauce can be made up to 5 days in advance and stored in an airtight container in the refrigerator.

TO MAKE THE BUCKWHEAT DUMPLINGS: Bring a medium saucepan of water to a boil. Add the soaked buckwheat and cook until it is tender, about 8 minutes. Drain the water. The buckwheat can be cooked and stored covered in the refrigerator up to 2 days before making the dumplings.

Heat a large pan over medium heat until a drop of water flicked on the surface sizzles gently on contact. Add 1 tbsp of the schmaltz with the salt, add the livers, and sauté until the livers are golden brown on both sides and medium-rare in the middle, about 2 minutes on each side. Add the cooked livers to a food processor with the remaining 5 tbsp chicken fat and the egg and purée until smooth. Transfer the mixture to a bowl. Add the cooked buckwheat and liver mixture in batches to the food processor and process to a smooth paste. The dumpling mixture can be made up to 3 days in advance and stored in an airtight container in the refrigerator.

Pour water into a steamer pan, place the steamer rack above the water, and bring to a boil over medium heat. While the water is heating, form the dumplings. Dust a clean work surface with buckwheat flour, transfer the dumpling mixture to the work surface, and divide the mixture into 6-oz/170-g portions. Using your hands, roll one portion into a log approximately 6 in/15 cm long and ¾ in/2 cm tall. Dust with additional buckwheat flour to prevent sticking. Cut the log into six pieces and place on a small heatproof tray that will fit in the steamer pan; do not let the dumplings touch. Steam the dumplings, covered, while you form the rest. Cook each batch for 10 to 12 minutes, until the dumplings hold together and are cooked through. Let the dumplings cool on the trays in the refrigerator, as they have a tendency to stick when warm. The dumplings can be made up to 3 days in advance and stored, covered with plastic wrap, in the refrigerator.

To serve, in a small saucepan over low heat, gently warm the paprikás sauce until it is hot. Heat two large sauté pans over medium heat until a drop of water flicked on the surface sizzles gently on contact. Add 1 tbsp schmaltz to each pan. To one pan, add the button mushrooms, cut-side down if the mushrooms are halved. Season the mushrooms with the salt and cook until browned, 5 to 6 minutes. To the other pan, add the buckwheat dumplings, cut-side down, and cook until browned, about 2 minutes. Turn the dumplings onto the second cut sides and continue to cook until browned, about 2 minutes longer. On a large serving platter, pool the paprikás sauce. Arrange the mushrooms and the dumplings on the sauce. Garnish with the sour cream, chives, and pepper. Serve immediately.

LENTIL CROQUETTES WITH WATERCRESS & KEFIR

This is a dish of addictive contrasts: crisp, warm, and spicy against cool, acidic, and refreshing. Inspired by *dahi vada*, a fried lentil dumpling served with spiced yogurt—and one of our favorite Indian snacks—flavorwise these croquettes skew more toward Budapest than Bombay. Of course, the spice trade that passed through India brought many of the spices that characterize Hungarian food, such as caraway and paprika. We like to think that this dish reflects that journey—an Indian dumpling from the banks of the Danube.

Makes 12 croquettes

KEFIR SAUCE

1 cup/240 ml kefir cream → 76 or drained yogurt → 74

1½ tsp fermented honey → 121, or honey

1 tsp kosher salt

WATERCRESS SAUCE

½ bunch watercress, large stems removed

½ cup/120 ml kombu dashi → 137

1 tsp coriander seeds, toasted and ground → 30

1 tsp caraway seeds, toasted and ground → 30

½ tsp kosher salt

LENTIL CROQUETTES

½ bunch green onions, white and tender green parts

1 cup/160 g lentil sprouts → 79

4 oz/115 g Danish-style rye or pumpernickel bread, crumbled

2 oz/56 g well-drained farmer's cheese → 67 or well-drained ricotta

3 garlic cloves

1 serrano chile, stemmed and chopped

1 tbsp sweet onion powder → 34

1 tsp caraway seeds, toasted and ground → 30

1 tsp sweet paprika → 42

1 tsp kosher salt

¼ cup/60 ml kombu dashi → 137

Rice bran oil for deep-frying

Sour cherry syrup → 129 for garnish

Lentil sprouts → 79 for garnish

Watercress leaves for garnish

Cilantro leaves for garnish

CONTINUED

TO MAKE THE KEFIR SAUCE: In a small bowl, combine the kefir cream, honey, and salt and mix well. The sauce can be made up to 1 day in advance and stored in an airtight container in the refrigerator.

TO MAKE THE WATERCRESS SAUCE: Chill a blender beaker in the freezer for at least 15 minutes. In the cold blender, combine the watercress, dashi, coriander seeds, caraway seeds, and salt and purée until smooth. Transfer to a bowl and let stand at room temperature while you prepare the croquettes. This sauce tastes best if eaten the day it is made.

TO MAKE THE LENTIL CROQUETTES: Heat a large cast-iron skillet over medium-high heat until a drop of water flicked on the surface sizzles gently on contact. Add the green onions to the hot skillet and press down on them with a weight or heavy pan. Cook until the onions begin to char, about 3 minutes. Turn the onions over, press down on them with the weight, and cook until charred on the second side, about 3 minutes. Continue until all sides are evenly charred but not completely black. Let cool to room temperature.

In a food processor, combine the lentil sprouts, bread, charred green onions, farmer's cheese, garlic, chile, onion powder, caraway seeds, paprika, salt, and dashi and process until a smooth paste forms.

Using your hands, gently shape the mixture into 2-in/5-cm balls and put them on a large plate or sheet pan. The croquettes can be shaped a day in advance, covered with plastic wrap, and refrigerated overnight; bring to room temperature before frying.

Pour the rice bran oil to a depth of 2 in/5 cm in a cast-iron or other heavy-bottomed saucepan and heat to 350°F/180°C. Line a sheet pan with paper towels and set a wire rack on the pan.

Add the croquettes to the hot oil a few at a time and fry until browned and crisp, about 2 minutes. Using a slotted spoon or a skimmer, transfer them to the prepared rack to drain. Repeat with the remaining croquettes.

To serve, add the watercress sauce to the kefir sauce and stir gently to mix the sauces slightly without incorporating them fully. The mixture should be a swirl of green and white. Transfer the croquettes to a serving platter and spoon the kefir-watercress sauce on top to cover the croquettes. Top with sour cherry syrup and garnish with the lentil sprouts, watercress, and cilantro.

STEAMED CELERY ROOT CAKE

This dish is inspired by Chinese turnip cakes, the dim sum standard. We put this on the menu during a dark period where we were experimenting heavily with white rice powder. Many root vegetables can be substituted for the traditional turnips, yielding a sweet or savory cake; see the parsnip dessert → 346. Celery root, the last cellared holdout from winter, is perfect with the first spring greens.

Serves 4 to 6

NETTLE SAUCE

1 lb/½ kg nettles

1 cup/235 g strong dashi → 138

1 tsp kosher salt

CELERY ROOT CAKE

1¼ lb/570 g celery root, peeled and quartered

½ cup/100 g lard → 93

1½ cups/280 g rice powder → 48 or rice flour, plus 2 tbsp

2 tsp sweet onion powder → 34

½ tsp freshly ground black pepper

2 tsp kosher salt

4 green onions, white and tender green parts, cut into thin slices

Pea shoots for garnish

Fava leaves for garnish

Kosher salt

Pork fat chile oil → 91 for garnish

Charred green onion powder → 36 for garnish

TO MAKE THE NETTLE SAUCE: Nettles are covered with minute fibers that can irritate skin, so be sure to wear sturdy gloves when working with them. (Once nettles are cooked, they lose their ability to sting.) Remove and discard any thick stems, as they are too fibrous to purée, then rinse the leaves thoroughly in water, drain, and set aside.

Prepare an ice bath and chill a blender beaker in the freezer for 15 minutes. Bring a large saucepan of salted water to a boil. Add the nettles and cook until they turn bright green and soften slightly, about 20 seconds. With a slotted spoon, immediately transfer the nettles to the ice bath. When they are cold, remove them from the ice bath, gently squeeze any excess water with your hands, and roughly chop. The nettles can be cooked a few hours in advance and stored in a covered container in the refrigerator.

Combine the nettles, dashi, and salt in the cold blender and purée just until smooth. Do not overblend or the mixture will heat up, which can spoil the color. Push the sauce through a fine-mesh sieve directly into an airtight container, cover, and refrigerate until ready to use. This sauce tastes best if eaten the same day it is made.

TO MAKE THE CELERY ROOT CAKE: Pour water into a steamer pan and place the steamer rack above the water. Bring the water to a boil over medium-high heat. Place the celery root wedges on the steamer rack; do not stack them. Cover the steamer and cook for 20 to 25 minutes, until the wedges are tender and easily pierced with a skewer. Be careful not to cook for too long, as extra moisture can affect the final texture of the cake.

In small batches in a blender, purée the celery root with 7 tbsp of the lard until completely smooth. Transfer the mixture to a medium bowl and add the 1½ cups/200 g of rice powder, the onion powder, pepper, and salt. Mix well with a spatula to combine, then stir in the green onions. Rub the inside of a small shallow baking pan or pans (with a ¾-in/19-mm rim or close to it) with 1 tsp lard. Pour the celery root mixture into the pan(s) and place immediately into the steamer pan. Steam for 30 to 40 minutes, until the cakes are hot throughout and the edges pull away from the sides of the pan(s). Remove the cakes from the steamer and refrigerate for 1 hour. At this point, they should be set in firm blocks.

Remove the celery root cake(s) from the pan(s) with a small spatula. Cut into 2- to 3-in/5- to 8-cm squares. Dust the outside of the cakes with the remaining 2 tbsp rice powder.

Heat a large cast-iron skillet over medium-high heat until a drop of water flicked on the surface sizzles gently on contact. Add the remaining 2 tsp lard and the celery root cakes, in batches if necessary so they are not touching in the skillet. Cook on medium heat until the cakes release easily from the pan when lifted with a spatula, 3 to 4 minutes. Flip the cakes and cook on the second side in the same manner. Transfer the cakes to a large plate. Add the pea shoots and fava leaves to the skillet, reserving a few raw shoots and leaves for garnish, and cook for about 15 seconds, until they just start to wilt, then transfer to a second plate. Season the greens with the salt. While browning the cakes, warm the nettle sauce in a small saucepan over low heat.

To serve, pour the nettle sauce into a shallow bowl, and place the warm celery root cakes over the sauce. Top the cakes with the cooked greens and pour the pork fat chili oil over the top. Garnish with the charred green onion powder and reserved raw shoots and leaves.

BAR TARTINE

SUNCHOKE CUSTARD WITH SUNFLOWER GREENS

Vast fields of sunflowers cover the Hungarian countryside. An important crop all over eastern Europe, the flowers are cultivated for their oil and their seeds. At Bar Tartine, we often cook with sunflower oil and seeds, which we add to salads, use to make milk, and even use in a tahini-like dip → 188. When we learned that one of our farmers was selling sunflower greens, we immediately began to experiment with them. In our first delivery, we discovered tiny flower buds intertwined with the leaves. Their arrival coincided with the first dry-farmed sunchokes of the season. Because the two are botanical cousins, both members of the Asteraceae family, we decided to pair them. We use the sunchokes in a riff on Japanese *chawan mushi* (savory custard), and serve the custard with *gomae*, the chilled Japanese salad that we make with sunflower leaves and seeds instead of spinach and sesame seeds. Get the salad ingredients ready and assemble while the custards are steaming so they will both be ready at the same time and can be served together.

Serves 4

SUNFLOWER VINAIGRETTE

1¾ cups/225 g sunflower seeds

1 cup/240 ml kombu dashi → 137

¼ cup/60 ml sunchoke oil → 90

2 tbsp mushroom reduction → 131

2 tbsp sweet white wine, such as Tokaji

2 tbsp fresh lemon juice

2 garlic cloves

⅛ tsp hot paprika → 42

2 tsp kosher salt

Freshly ground black pepper

SUNCHOKE CUSTARD

8 oz/225 g sunchokes

1 cup/240 ml kombu dashi → 137

2 tbsp sweet white wine, such as Tokaji

1 tbsp mushroom reduction → 131 or soy sauce

Kosher salt

2 eggs, lightly beaten

2 tbsp poached sunflower seeds (reserved from vinaigrette)

Sweet paprika → 42 for garnish

1 lb/455 g sunflower greens or bunched spinach

10 small sunflower buds

2 tbsp amaranth, plus ¼ cup/60 g amaranth, sprouted → 80

2 green onions, white and tender green parts, thinly sliced

2 tbsp sunflower seeds, toasted

1 tbsp sunchoke oil → 90

Freshly ground black pepper

CONTINUED

TO MAKE THE SUNFLOWER VINAIGRETTE: In a medium saucepan over medium heat, combine the sunflower seeds and dashi, bring to a simmer, and poach gently until the seeds are soft, about 8 minutes. Drain, reserving both the seeds and the poaching liquid. Set aside 2 tbsp of the seeds for use in the custard.

In a blender, combine the remaining poached seeds and the poaching liquid with the sunchoke oil, mushroom reduction, wine, lemon juice, garlic, paprika, salt, and pepper and process until smooth. The vinaigrette should resemble thin tahini. If it is too thick, add a little more dashi if you have some on hand or some water to create a smooth texture. Transfer to an airtight container and refrigerate until ready to use, or for up to 1 week.

TO MAKE THE SUNCHOKE CUSTARD: Scrub the sunchokes, making sure to break off any small knobs and check between tight crevices. Sunchokes can be quite dirty, so be diligent.

Pour water into a steamer pan, place the steamer rack above the water, and put the sunchokes on the rack. Cover the steamer, bring the water to a boil over medium-high heat, and steam until the sunchokes are easily pierced with a skewer, about 20 minutes. Set aside two large sunchokes. Put the remaining sunchokes in the blender and purée until smooth.

In a large bowl, combine the sunchoke purée, dashi, wine, mushroom reduction, and 1 tsp salt. If you are going to bake the custard the day you make this mixture, stir in the eggs and then pass the mixture through a fine-mesh sieve to distribute the eggs evenly. Taste the batter; if you are uneasy tasting raw egg, fill a small ramekin with the mixture and bake in a 300°F/150°C oven for about 5 minutes to heat through before tasting. Add more salt if necessary. Otherwise, wait to add the eggs, as the salt will start to cure them. One day ahead is fine but no more.

Set up the steamer over medium heat and bring the water to a simmer. While the water heats, gather four 1- to 1½-cup/240- to 360-ml bowls. Cut the reserved sunchokes in half and place a half in the bottom of each bowl. Distribute the poached sunflower seeds evenly among the bowls. Pour ½ cup/120 ml of the custard mixture into each bowl. Place the custards on the steamer rack and steam, covered, until set around the edges and firm yet wobbly in the center, 12 to 15 minutes. They will look like silken tofu. Do not overcook the custards, steam them at too high a temperature, or cook them too quickly because overcooked eggs will alter the luscious texture you are trying to achieve. Remove from the steamer and keep warm.

While the custards are cooking, prepare an ice bath. Bring a large pot of salted water to a boil. Add the sunflower greens and sunflower buds and cook just until tender, about 3 minutes. Immediately transfer the greens and buds to the ice bath. When cool, squeeze the water from the greens and buds with your hands. Cut the buds in half and chop the greens into bite-size pieces.

Heat a large saucepan over high heat until a drop of water flicked on the surface sizzles on contact. Add 1 tbsp of the amaranth, cover, and shake the pan several times to distribute the grains evenly. Cook until the grains have popped, about 15 seconds. Transfer the popped amaranth to a bowl and repeat with the remaining 1 tbsp amaranth.

To serve, garnish each of the warm custards with sweet paprika and two or three of the blanched bud halves. Combine the chopped sunflower greens, remaining sunflower buds, and green onions in a large bowl. Add the vinaigrette and toss to coat evenly. Divide the salad among individual plates and garnish with the toasted sunflower seeds, sunchoke oil, and pepper. Divide the puffed amaranth and sprouted amaranth evenly among the salads. Serve immediately with the warm custards.

CLAMS IN CHILLED BROTH

This dish was influenced by our Laotian sous chef, Harry Kongvongxay. When he was a kid, his mother would sometimes make *laap tao*, a Laotian salad that combines fresh snails and a pungent chrysanthemum broth. This is an homage to that dish. We love Laotian food and often comment that sticky rice and chile paste would be at the center of our last meal. Cherrystones, large, hard-shell clams from the Atlantic coast, have an intense, briny flavor that goes especially well with pungent herbs like marjoram, cilantro, and sage.

Serves 4 to 6

2 bunches baby radishes, with greens and bulbs reserved separately

8 oz/225 g Bloomsdale spinach, tough stems removed

1 cup/240 ml strong dashi → 138, chilled

Leaves from 1 bunch fresh flat-leaf parsley

Leaves from 1 bunch fresh cilantro

1 tsp kosher salt

12 cherrystone clams, scrubbed in cold water

2 tbsp parsley oil → 87

Leaves from ¼ bunch each fresh chervil, curly parsley, and marjoram

8 fresh sage leaves, torn into small pieces

½ bunch fresh chives, chopped or torn into ¼-in/6-mm pieces

Prepare an ice bath. Bring a large pot of salted water to a boil. Add the radish bulbs and cook until they start to look translucent and are still firm, about 30 seconds. With a slotted spoon, immediately transfer the radishes to the ice bath. When the radishes are cold, remove them from the ice bath, pat dry, and, if larger than bite-size, cut in half lengthwise. Place on a plate, cover with a damp kitchen towel, and refrigerate until ready to use.

Bring the water back to a boil. Put the spinach in a colander or sieve and dip the colander in the boiling water just until the spinach is wilted, about 3 seconds. Immediately transfer the spinach to the ice bath to preserve its bright color. When cool, remove the spinach from the ice bath and squeeze out the excess water with your hands. Put the radish greens in the colander or sieve and dip them in the boiling water just until wilted, about 3 seconds. Immediately transfer the radish greens to the ice bath. When cool, remove the radish greens from the ice bath and squeeze out the excess water with your hands. Keep the spinach and radish greens separate, and refrigerate until ready to use, or for up to 2 hours.

Chill a blender beaker in the freezer for at least 15 minutes. Combine the dashi, flat-leaf parsley, cilantro, radish greens, and salt in the cold blender and purée just until smooth. Do not overblend or the mixture will heat up, which can spoil the color. Push the sauce through a fine-mesh sieve directly into an airtight container, cover, and refrigerate for up to 2 hours until ready to use.

Just before serving, working over a bowl to catch any liquid, wedge a short, sturdy knife blade between the shells of a clam to open the clam. Cut the upper and lower adductor muscles away from the shells to loosen the meat and transfer the meat to a plate. Repeat with the remaining clams. Refrigerate the clam meat while you finish the dish. Strain the captured clam juice through a fine-mesh sieve into a small bowl, then stir the juice into the chilled herb broth. Set aside the better-looking half of each pair of shells for

serving, removing any shell fragments that may have chipped off during shucking.

Place the cooked spinach on a platter. Arrange a clam and 2 radish halves on each reserved clam shell and set on the platter. Pour chilled broth into each shell until it begins to overflow the rim. Top the clams and vegetables with the parsley oil and garnish with the chervil, curly parsley, marjoram, sage, and chives. Serve immediately.

SALMON IN CLEAR BROTH

We sometimes call this dish a *suimono*, though that's not completely accurate. A classic suimono is a warm, very clear broth with elegant, carefully arranged vegetables, seafood, or poultry. It is typically served in and sipped from a deep bowl. Our version is cold and served in a shallow bowl, but it's still all about the clear broth, the best vegetables, and our local king salmon. We poach the fish briefly in oil at a low temperature, leaving the flesh with a raw appearance and tender texture. The poaching oil can be used again for poaching fish, for making anchovy vinaigrette for the chicory salad → **184**, or for the tonnato sauce → **272**.

Serves 4 to 6

1 lb/455 g skinless center-cut sashimi-grade king salmon fillet, cut into 4 to 6 pieces

1 tsp kosher salt

2 cups/480 ml extra-virgin olive oil

1 bunch baby turnips, halved lengthwise with tender greens attached to both halves

1 cup/240 ml strong dashi → **138**, chilled

Fresh peppercress, chives, chervil, dill, shiso, and nasturtium leaves and flowers for garnish

Thinly sliced cucumber and kohlrabi for garnish

Season the salmon with the salt and let stand at room temperature for about 20 minutes. Pour the olive oil into a wide, shallow stainless-steel saucepan that will accommodate the salmon pieces in a single layer. Place over low heat and warm the oil to 104°F/40°C. Immerse the salmon in the oil and poach until an instant-read thermometer inserted into the center registers 104°F/40°C, about 20 minutes. The color should not change but the fish should be tender to the touch.

Remove from the heat, then remove the salmon from the oil. Refrigerate the salmon and oil separately until ready to serve. The salmon can be poached up to 1 day in advance.

Prepare an ice bath. Bring a large pot of salted water to a boil. Add the turnips and cook until they start to look translucent and are still firm, about 30 seconds. With a slotted spoon, immediately transfer the turnips to the ice bath. When the turnips are cold, remove them from the ice bath, gently squeeze the excess water from the greens with your hands, and pat the bulbs dry. Place in a covered container and refrigerate until ready to use. The turnips can be cooked up to a few hours in advance.

Chill individual shallow bowls in the refrigerator for at least 15 minutes. Pour dashi into each chilled bowl to a depth of ¼ in/6 mm. Cut the salmon into slices ½ in/12 mm thick and divide the slices evenly among the bowls. Arrange the radishes next to the salmon. Pour a little of the reserved poaching oil over the dashi. Garnish with peppercress, chives, chervil, dill, shiso, nasturtium leaves and flowers, cucumber slices, and kohlrabi slices. Serve immediately.

PICKLED HERRING WITH SOUR CREAM & ONION

Serves 6 to 8

1 lb/455 g fresh or frozen herring fillets

½ cup/90 g kosher salt, plus 1 tbsp

2 cups/480 ml rice wine vinegar → 95

1 cup/200 g firmly packed light brown sugar

4 garlic cloves, smashed

1 tbsp black peppercorns, ground → 30

1 tbsp brown mustard seeds, ground → 30

2 bay leaves

1 sweet white onion, sliced paper thin

1 cup/240 ml sour cream → 71

Sliced dark bread, such as pumpernickel or Danish-style rye

Fresh dill leaves for garnish

Freshly ground black pepper

The local herring season in San Francisco arrives in December or January, and we fillet, salt, and pickle thousands of these tasty baitfish during their short season. We make a big bucket of fish sauce every year with the remnants of the herring that didn't get pickled. If you choose to do so, we highly recommend that you go way out in the country away from neighbors. We cover the bones with solé → 62 and let it sit for a year at room temperature. Then we strain it and let it age for another 6 months. It can be used in just about anything; we like it in the green chili fish stew → 176.

There are many variations of pickled herring, including one seasoned with curry, but this sour cream version is our favorite. We like it with dark bread and fresh dill.

Sardines or mackerel are good substitutes for herring. Salted herring, which is available from specialty food stores and some well-stocked supermarkets, can also be substituted for fresh herring. It has a higher salt content than the herring in this recipe, however, so soak it overnight in 4 cups/960 ml water or milk and go directly to making the brine, skipping the step of salting the fish overnight.

Arrange the herring fillets flesh-side up in a single snug layer in a small baking dish. Season the flesh side with 1 tbsp of the salt. Cover the dish and refrigerate for 24 hours.

In a small nonreactive saucepan over low heat, combine the vinegar, brown sugar, garlic, peppercorns, mustard seeds, bay leaves, and remaining 1 tbsp salt. Bring to a simmer and cook, stirring occasionally, to steep the aromatics and dissolve the sugar to create a brine, about 15 minutes. Strain the mixture through a fine-mesh sieve into a nonreactive container. Add the onion to the brine, cover, and refrigerate until cold, about 2 hours.

If you have a butane kitchen torch, gently run the flame over the skin of the fillets to tenderize. If you don't have one, the herring will still be good, but just a bit less tender on the skin side. Add the herring to the cold brine, cover, and refrigerate for 2 days.

Pour off the brine from the herring and onion and discard the bay leaves. Cover and refrigerate the herring. Transfer the onion to a large nonreactive bowl, add the sour cream, and stir gently to mix well. Cover and refrigerate for at least 1 hour before serving. The pickled herring and the onion

mixture can be stored in the refrigerator for up to 1 week.

Spoon pickled onion onto sliced rye bread and top with herring fillets. Garnish with dill and pepper. Serve immediately.

PRESERVED RAINBOW TROUT WITH GREENS & MUSHROOMS

Nare zushi is a method of preserving fish in rice, the original form of sushi. The traditional method can be funky, as the fish ferments with the rice. It is not for timid palates. This version is adapted from the original. We combine naturally soured pickle brine, cooked brown rice, and lightly salted fish and let the mixture gently ferment, allowing the fish to pick up the mild acidity and nuttiness of the rice. Although in this recipe the fish cures in the refrigerator, at the restaurant, we let the trout cure at room temperature for several days before moving it to the refrigerator. This activates the fermentation process and intensifies the flavors of the fish, but is not necessary to make a delicious dish. A variety of different types of fish, including rainbow trout, salmon, and sturgeon, can be cured using this method.

Serves 4 to 6

Two 10-oz/285-g rainbow trout fillets with skin intact, pin bones removed

1 tbsp kosher salt

2 cups/400 g short-grain brown rice

2½ cups/600 ml water

2 qt/2 L mustard green pickle brine → 109 or other brine from lacto-fermented vegetables

6 oz/170 g baby or large shiitake mushrooms, stems removed, sliced into quarters if large

1 cup/150 g drained brined mustard greens → 109, chopped into 1-in/2.5-cm pieces

4 green onions, white and tender green parts, thinly sliced

2 cups/240 ml strong dashi → 138, chilled

Chile oil → 89 for garnish

Finishing salt

Season the trout fillets with 2 tsp of the kosher salt and refrigerate covered for at least 12 hours before pickling.

Put the rice in a medium bowl, add cold water to cover, and agitate with your hand until the water becomes cloudy. Drain and rinse the rice, then cover with fresh cold water and repeat the swishing and draining until the water is clear, about three times. Transfer the rice to a medium heavy-bottomed saucepan, add the 2½ cups/600 ml water, and let stand for 30 minutes.

Place the rice over medium heat, bring to a simmer, cover, turn the heat to low, and cook until the water has been absorbed and the rice is tender, about 30 minutes. Spread the cooked rice on a rimmed baking sheet and gently break

CONTINUED

BAR TARTINE

up any clumps with a spatula, stirring in the remaining 1 tsp kosher salt. Let cool to room temperature and refrigerate until chilled, about 1 hour. The cooked rice can be made the day before pickling the fish.

Spread a layer of the cooked rice on the bottom of a deep baking dish that is the size of a single trout fillet. Top with a fillet, another layer of rice, and the final fillet. Cover with the remaining rice and pour the brine over the top. Place a plate on top, cover, and refrigerate for 1 week. Make sure the fish and rice remain submerged for the entire time.

Remove the trout from the rice, carefully wiping off the grains with a towel. (Use the leftover rice for a second batch of cured trout or to make a slightly sour congee that is also good with the trout, mustard greens, and mushrooms!)

The trout is now ready to eat but you may want to tenderize the fish. Use a small butane kitchen torch or boiling water to quickly scald the skin side. The cured trout should be eaten within 1 day of removing from the rice and brine mixture.

Prepare an ice bath. Bring a small saucepan of lightly salted water to a boil. Add the mushrooms and cook until tender, about 30 seconds. Immediately drain and place the mushrooms in the ice bath. When cool, remove them from the ice bath and gently pat dry with a towel.

To serve, slice the trout on a slight bias, cutting with the knife angled toward the tail of the fillet. Arrange the mustard greens, mushrooms, and green onions in a shallow bowl and top with the slices of fish. Pour the dashi around the bowl and top with the chile oil. Garnish with finishing salt and serve immediately.

GRILLED RAINBOW TROUT WITH CUCUMBERS & BUTTERMILK

We both have memories of fishing for rainbow trout in the Midwest, cooking them in a frying pan, and eating them with nothing more than a squeeze of lemon juice. These days, we source farmed rainbow trout from Kenny Belov of TwoXSea in Sausalito, California. A model of sustainable aquaculture, Belov's McFarland Springs trout are fed an entirely vegetarian diet. Rainbow trout tend to be lean and thus benefit from a creamy, acidic sauce like this one.

Serves 4 to 6

Two 10-oz/280-g rainbow trout fillets with skin intact, pin bones removed

Kosher salt

BUTTERMILK CUCUMBER SAUCE

2 oz/55 g Yukon gold potato, chopped into large dice

1½ cups/360 ml kefir buttermilk → 76

1 sweet white onion, coarsely chopped

2 tbsp apple cider vinegar → 95

1 tbsp fermented honey → 121, or honey

1 tbsp kosher salt

1 cup/240 ml sour cream → 71

2 lb/910 g cucumbers, cut into ¼-in/6-mm dice or thinly sliced

Fresh curly parsley, torn, for garnish

Fresh dill, torn, for garnish

Fresh chives, minced, for garnish

Green coriander seeds for garnish

Sliced cucumbers and halved mouse melons for garnish

Chive oil → 87 for garnish

Season the trout with 2 tsp salt and refrigerate for at least 1 hour before cooking.

TO MAKE THE BUTTERMILK CUCUMBER SAUCE: In a small saucepan cover the potato with about 1 in/2.5 cm of water and bring to a simmer over medium heat. Cook until the potato is tender and easily pierced with a skewer, 10 to 15 minutes. Drain and let cool to room temperature.

In a blender, combine the buttermilk, onion, and vinegar and process until smooth. Add the potato, honey, and salt and process until the sauce is creamy and the potato is completely incorporated. On low speed, add the sour cream and process just until mixed. Transfer to a bowl and stir in the cucumbers. Cover and refrigerate for at least 1 hour before using, to marinate the cucumbers and allow them to soften. The sauce can be made up to 1 day in advance and stored in an airtight container in the refrigerator.

Prepare a medium-hot fire for direct-heat cooking in a charcoal or gas grill. Using a paper towel, pat dry the skin side of each fish fillet to ensure a nice char. Season with 1 to 2 tsp salt. Place the fillets, skin-side down, on the grate directly over the fire and grill until the flesh side of each fillet starts to turn opaque and the skin easily releases from the grate, about 2 minutes. Rotate the fish 90 degrees and grill about 2 minutes longer. At this point the fish should be partially cooked and the flesh side should be warm to the touch. Remove the fillets from the grill and cut into thick slices if desired.

To serve, pour the sauce in an even layer on a large serving platter. Top with the fish fillets, skin-side up. Garnish with the parsley, dill, chives, coriander seeds, sliced cucumbers, and the chive oil. Serve immediately.

CATFISH CABBAGE ROLLS WITH CARAWAY & PICKLED DILL SEEDS

This dish makes use of *kamaboko*, a Japanese steamed fish cake that is popular in ramen, in soups, and as a simple snack. In Japan, it is steamed into logs and then sliced. For this dish, we marry the flavors of this fish sausage and dashi broth with beets, caraway, and dill. It is important to keep everything very cold throughout this process, as this will guarantee the best texture for the finished kamaboko.

Serves 4 to 6

BROTH

1½ cups/360 ml strong dashi → 138

1 tsp caraway seeds, toasted and crushed

½ cup/120 ml beet juice → 129

CATFISH ROLLS

1 head savoy cabbage

1 lb/455 g catfish fillet, large sinew, bones, and skin removed, diced

¼ cup/60 ml strong dashi → 138

2 tbsp fish sauce

2 tsp kosher salt

Greens from 2 bunches beets

Caraway oil → 87 for garnish

Dill flower vinegar → 99 for garnish

Sour cream → 71 for garnish

Poppy seeds for garnish

Fresh dill for garnish

Pickled dill seeds → 115 for garnish

Freshly ground black pepper

TO MAKE THE BROTH: In a small saucepan over medium heat, combine the dashi with the caraway seeds and simmer for 5 minutes. Cover, remove from the heat, and let steep until the dashi is infused with the flavor of the seeds, about 30 minutes. Strain the dashi through a fine-mesh sieve or cheesecloth into a container. Discard the solids. Add the beet juice to the infused dashi. Refrigerate until ready to use, or for up to 4 days.

TO MAKE THE CATFISH ROLLS: Bring a large pot of salted water to boil over high heat, and prepare an ice bath. Separate the leaves of the cabbage, keeping them as intact as possible by cutting around the core with a paring knife to release them. Trim any large, tough stems from the cabbage leaves. Add the leaves to the

CONTINUED

boiling water and blanch until the leaves are just tender enough to pinch through, but are still holding together, about 1 minute. Immediately transfer the leaves to the ice bath. When cool, remove the leaves from the ice bath and pat them dry.

Chill the catfish, dashi, and the bowl and blade of a food processor in the freezer until the outside of the fish begins to harden, about 20 minutes. In the chilled food processor, combine the fish, fish sauce, and salt and process until the fish pieces come together in a single mass, about 2 minutes. Add the chilled dashi and purée until the broth is incorporated into the fish and the mixture is smooth and tacky, 3 to 5 minutes. You want it to be very sticky so that the cabbage leaves adhere to it.

On a work surface, spread out two large sheets of good-quality plastic wrap, each 8 in/20 cm wide by 12 in/30 cm long. Lay out cabbage leaves on each sheet of plastic, covering the entire surface. Divide the fish mixture between the two sheets, and, with a spatula, shape into logs about 6 in/15 cm long and 1½ in/4 cm in diameter. Fold the sides of the leaves in around the fish and then roll the leaves lengthwise around the fish mixture, as if making a burrito; use the plastic wrap to tighten down on the roll. Tightly wrap the logs in the plastic, being careful to push out any air bubbles. Twist the excess plastic on each end

to secure the ends and fold them under the roll. Roll each log in a second sheet of plastic.

Set up a steamer and prepare an ice bath. Steam the rolls for 15 to 20 minutes, until they are firm to the touch and a small knife blade inserted into the center comes out warm. Transfer the rolls to the ice bath to cool. The rolls can be used right away or refrigerated wrapped in plastic wrap for up to 4 days.

Bring a pot of salted water to a boil over high heat and prepare an ice bath. Add the beet greens and cook until tender, about 1 minute. Transfer the greens to the ice bath. When cool, remove the greens from the ice bath and gently squeeze out the excess water with your hands.

Set up a steamer. Warm the broth in a small saucepan over medium heat. Slice the catfish rolls into ½-in/12-mm slices, being careful to keep the cabbage leaves intact. Place the slices and the beet greens on a small sheet pan or plate that fits in your steamer. Steam for 3 minutes, until warm.

To serve, ladle about ¼ cup/60 ml of the warm broth into serving bowls and add the warm catfish roll slices. Form the beet greens into four to six small balls and place a ball in each bowl. Spoon on some of the caraway oil and vinegar, garnish with a small spoonful of sour cream, the poppy seeds, fresh dill, dill seeds, and pepper.

TUNA WITH BLACK BEER PONZU & RADISH

Our friends at Linden Street Brewery in Oakland, California, isolated the yeast from the starter used for Tartine bread and now brew a beer with it to great success. One particular batch of beer was a black lager; when a keg accidently went flat, we decided to reduce it to use as a sauce, adding some kombu to it as it cooked. The resulting syrup tasted a bit like soy sauce, and our first thought was to make ponzu, the Japanese staple traditionally made with soy sauce, dashi, citrus, and sugar. We liked the result and never looked back. We now use our beer ponzu on grilled vegetables, beef, lamb, and fish. A porter or a stout is perfect here. The less hoppy the better, as very bitter beer makes an even more bitter sauce. This dish is similar to tataki, a Japanese favorite in which fish or meat is seared very briefly and sliced thin.

Our local Pacific Coast albacore is a true delicacy. It has a unique buttery texture that is unlike any other fish we know. The best substitute for it is skipjack tuna, the classic tataki fish. Seared and sliced beef can work in this recipe, too.

BLACK BEER PONZU

2 qt/2 L dark beer (see headnote)

4 sheets dried kombu, each 3 by 6 in/ 7.5 by 15 cm

2 cups/50 g packed katsuobushi flakes

2 tbsp malt syrup or light brown sugar

¼ cup/60 ml fresh lemon juice

1 tbsp kosher salt

1 lb/455 g center-cut sashimi-grade tuna fillet, skinned

Kosher salt

1 watermelon radish, peeled and grated

4 green onions, white and tender green parts, sliced thinly

1 small piece fresh ginger, peeled

TO MAKE THE BLACK BEER PONZU: In a medium saucepan over medium heat, simmer the beer until the liquid has reduced by half, about 1 hour. Add the kombu, reduce the heat to low, and cook until it is tender enough to pierce with a chopstick, about 1½ hours. Remove the kombu, remove the pan from the heat, add the katsuobushi, and let steep for 5 minutes.

Strain the liquid through a fine-mesh sieve and press firmly to extract the liquid from the katsuo-bushi. Discard the flakes. Stir in the malt syrup, lemon juice, and salt. Transfer to an airtight container, let cool, cover, and refrigerate for up to 3 months.

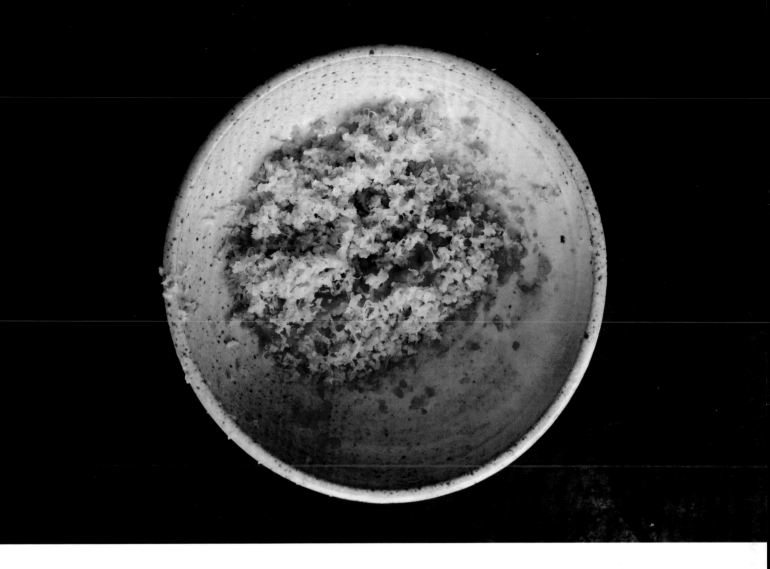

This next step can generate some smoke, so be sure to open a window or turn on a fan before beginning. Heat a cast-iron skillet over high heat until very hot, 4 to 5 minutes. Season the tuna on all sides with salt, transfer to the hot skillet, and press down on the fish. Cook until the fish is charred, about 15 seconds. Turn the fish over, press down on it, and cook until charred on the second side, about 15 seconds. Continue until all sides are seared. Transfer the fish to a rack and refrigerate immediately. Chill for at least 30 minutes or until you are ready to serve. The fish should be served the day it is seared.

To serve, cut the tuna into slices ¼ in/6 mm thick, being careful not to tear the flesh. Pour the ponzu on a large serving platter and arrange the tuna slices, radish, and green onions around the plate. Grate the ginger with a fine-tooth grater into the exposed sauce. Serve immediately.

BAR TARTINE

TOMATOES WITH TONNATO SAUCE & NORI

This dish is a great one to pair with Tuna with Black Beer Ponzu & Radish → 268. The center cut of the tuna is seared for the latter while the scraps are used in this recipe for tuna mayonnaise, or *tonnato*, as it is called in Italy. We sometimes serve the mayonnaise with vegetables, such as green beans, potatoes, or summer squashes, but it's traditionally paired with tomatoes. The "crazy water" vinaigrette for this recipe is influenced by *acqua pazza*, a rustic Italian fisherman's sauce.

Serves 4 to 6

TONNATO SAUCE

2 oz/55 g Yukon gold potato

4 oz/115 g tuna scraps, cut into ¼-in/ 6-mm dice

2 dried shiitake mushrooms

6 garlic cloves, smashed

¾ cup/180 ml unfiltered grapeseed oil

12 oil-packed anchovy fillets

2 tsp fish sauce

2 egg yolks

1 tbsp fresh lemon juice

2 tsp kosher salt

1 tbsp freshly ground black pepper

CRAZY WATER

¼ cup/60 ml tomato water → 131

¼ cup/60 ml brine from a jar of green olives or from brined green beans → 110

2 tsp fish sauce

2 tsp fresh lemon juice

2 garlic cloves, minced

1 tsp fermented honey → 121, or honey

½ tsp kosher salt

4 ripe tomatoes

3 sheets toasted nori, or 2 oz/55 g wild nori plus 2 tbsp unfiltered grapeseed oil

Purslane, arugula, or mizuna for garnish

8 shiso leaves, torn into pieces

Extra-virgin olive oil for garnish

Green onions, white and tender green parts, thinly sliced, for garnish

Finishing salt and freshly ground black pepper

TO MAKE THE TONNATO SAUCE: In a small saucepan, cover the potato with about 1 in/ 2.5 cm of water and bring to a simmer over medium heat. Cook until the potato is tender enough to be easily pierced with a skewer, 10 to 15 minutes. Drain well and set aside.

In a small saucepan over very low heat, combine the tuna scraps, mushrooms, garlic, and grapeseed oil. Drain any oil from the anchovies into the pan. Cook until the garlic is tender enough to be easily pierced with a skewer, about 30 minutes. Remove from the heat, transfer to a bowl, and refrigerate until well chilled, about 30 minutes. Remove the mushrooms and discard.

TO MAKE THE CRAZY WATER: In a small bowl, combine the tomato water, olive brine, fish sauce, lemon juice, garlic, honey, and kosher salt and mix well. The broth can be made up to 5 days in advance and stored in an airtight container in the refrigerator.

Using a paring knife, core the tomatoes, then cut a small, shallow X in the blossom end. Bring a large pot of water to a boil and set up an ice bath. Add the tomatoes and boil just long enough to loosen their skins, about 15 seconds. Do not overcook. Using a slotted spoon, transfer the tomatoes to the ice bath. When cool, peel the tomatoes. Then, using the paring knife, cut each tomato into four wedges, starting at the stem but not cutting all the way through the blossom end.

If using toasted nori, if you have a gas stove, turn on a burner to low, then hold the nori sheets directly over the flame and toast for about 2 seconds on each side. Alternatively, preheat the oven to 450°F/230°C, place the nori on a baking sheet, and bake for 5 minutes. If using wild nori, preheat the oven to 350°F/180°C. On a sheet pan, toss the wild nori with the grapeseed oil and bake until crisp, 3 to 5 minutes.

To serve, stand the tomatoes, cut-side up, on a serving platter and carefully spread the wedges apart. Spoon the tonnato sauce into the tomatoes. Arrange the greens around the tomatoes and scatter the shiso over the top. Pour the crazy water and a genreous amount of olive oil over everything. Crumble the nori directly over the tomatoes, then garnish with the green onions, finishing salt, and pepper.

Strain the chilled mixture, reserving the tuna mixture and oil separately. In a food processor, combine the cooked potato, tuna mixture, anchovies, fish sauce, egg yolks, and lemon juice and purée until smooth, about 1 minute. With the processor running, slowly pour in the strained oil. Do not overprocess or the mixture will heat up, which can cause the emulsion to break. The sauce should be quite thick. Season with the kosher salt and pepper, then transfer to an airtight container and refrigerate for up to 3 days.

BRUSSELS SPROUTS WITH DRIED TUNA & TONNATO SAUCE

In this autumnal dish, the Brussels sprout leaves are separated from the cores. The leaves are cooked briefly so that they remain crunchy, while the sweet middles are roasted until tender. We layer tuna flavor into the dish in a couple of different ways: an ever-versatile and satisfying tonnato sauce provides nice rich-ness, and by salting and drying the tuna loin, we concentrate the fish's flavor, creating a bottarga-like product that we grate and use, in effect, to season the sprouts.

Serves 4 to 6

2 lb/910 g Brussels sprouts, ends trimmed

2 tbsp unfiltered grapeseed oil

2 tsp kosher salt

Tonnato sauce → 272

Juice of 2 lemons

2 tbsp sunchoke oil → 90 or extra-virgin olive oil

One ½-oz/15-g chunk of dried tuna (see Dry-Cured Meat or Fat → 61)

Fresh chervil for garnish

Freshly ground black pepper

Pick the leaves off the Brussels sprouts until the sprouts are about half of their original size. Cut the sprouts in half and reserve the leaves separately.

Preheat the oven to 350°F/175°C. Prepare an ice bath. Bring a large pot of salted water to a boil. Add the Brussels sprouts leaves and cook until they are bright green and still firm, about 20 seconds. With a slotted spoon, immediately transfer the leaves to the ice bath. When the leaves are cold, remove them from the ice bath, gently squeeze the excess water with your hands, and pat dry with a clean kitchen towel. Place in a covered container and refrigerate until ready to use. The leaves can be cooked up to a few hours ahead of serving.

In a large bowl, gently toss the halved Brussels sprout cores with the grapeseed oil and 1½ tsp of the salt. Lay out the sprouts on a sheet pan, cut-side down. They can be touching, but not stacked. Roast for 15 to 20 minutes, until the cut surfaces of the sprouts are light golden brown. Remove from the oven and let the sprouts cool to just above room temperature.

Spread the tonnato sauce on a serving platter. Place the roasted sprouts browned sides facing up on top of the tonnato sauce. In a medium bowl, toss the sprout leaves with the lemon juice, sun-choke oil, and the remaining ½ tsp salt. Arrange the leaves over the charred sprouts, pouring any sunchoke oil from the bowl over the sprouts. With a fine-tooth grater, generously grate the dried tuna over the entire plate. Garnish with the chervil, and top with plenty of pepper. Serve immediately.

RYE BREAD WITH SALMON ROE & CULTURED BUTTER

This is a northern European ode to *ikura nigiri*, the classic sushi of salmon roe and rice. The Danish-style rye bread that Chad makes with sprouted rye berries and our buttermilk is dense and quite moist, and though it may sound like a stretch, its texture is a little like Japanese sushi rice. The bread is toasted with some of our cultured butter and then topped with radish slices and a generous spoonful of briny, local salmon roe. We have the best luck finding local fish roe in the late summer through early winter. After salmon season ends, we usually find roe in black cod for a couple of months. We also cure farmed McFarland Springs rainbow trout roe when it is available. If you are curing a larger amount of roe, work in batches of 1 lb/455 g for the best result.

Serves 4

2 tbsp kefir butter → 76, plus more for toasting

4 slices Danish-style rye bread, ¼ in/6 mm thick and about 6 in/15 cm long, crust removed

4 radishes, trimmed and thinly sliced

Finishing salt

4 oz/110 g cured fresh fish roe (recipe follows), or cod roe in beet brine (recipe follows)

Spread a thin layer of butter on both sides of the bread slices. Place a large skillet over medium heat. When the pan is hot, add the bread slices and sear, turning once, for about 30 seconds on each side. The surfaces should be browned but the centers should remain soft. Transfer the bread to a paper towel to absorb any excess butter and let cool for about 5 minutes.

Spread the 2 tbsp butter on one side of each of the half-cooled slices, evenly dividing the butter. Cover with the radish slices and season with salt. Cut the bread slices into bite-size pieces, keeping them close together. Cover completely with a dense layer of salmon roe and serve immediately.

CURED FRESH FISH ROE

Makes 1 pt/450 g

1 cup/140 g kosher salt

3 qt/2.8 L water

1 lb/455 g fresh salmon or trout roe in sacs

2 tbsp Tokaji aszù or other sweet white wine

In a medium bowl, dissolve ½ cup/70 g of the salt in 1 qt/960 ml of the water. Add the roe sacs, cover, and refrigerate to cure and set the eggs, 5 to 10 minutes.

In a medium saucepan over low heat, warm 1 qt/960 ml water to 110°F/43°C. Remove the sacs from the salted water, discard the water, and return them to the bowl. Pour the warm water over the sacs and let stand for 5 minutes. This helps release the eggs. Gently rub the eggs from the sacs, being careful not to puncture them. When all of the roe has been freed, discard the empty sacs and let the roe drain in a fine-mesh sieve. Gently rinse under cold running water.

Mix a fresh brine with the remaining ½ cup/70 g salt and 1 qt/960 ml water, stirring until the salt dissolves. Add the roe to the brine and refrigerate for 20 minutes. Drain it again in the sieve. Transfer the roe to a medium bowl, add the wine, and let stand for 15 minutes. The wine balances the briny nature of the eggs. (Experiment with the type of wine if you would like a sweeter flavor.) Place the roe on a clean kitchen towel, and holding the towel by both the ends, roll the roe back and forth to remove empty sacs and sinew. Transfer the roe to an airtight container and refrigerate for up to 3 days. If storing, you may need to pat the roe dry or drain it on a clean kitchen towel before serving, as it will release more liquid over time.

COD ROE IN BEET BRINE

Makes 1 pt/450 g

¼ cup/35 g kosher salt

2 cups/480 ml beet juice → 129

1 lb/455 g fresh cod roe in sacs

In a medium bowl, dissolve the salt in the beet juice. With a knife, carefully split each roe sac, being cautious not to puncture the eggs. With the back of the knife or a plastic dough scraper, free the roe from each sac into the beet brine.

Cover and refrigerate to cure the eggs, about 20 minutes.

Line a fine-mesh sieve with cheesecloth and set out a medium bowl. Transfer the roe to the sieve to drain, then place the sieve-and-bowl setup in the refrigerator until the roe is free of moisture, about 1 hour. Use immediately, or refrigerate in an airtight container for up to 3 days. If storing, you may need to pat the roe dry or drain it on a clean kitchen towel, as it will release more liquid over time.

BAR TARTINE

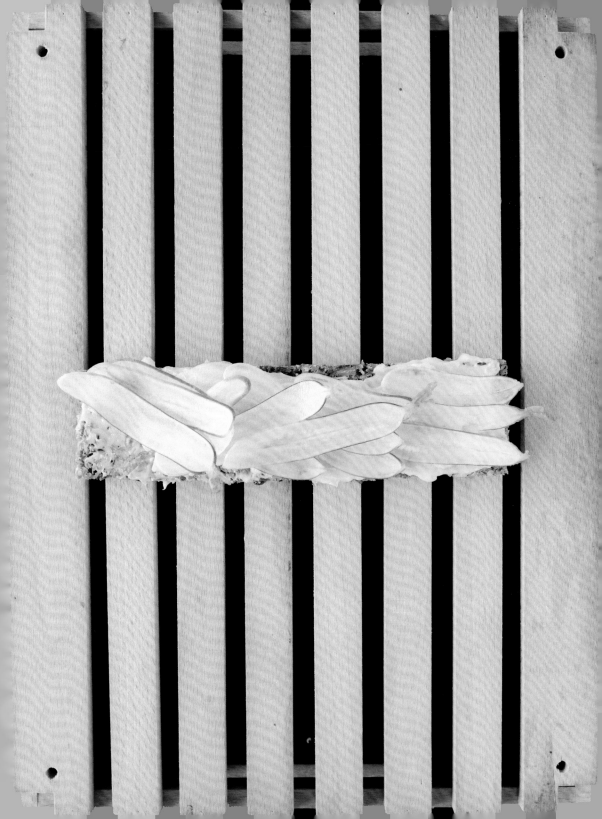

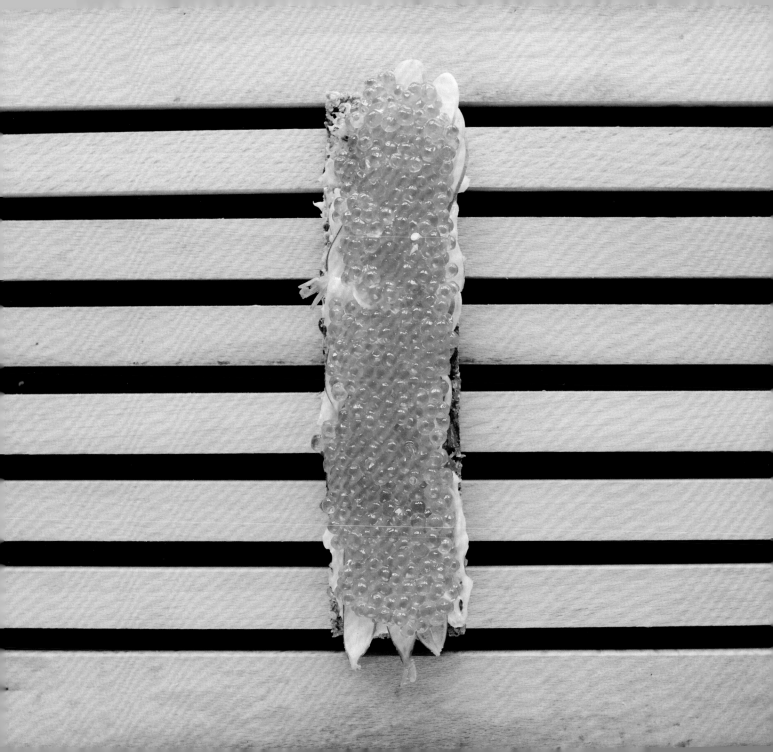

BEEF TARTARE TOAST WITH BOTTARGA

The simplicity of this dish gives little hint to its broad spectrum of flavors. Chad makes the bread with our homemade rice koji, which adds a sweet, nutty aroma to the loaves. We cure the mullet roe that we get from Nick's uncle, a fisherman in Florida, and finally the grass-fed beef is from our friend Claire Herminjard at Mindful Meats. Sourced from dairy cows, which are older than traditional beef cattle, the beef is deeply flavored and quite lean, making it an excellent choice for tartare.

Any good, crusty bread will work for this dish.

Serves 4

KOJI SAUCE

2 oz/55 g Yukon gold potato

¼ cup/60 ml strong dashi → 138

3 tbsp tallow → 94, at room temperature

2 tbsp salt koji → 124 or white miso

3 tbsp sour cream → 71

1 tsp kosher salt

4 tbsp/55 g tallow → 94, at room temperature

2 thick slices good-quality crusty country-style bread

4 small turnips, peeled and sliced paper-thin

Finishing salt

8 oz/225 g freshly ground or finely chopped grass-fed eye of round or beef shoulder

1 oz/30 g bottarga → 62

Peppercress or arugula for garnish

Garlic chives for garnish

Freshly ground black pepper

TO MAKE THE KOJI SAUCE: In a small saucepan, cover the potato with about 1 in/2.5 cm of water and bring to a simmer over medium heat. Cook until the potato is tender enough to be easily pierced with a skewer, 10 to 15 minutes. Drain well.

In a blender, combine the warm potato, dashi, tallow, and salt koji and process until smooth. Add the sour cream and kosher salt and process until all of the ingredients are fully incorporated. Transfer to an airtight container and refrigerate for up to 3 days.

Spread the tallow on one side of the bread slices, dividing it evenly. Heat a cast-iron skillet over medium heat until a drop of water flicked on the surface sizzles gently on contact. Add the bread, tallow-side down, to the pan, and cook, turning once, just until the surface is browned but the center of each slice is still soft, about 4 minutes. Let the bread slices cool for 5 minutes.

Spread the koji sauce in an even layer on the tallow side of the bread slices, evenly dividing the sauce. Cover with a thin layer of the turnip slices and season with finishing salt. Spread the ground beef over the turnips as evenly as possible. Liberally grate the bottarga over the beef and season with more finishing salt. Garnish with the peppercress and garlic chives and season with pepper. Slice each toast into two or four pieces, transfer to a large plate or tray, and serve immediately.

KOHLRABI WITH HAM & TURNIPS

Circumstance is often the mother of invention at Bar Tartine. This dish came together one day after we had simmered a large batch of kohlrabi and turnips in dashi. We also had some Mangalitsa hams that had been aging for a few years that were ready to slice. The combination worked. We emulsified some of the cooking dashi with the ham fat to make a light yet creamy sauce, creating a dish unexpectedly reminiscent of scalloped potatoes.

Butcher shops and specialty food stores often have prosciutto scraps that too frequently go to waste. Ask for the trimmings to use in soup bases, pasta fillings, and dishes like this one.

Serves 4 to 6

6 cups/1.5 L katsuo dashi → 137

1 lb/455 g kohlrabi, peeled

2 tsp kosher salt

12 to 15 baby turnips, peeled, with greens removed and reserved

10 oz/280 g Yukon gold potato, peeled and chopped

2 medium turnips, peeled and chopped

1 sweet white onion, chopped

4 oz/115 g prosciutto fat trimmings or whipped cured pork fatback → 94, chopped

1 tbsp apple cider vinegar → 95

4 oz/115 g thinly sliced prosciutto

1 bunch fresh chives, cut into ½-in/ 12-mm pieces

Leaves from 1 bunch fresh curly parsley

Lamb's quarters for garnish

In a large pot narrow enough so that the kohlrabi is completely submerged in liquid, combine the dashi, kohlrabi, and salt. Bring to a boil over high heat, lower the heat to a gentle simmer, and cook until the kohlrabi is almost tender, about 20 minutes. Add the whole baby turnips to the saucepan, remove from the heat, and let the vegetables steep in the warm broth until the turnips are just beginning to become tender, about 10 minutes. Remove the kohlrabi and turnips from the broth and reserve at room temperature.

Return the broth to medium-high heat, bring to a simmer, and cook until reduced by half. Scoop out ¼ cup/60 ml of the broth and reserve. Add the potato, chopped turnips, onion, and prosciutto trimmings to the remaining broth in the saucepan and simmer until the vegetables are quite tender, about 45 minutes. Add the vinegar, remove from the heat, and let cool slightly.

Transfer the contents of the saucepan to a blender, working in batches so the machine is no more than half full, and purée until very smooth. Strain through a fine-mesh sieve into a medium saucepan and keep warm over

low heat. If not using the sauce right away, let cool, transfer to an airtight container, and refrigerate for up to 5 days; reheat over low heat just before serving.

To serve, preheat the oven to 300°F/150°C. With a mandoline or a sharp knife, cut the kohlrabi into thin rounds. Spread the kohlrabi slices and the baby turnips in a single layer on a sheet pan and moisten with some of the reserved broth. Warm in the oven for about 5 minutes.

Spread the warm turnip sauce on a large serving platter. Arrange the reserved turnip greens on the sauce, then arrange the prosciutto slices on the greens. Top with the chives and parsley. Cover the prosciutto and herbs with a thin layer of warmed kohlrabi slices and top with the baby turnips. Pour the remaining reserved broth over everything and garnish with lamb's quarters. Serve immediately.

GAI LAN WITH AIR-DRIED BEEF

There is a whole world of Asian greens grown in California that are almost completely ignored by most non-Asians. They are usually half the price of their downtown farmers' market counterparts. Most important, these vegetables are delicious. Gai lan (Chinese broccoli) in particular makes frequent appearances on our menu. The leaves remind us of spinach, the small stems of broccoli, and the larger stems of asparagus. Here, we give this versatile green a meaty flavor, with a broth infused with beef fat and a garnish of grated dried beef. We use a katsuobushi grater to shave our dried beef, but a very sharp cheese grater also works well.

Serves 4 to 6

1 lb/455 g beef marrowbones

1 lb/455 g beef trimmings or lean beef

2 qt/2 L kombu dashi → 137

3 cups/75 g packed katsuobushi flakes

2 tbsp white soy sauce, or 4 tsp kosher salt

1 lb/455 g gai lan, large stems peeled, then stalks cut crosswise into 2-in/5-cm lengths

Kosher salt

1 tbsp water

4 oz/115 g daikon radish, peeled

4 oz/115 g dry-cured beef → 61 or bresaola

Finishing salt and freshly ground black pepper

Preheat the oven to 350°F/180°C. Lightly oil a sheet pan, then arrange the marrowbones and beef trimmings in a single layer on the prepared pan. Roast until fragrant and beginning to brown, 20 to 25 minutes.

Transfer the bones and trimmings to a heavy-bottomed stockpot and place over very low heat. Add the dashi and simmer until the liquid is reduced by half, about 3 hours. Remove from the heat and add the katsuobushi flakes. Allow to steep for 5 minutes. Strain the broth, bones and all, through a fine-mesh sieve into a medium bowl. Using a large spoon, skim the fat from the surface and reserve the fat for garnishing the gai lan.

Prepare an ice bath. Season the broth with the soy sauce, nest the bowl in the ice bath, and chill well.

Heat a large cast-iron skillet over medium-high heat until a drop of water flicked on the surface sizzles on contact. Add the gai lan to the hot skillet and season with a pinch of kosher salt. Top with a heavy pan or other weight, pressing the greens into the pan. Cook until they start to char slightly, about 2 minutes. Flip the greens and press for 1 minute longer to char a bit on the other side. Add the water to the pan to briefly

steam the greens, flip one last time, and remove the greens from the skillet.

In a medium saucepan over medium heat, bring the broth to a simmer. Put the gai lan in a large, shallow serving bowl and pour the hot broth over the top. Garnish with 1 tbsp of the reserved beef fat. Grate the daikon radish onto a small plate, then top the gai lan with mounds of the grated daikon. Shave the dried beef over the gai lan to cover completely. Season the greens with finishing salt and pepper. Serve immediately.

GRILLED TRIPE WITH PAPRIKA & FENNEL

Similar to a Hungarian classic known as *pacalpörkölt*, this is the dish for people who don't think they like tripe and for those who know they do. The old-world version is often made with pork knuckle, and we sometimes serve it that way, but this recipe includes bacon instead. Our take on this dish differs also in how we cook the tripe. Traditionally it would be simmered for a long time, yielding a soft texture. Here, the tripe is braised, quickly deep-fried, and finally grilled before it is sliced and served in a paprika stew. The result is a crisp surface, tender interior, and smoky aroma. Serve with Smoked Potatoes with Ramp Mayonnaise → 226.

Serves 4 to 6

6 dried árbol chiles

4 oz/115 g bacon, cut into ¼-in/6-mm pieces

8 garlic cloves, chopped

4 dried tomatoes → 40, dried for 24 hours

2 sweet white onions, thinly sliced

2 fennel bulbs, halved, cored, and thinly sliced

2 serrano chiles, stemmed and thinly sliced

¼ cup/75 g sweet or hot paprika → 42

1½ lb/680 g cleaned honeycomb tripe, in a single piece

1 tbsp kosher salt

2 qt/2 L beef broth → 142

2 tsp freshly ground black pepper

Rice bran oil for deep-frying

Fresh cilantro leaves for garnish

Green onions, white and tender green parts, thinly sliced, for garnish

2 limes, halved

Heat a cast-iron skillet over high heat until a drop of water flicked on the surface sizzles on contact. Add the árbol chiles to the hot skillet and char, turning as needed, until blackened on all sides, about 3 minutes total. Let the chiles cool, crumble into flakes, and set aside.

Heat a heavy-bottomed Dutch oven over medium heat until a drop of water flicked on the surface sizzles gently on contact. Add the bacon and stir until it renders most of its fat, about 5 minutes. Add half of the garlic, the dried tomatoes, onions, fennel, and serranos and continue to stir until the onions begin to brown, about 5 minutes longer. Add the paprika and stir until fragrant, about 1 minute. Add the tripe, salt, and broth and bring to a simmer. Turn the heat to low and cook, covered, until the tripe is tender, 4 to 4½ hours.

Remove the pot from the heat, then remove the tripe from the broth. With a paper towel, pat the tripe dry, wiping off any vegetables that may have stuck to it. Divide the tripe into four to six equal pieces. The broth can be cooled to room temperature, then transferred to an airtight

container and refrigerated for up to 4 days. The tripe pieces can also be transferred to an airtight container and refrigerated for up to 4 days.

Pour the broth into a medium saucepan, add the remaining garlic, árbol chile flakes, and pepper and bring to a simmer over medium-high heat. Simmer for 15 minutes. Adjust the heat to keep the broth hot while you fry the tripe.

Pour the rice bran oil to a depth of 1 in/2.5 cm in a cast-iron or other heavy-bottomed skillet and heat to 350°F/180°C. Heat a stove-top cast-iron grill pan or skillet over medium-high heat. Add the tripe, one or two pieces at a time, to the hot oil and fry until lightly browned, 1 to 2 minutes.

Using tongs, immediately transfer the fried tripe to the hot grill pan and cook, turning once, until the tripe is crisp on the outside but still soft in the center, about 4 minutes.

When all of the tripe pieces are ready, cut them into strips ¼ in/6 mm wide. Ladle the warm broth into a serving bowl, add the tripe strips, and garnish with the cilantro and green onions, then squeeze the lime halves over the top. Serve immediately. The texture of the tripe is best if it is eaten immediately after the ingredients are combined, but any leftover tripe stew can be stored in an airtight container in the refrigerator for up to 4 days.

PORK KNUCKLE & SAUSAGE- STUFFED VEGETABLES

This dish is as much fun to prepare as it is to eat. Stewed sauerkraut is the perfect vehicle for sausage-stuffed vegetables and a roasted pork knuckle. The knuckle is the part of the leg that includes the hock. It is a delicacy in many parts of the world, and to our minds, one of the most delicious cuts.

The cooking of the stuffed vegetables, mashed potatoes, and pork knuckle will happen simultaneously. It's helpful to have the table set, the other dishes ready to go, and the serving platters warm before beginning the final cooking.

The vegetables require quite a bit of trimming, but there's no reason to do the job alone. Lure your guests to the kitchen with a glass of wine. Pass out some paring knives and cutting boards and get everyone involved. The youngest guests can stuff the vegetables with sausage.

Serves 6 to 8

PORK KNUCKLE

2 qt/2 L onion brine → 115

1 pork knuckle, 3 to 5 lbs/1.4 kg to 2.25 kg

1 tsp kosher salt

PORK SAUSAGE

1 cup/200 g short-grain brown rice

1¼ cups/300 ml water

4 oz/115 g bacon, minced

2 sweet white onions, minced

3 serrano chiles, stemmed and minced

12 garlic cloves, minced

1 tbsp kosher salt, plus 1 tsp

1 lb/455 g ground pork

1 tbsp sweet or hot paprika → 42

½ bunch each fresh thyme, marjoram, flat-leaf parsley, and dill, minced

Freshly ground black pepper

STEWED SAUERKRAUT

8 dried tomatoes → 40, dried for 24 hours

4 cups/960 ml chicken broth → 139

12 oz/335 g sliced bacon, cut into small strips

3 large sweet onions, julienned

25 garlic cloves, thinly sliced

3 tbsp sweet paprika → 42

2 tbsp hot paprika → 42

4 cups/960 ml sauerkraut with brine →111

2 tsp kosher salt

CONTINUED

STUFFED VEGETABLES

2 kohlrabies

1 small kabocha squash, about 12 oz/340 g, or a
    similar winter squash, such as buttercup

2 large sweet white onions, peeled

1¼ lb/570 g pork sausage

8 button mushrooms, stems removed

CABBAGE ROLLS

2 heads savoy cabbage

1¼ lb/570 g pork sausage

4 russet potatoes

Kosher salt

¾ cup/180 ml sour cream → 71, at room
    temperature, plus more for garnish

1 tbsp kefir butter → 76, at room temperature

Chopped fresh flat-leaf parsley for garnish

Chopped fresh chives for garnish

Chopped fresh dill for garnish

Coarsely ground black pepper

TO PREPARE THE PORK KNUCKLE: In a large nonreactive container, combine the onion brine and pork knuckle. Cover and refrigerate for 12 hours. Remove the knuckle from the brine and discard the brine. Pat the knuckle dry, cover, and refrigerate for up to 4 days.

TO MAKE THE PORK SAUSAGE: Put the rice in a medium bowl, add cold water to cover, and swish the rice with your hand until the water becomes cloudy. Drain and rinse the rice, then cover with fresh cold water and repeat the swishing and draining. Repeat this action until the water is clear, about three times. Transfer the rice to a medium heavy-bottomed saucepan, add the 1¼ cups/300 ml water, and let stand for 30 minutes.

Place the rice over medium heat, bring to a simmer, cover, turn the heat to low, and cook until the water has been absorbed and the rice is tender, about 30 minutes. Spread the cooked rice in a baking pan and gently break up any clumps with a spatula. Let cool to room temperature.

Heat a large pan over medium heat until a drop of water flicked on the surface sizzles gently on contact. Add the bacon and cook until it begins to render some of its fat, about 1 minute. Stir in the onions, chiles, and garlic and cook, stirring, for 2 minutes. Add the 1 tbsp salt and continue cooking, stirring occasionally, until the onions are translucent, about 20 minutes longer. Let cool to room temperature.

In a large bowl, combine the cooled bacon mixture and the cooled rice with the ground pork, paprika, thyme, marjoram, parsley, dill, remaining 1 tsp salt, and pepper. Cover and refrigerate until well chilled, about 1 hour. With your hands, thoroughly mix the chilled ingredients. You should have 2½ lb/1.2 kg of sausage, just enough for the stuffed vegetables and the cabbage rolls. Re-cover and refrigerate for up to 4 days.

TO MAKE THE STEWED SAUERKRAUT: In a small saucepan over low heat, combine the tomatoes and broth and bring to a simmer. Remove from the heat and let stand until the tomatoes begin to soften and rehydrate, about 15 minutes. Transfer to a blender and purée until smooth.

Heat a stockpot over medium heat until a drop of water flicked on the surface sizzles gently on contact. Add the bacon and stir until it renders most of its fat, about 5 minutes. Add the onions and garlic, turn the heat to low, and continue to stir until translucent, about 20 minutes longer. Add the sweet paprika and hot paprika and stir until fragrant, about 1 minute. Add the sauerkraut, puréed tomatoes, and salt. Bring to a simmer and cook, stirring frequently, until the sauerkraut

softens, about 30 minutes. There should be about half as much liquid as there are stewed vegetables. Transfer to a container and let cool. Cover and refrigerate for up to 4 days.

TO MAKE THE STUFFED VEGETABLES: Preheat the oven to 350°F/180°C. With a vegetable peeler, peel the kohlrabies. Make sure the skin is completely removed, including the thin, tough layer of flesh attached to the peel. Using a paring knife, and working from the stem, carefully carve out the center of each kohlrabi, leaving a ½-in/12-mm layer of flesh on the sides and the bottom.

Cut the top off the squash and scoop out the seeds. Scrape off any scales on the skin. (The skin is edible once the squash is cooked.) Set the onions, stem-end up, on a kitchen towel to secure them. Using the paring knife, carefully carve out the center of each onion, leaving a ½-in/12-mm layer of flesh on the sides and bottom. Stuff the kohlrabies, squash, onions, and mushrooms with about half of the sausage, filling each vegetable until the meat protrudes about ¼ in/6 mm above the top. Set the stuffed vegetables on a large plate, cover, and refrigerate for up to 4 hours.

TO PREPARE THE CABBAGE ROLLS: Bring a large pot of water to a boil over high heat. Prepare an ice bath. Line a sheet pan with a clean kitchen towel. Pull the leaves from the cabbage, being careful not to tear them. You will need six to eight large leaves. With a knife, cut out any large ribs. Add the leaves to the boiling water and cook just until they begin to soften, 1 to 2 minutes. With a slotted spoon, transfer the leaves to the ice bath. When cool, remove the leaves and pat dry.

CONTINUED

On a work surface, spread a cabbage leaf with a wide edge facing you. Spoon about 3 oz/85 g of the sausage in the center of the leaf and use your fingers to shape it into a log about 3 in/7.5 cm wide. Fold in the sides of the leaf; then, starting from the edge nearest you, roll up the leaf as tightly as possible, enclosing the sausage. Repeat to make six to eight rolls. Set the rolls aside.

Preheat the oven to 350°F/180°C. Place the pork knuckle and potatoes in a baking pan, lightly season the knuckle with salt, and place in the oven uncovered. Bake for 20 minutes. Meanwhile, in a large saucepan over medium heat, warm the stewed sauerkraut until just heated through. In a large nonreactive baking pan or roasting pan, arrange the cabbage rolls in a single layer, pour the warm stewed sauerkraut over them, and cover. Place the stuffed kohlrabies, squash, and onions in a separate baking pan; do not cover. Put both pans into the oven with the knuckle and potatoes and bake for 30 minutes.

After the cabbage rolls and stuffed vegetables have baked for 30 minutes, and the knuckle and potatoes have baked for 50 minutes, remove all pans from the oven. Transfer the potatoes to a plate and set aside. Uncover the cabbage rolls and transfer the cooked stuffed vegetables from their pan to the pan containing the cabbage rolls, setting the stuffed vegetables on top. Transfer the pork knuckle as well, and then add the stuffed mushrooms. Return the pan, uncovered, to the oven and bake until the vegetables are tender enough to be easily pierced with a skewer, and an instant-read thermometer inserted into the filling of a stuffed vegetable or into the pork knuckle registers at least 145°F/63°C, 20 to 30 minutes longer.

After removing the potatoes from the oven, allow them to rest at room temperature for about 10 minutes, until just cool enough to handle, then peel them. Immediately pass the peeled potatoes through a food mill into a medium bowl, or put them in the bowl and mash with a wooden spoon. Add the sour cream and butter, season with salt, and stir just enough to mix. Cover to keep warm until ready to serve.

After removing the roasting pan from the oven, spread the mashed potatoes on the bottom of a large serving platter or shallow bowl. Arrange all of the stuffed vegetables and the pork knuckle on top, then arrange the cabbage rolls, covering the potatoes. Spoon the sauerkraut from the roasting pan over and around the vegetables and pork. Garnish with a few scoops of sour cream; the dill, parsley, and chives; and pepper.

HARVEST PARTY

Mindy and Juston Enos of Full Table Farm in the Napa Valley work their plot of land with unequaled respect and passion. They grow uncommon crops, such as celtuce, black soybeans, Asian greens, and tiny cucumbers known as mouse melons or prickly burr gherkins. They also grow more common items extraordinarily well. Every time they make a delivery, we find ourselves saying at least once that whatever vegetable they have brought is the best of its kind we have tasted and seen. They also love good food and drink and know how to throw a party.

The farm has a couple cranky roosters that have been harassing the chickens all summer. These old cocks need to be dispatched, and now is the time to do it. What's left of the tomatoes and peppers must be picked before they fall to the ground. The apples and pears are at their peak, and the last of the figs are bursting at their seams. As we help clear the fields, we know that we are harvesting more than we can eat, but that's okay. Anything that doesn't go into the dinner will be pickled, cured, smoked, or dried to be used later in the year.

The weather will soon be cold and the summer vegetables will be gone. It's time to celebrate another abundant season.

ROOSTER BOIL

One-pot cooking at its finest, this is not a restaurant dish, but something to serve at a party. We like to cook this outdoors over a wood fire in a traditional *bogrács* (cast-iron pot). The Hungarians use it most often for gulyas, but it is also great for ornery roosters. The bird should be dispatched at least two days before the event, so the meat can age and then brine before it is cooked. The meat on older, larger birds can be a bit more toothsome than on young chickens. It is also much more flavorful.

This dish starts with a base that is similar to the popular Hungarian dish known as *lecsó*, a stew of peppers and onions roasted in fat, usually bacon drippings, and mixed with paprika, garlic, and tomato. In the end, this recipe takes on a mole-like flavor with the addition of sweet dried vegetables and the smokiness of the paprika and burnt bread. The whole bird makes a dramatic presentation, but it can be awkward to handle. Alternatively, cut the bird into quarters and cook as directed. If you cannot find a rooster, substitute a pair of large roasting chickens.

Serves 6 to 8

One 8-lb/5.4-kg rooster, plucked, gutted, and aged 1 to 5 days, or two 4- to 6-lb/1.8- to 2.7-kg chickens

4 qt/3.8 L onion brine → 115

8 oz/225 g slab bacon, cut into ¼-in/6-mm dice

4 large sweet white onions, quartered

3 green bell peppers, stemmed, seeded, and cut into ½-in/12-mm dice

3 red paprika peppers, stemmed and cut into ½-in/12-mm dice

6 serrano chiles, stemmed and chopped

20 garlic cloves, sliced

3 tbsp sweet paprika → 42

10 charred árbol chiles → 47

3 tbsp burnt bread powder → 48

One 750-ml bottle dry red wine

1 gl/3.8 L chicken broth → 139

6 fresh tomatoes, cored and halved

12 dried tomatoes → 40, quartered

12 dried zucchini → 41, broken into pieces

2 tbsp kosher salt

Fresh marjoram for garnish

Overgrown garden pickles → 105 to accompany

Country-style bread to accompany

Put the rooster in a large stockpot, add brine to cover, and refrigerate for 12 hours. Drain, discard the brine, and pat the bird dry.

Rig a 3-gl/11-L kettle over hot embers (or on a stove top). If cooking over embers, the intensity of the heat should be equivalent to a stove-top burner turned to medium-high heat. When a

drop of water flicked on the surface of the kettle sizzles on contact, add the bacon and stir until much of the fat has rendered and the bacon is beginning to brown, about 2 minutes. Using a slotted spoon, transfer the bacon to a small bowl. Add the rooster to the bacon fat and baste until the skin starts to render, about 2 minutes. Add the onions, bell peppers, paprika peppers, serranos, and garlic and stir until the vegetables begin to brown, about 2 minutes. Add the sweet paprika and stir until fragrant, about 1 minute. Add the árbol chiles, burnt bread powder, wine,

broth, fresh and dried tomatoes, zucchini, and salt. Bring to a gentle simmer and cook until the bird is cooked through and just tender, about 1½ hours for a rooster, 1 hour for two chickens.

To serve, carve the bird and assemble in a large serving bowl or on a large, deep serving platter. Ladle the broth over the top. Garnish with the fresh marjoram leaves. Serve immediately with the pickles on the side and fresh bread. Any leftover soup can be stored in an airtight container and refrigerated for up to 4 days.

GRILLED WHOLE EGGPLANT WITH TOMATO JAM & SPICED HAZELNUTS

When we first started grilling whole eggplants, we figured we would slice them and use them in salads. Then we discovered that by marinating them first, then grilling and roasting them, we ended up with fork-tender eggplants with a meaty texture. The texture is tender enough that you can cut it with a fork. It's a dish that we believe can stand on its own. Serve it alongside a platter of your favorite grilled meat and be prepared for it to steal the show.

Serves 6 to 8

SPICED HAZELNUTS

1 tsp unsalted butter

1½ tsp honey

1 tsp kosher salt

1 cup/130 g blanched hazelnuts

1 tsp hot paprika → 42

GRILLED EGGPLANTS

3 large globe or Rosa Bianca eggplants

1 bunch each fresh cilantro and flat-leaf parsley, chopped

4 garlic cloves

2 green serrano chiles, stemmed

2 limes from the lime pickle → 115, seeded and coarsely chopped

1 tbsp honey

1 tbsp kosher salt

1 cup/240 ml drained yogurt → 74

¼ cup/80 g tomato jam → 126

¼ cup/65 g lime pickle condiment → 117

Fresh dill, cilantro, and parsley leaves for garnish

Fresh chives for garnish

Finishing salt and freshly ground pepper

TO MAKE THE SPICED HAZELNUTS: Preheat the oven to 350°F/180°C. In a small saucepan over medium heat, melt the butter with the honey and salt.

In a small bowl, toss the hazelnuts with the butter mixture, then spread the nuts in a single layer on a sheet pan. Toast in the oven until slightly browned, about 15 minutes.

Remove from the oven, toss with the paprika, and let cool. The nuts can be stored in an airtight container at room temperature for up to 2 weeks.

TO MAKE THE GRILLED EGGPLANTS: With a vegetable peeler, peel lengthwise strips of skin ½ in/12 mm wide from the eggplants, alternating them with intact strips of equal width.

In a blender or food processor, combine the cilantro, parsley, garlic, serranos, lime pickle, honey, and kosher salt and process until a coarse paste forms. Set aside 1 tbsp of the mixture and rub the rest of it onto the eggplants. Place the eggplants in a container, cover, and refrigerate, turning the eggplants occasionally, for 12 hours.

Prepare a medium-hot fire for indirect-heat cooking in a charcoal or gas grill. Wipe the excess marinade from the eggplants and place them on the grate opposite the fire. Grill the eggplants, turning them every 5 minutes and being careful not to burn the skin, until tender and easily pierced with a skewer but not falling apart, 30 to 45 minutes. Remove from the grill.

To serve, spoon the yogurt on the bottom of a serving platter. Put the grilled eggplants on top, and spread the reserved 1 tbsp marinade evenly over the eggplants. Garnish with the spiced hazelnuts, the tomato jam, the lime pickle condiment, all of the herbs, and finishing salt and pepper.

TOAST WITH LARD, ONION & PAPRIKA

Remove the whipped cured pork fatback from the refrigerator 20 minutes before serving so it will spread more easily.

Spread the fatback on the bread slices, then top with the onion slices, paprika, and finishing salt. Cut each bread slice into smaller portions for serving.

Hungarians love raw onions. It's said that Hungary is the only place in the world where onion breath is an attractive attribute. Here, we spread a thick layer of whipped lard on a piece of toast and top it with raw onion slices and good-quality Hungarian paprika. If cured pork fatback is not available, fresh rendered lard can be used in its place.

Serves 6 to 8

4 oz/110 g whipped cured pork fatback → 94 or lard → 93

3 thick slices crusty country-style bread, toasted and cooled to room temperature

1 small sweet white onion, sliced paper-thin

1 tsp sweet paprika → 42

Finishing salt

FARMER'S CHOP SUEY

Cortney's grandmother Ethel came to America from Lithuania in 1906. A frugal shopper, Ethel thought nothing of going to three different grocers looking for the best deal on cabbage. She would often buy less-than-perfect vegetables from the bargain bin to use in this classic salad. It's one of Cortney's mother's favorite dishes from her childhood, and one beloved by Ethel's grand-daughter, as well.

Serves 6 to 8

8 eggs

2 pt/740 g cherry tomatoes, halved

2 cucumbers, cut into ½-in/12-mm chunks

1 lb/455 g button mushrooms, stems trimmed and quartered

2 red sweet peppers, cut into large pieces

1 red onion, cut in ¼-in/6-mm dice

1 tbsp sweet onion powder → 34

1 tsp dry mustard

1 tsp sugar

¼ tsp celery seeds

2 tbsp red wine vinegar → 95

Kosher salt and freshly ground black pepper

2 cups/450 g cottage cheese → 69

1 lemon, halved and seeded

Fresh dill, chopped, for garnish

Freshly ground black pepper

Finishing salt

Bring a medium saucepan of water to boil over high heat. Gently slide the eggs into the pot and bring back to a boil. Boil for 8 minutes. While the eggs are cooking, set up an ice bath. After 8 minutes, remove the eggs from the water, place in the ice bath, and let cool for 10 minutes. Remove the eggs from the ice bath, peel them, and set aside until ready to use.

In a large bowl, combine the tomatoes, cucumbers, mushrooms, sweet peppers, and onion. Add the onion powder, dry mustard, sugar, celery seeds, and vinegar; season with kosher salt and pepper; and toss well. Let stand for at least 15 minutes, or for up to 1 hour, before serving.

To serve, quarter the eggs and season them with salt. Spread a thick layer of cottage cheese onto a serving platter and arrange the vegetables and eggs on top. Squeeze the lemon halves over everything, garnish with the dill, and season with finishing salt and pepper. Leftover salad can be stored in an airtight container in the refrigerator for up to 2 days.

KRUMKAKE WITH GRILLED FIGS, WALNUT BUTTER & LEMON-SOUR CREAM SAUCE

This is a great dish for the early fall harvest, when the figs are on their last fruiting, walnuts are ready to be shelled, and lemons are just becoming juicy and tart. Juston and Mindy Enos grow all of these on their farm. Prepare the batter, lemon cream, jam, and walnut butter ahead of time and this becomes a dessert you can make for the masses and never leave the warmth of the fire.

Serves 6 to 8

FIG JAM

2 lb/910 g figs (black mission, Kadota, or other variety), stemmed and quartered

1¾ cups/340 g sugar

2 tbsp fresh lemon juice

3 fig leaves

KRUMKAKE

½ cup/110 g kefir butter → 76, at room temperature

½ cup/100 g sugar

3 eggs

1 cup/125 g all-purpose flour

1 tsp kosher salt

⅛ tsp freshly ground black pepper

6 tbsp/90 ml milk kefir → 75 or whole milk

LEMON-SOUR CREAM SAUCE

2 whole eggs, plus 2 egg yolks

½ cup/120 ml fermented honey → 121, or plain honey

½ cup/120 ml fresh lemon juice

½ tsp kosher salt

4 tbsp/55 g kefir butter → 76, cut into pieces and well chilled

½ cup/120 ml sour cream → 71

GRILLED FIGS

8 to 12 figs

Filtered grapeseed oil for brushing

1 lb/455 g black or English walnut pieces, made into walnut butter → 83

¼ cup/30 g toasted walnuts

CONTINUED

TO MAKE THE FIG JAM: Put four small spoons in the freezer. In a large, wide, heavy pot over medium heat, combine the figs, sugar, and lemon juice and bring to a simmer, stirring continuously to dissolve the sugar. When the sugar has dissolved, increase the heat to medium-high and bring to a boil. Add the fig leaves to the pot and cook until they have infused the mixture with their perfume, about 10 minutes.

Remove and discard the leaves, then continue to cook the jam, stirring occasionally. When it begins to thicken, after about 25 minutes, place a small amount of the jam on a chilled spoon. Return the spoon to the freezer for about 4 minutes, then test the jam for doneness. If it wrinkles slightly when you press it with a fingertip and is thick rather than runny and thin, it is ready. If not, continue to cook for a few minutes longer and test again. The jam can be stored in an airtight container in the refrigerator for up to 2 months.

TO MAKE THE KRUMKAKE: In a stand mixer fitted with the paddle attachment, combine the butter and sugar and mix on medium speed until pale, about 8 minutes. Add the eggs, one at a time, mixing well after each addition. Remove the bowl from the stand and stir in the flour, salt, and pepper. Add the kefir and stir to form a thin batter. The batter can be stored in an airtight container in the refrigerator for up to a week.

Preheat a krumkake mold according to the manufacturer's instructions. Add about 1 tsp of the krumkake batter to the hot mold and cook until golden brown on both sides, about 2 minutes. Remove the krumkake from the mold and let cool on a wire rack. Repeat with the remaining batter. Krumkakes are best the day they are made.

TO MAKE THE LEMON-SOUR CREAM SAUCE: Prepare an ice bath. Bring 2 in/5 cm of water to a simmer in a medium saucepan. In a medium heatproof bowl, combine the whole eggs, egg yolks, honey, lemon juice, and salt and set the bowl over (not touching) the simmering water. Cook, stirring continuously and alternating between a whisk and a spoon or spatula so as to not incorporate too much air, until the custard is thick enough to coat the back of a spoon and holds a line when a finger is drawn through it, about 15 minutes. Do not allow the custard to boil.

Remove from the heat, let stand for 10 minutes, and then whisk in the butter a few pieces at a time. Press a sheet of plastic wrap directly onto the surface of the sauce to prevent a skin from forming. Nest the bowl in the ice bath and let the sauce cool completely. The sauce can be prepared up to this point 4 days in advance and refrigerated in an airtight container. Just before using, fold in the sour cream.

TO MAKE THE GRILLED FIGS: Prepare a medium-hot fire for direct-heat cooking in a charcoal or gas grill, or right over the fire. Lightly brush the figs with grapeseed oil and place them on the grate directly over the fire. Grill, turning as needed to cook evenly, until softened and lightly charred on all sides, 8 to 10 minutes. Transfer to a platter and set aside until ready to assemble the dessert.

To serve, spread walnut butter on one side of a krumkake and top with some of the fig jam. Top with a second krumkake to create a sandwich cookie. Repeat until the cookies are used up. Put the lemon sauce in a bowl or on a coupe plate, and place the grilled figs on and in it. Spoon the toasted walnuts over the top and enjoy the sauce and figs with the cookies.

SWEETS

We don't think of dessert as a separate course. It is an extension of the meal. For this reason, overly sweet desserts don't make sense on our menu. Ours usually have a savory bent. They are gently sweetened, focusing on textures and flavors that complement the overall experience of a meal. Honey, koji, dairy, fruit, vegetables, and some legumes contain natural sugars that add not only sweetness but also flavor. Refined sugars have their place— we don't outlaw them completely—but there are many other ways to approach the world of desserts.

As with everything we cook, these desserts are influenced by many cultures. Japanese mochi, Hungarian farmer's cheese, and Danish rye porridge are all from different places and somehow work together. Some of the recipes here have come about by playing with kefir and koji, experimenting with flavor and temperature, and some, like the pound cake and the rice pudding, are just comforting.

RYE POUND CAKE WITH PEAR SHERBET & CHESTNUTS

Pears, chestnuts, and vinegar make us think of autumn, harvest time, cooler days, and the coming of winter. Just as the season asks us to make do with less, this dessert relies on a few simple flavors. The pear skins give the sherbet a slightly granular texture that feels like biting into a fresh fruit, and roasting the pears on rock salt locks in the moisture and flavor and gently seasons them. The technique of mixing the butter into the flour is an unusual one for cake making. It helps create a tender cake, as it minimizes gluten development.

Serves 6 to 8

VINEGAR MERINGUE

1 egg white

2 tbsp fermented honey → 121, or honey

2 tsp pear vinegar → 95

PEAR SHERBET

3 lb/1.4 kg rock salt

1 lb/455 g firm ripe pears, such as Warren

½ cup/120 ml kefir buttermilk → 76

2 tbsp fermented honey → 121, or honey

2 tbsp sugar

2 tbsp fresh lemon juice, plus grated zest of 1 lemon

CHESTNUT CREAM

½ cup/120 ml goat or cow milk

1 cup/190 g roasted and peeled chestnuts

1 tsp fermented honey → 121, or honey

RYE POUND CAKE

½ cup/100 g sugar

7 tbsp/50 g Kamut flour or 6 tbsp/50 g all-purpose flour

6 tbsp/35 g light rye flour

½ tsp baking powder

¾ tsp kosher salt

½ cup plus 1 tbsp/130 g kefir butter → 76, at cool room temperature

2 eggs

1 tbsp apple or pear cider vinegar → 95

BUTTERMILK CRÈME ANGLAISE

1 cup/240 ml heavy cream

1 cup/240 ml kefir buttermilk → 76

4 egg yolks

¼ cup/60 ml fermented honey → 121, or honey

3 large firm ripe pears, such as Warren

6 roasted and peeled chestnuts

TO MAKE THE VINEGAR MERINGUE: Bring about 2 in/5 cm water to a simmer in a medium saucepan. Combine the egg white and honey in the bowl of a stand mixer and set the bowl over (not touching) the simmering water. Whisk continuously until the sugar dissolves and the mixture registers 120°F/48°C on an instant-read thermometer. Remove from the heat and whisk in the vinegar.

Fit the stand mixer with the whip attachment and beat the warm egg-white mixture on low speed for 5 minutes. Increase the speed to medium-high and continue to beat until the meringue is very stiff and shiny and the bowl feels cool to the touch, about 10 minutes. If not using right away, transfer the meringue to an airtight container and refrigerate for up to 4 days or freeze for up to 1 month. Rewhip just before using.

TO MAKE THE PEAR SHERBET: Preheat the oven to 300°F/150°C. Spread the rock salt in an even layer about 1 in/2.5 cm deep in a shallow baking dish. Lay the pears on the rock salt and roast, turning once halfway through the cooking time, until tender when pierced with a knife tip, 30 to 45 minutes. Remove the pears from the oven and let cool until they can be handled. When cool, cut in half and remove the stem and core.

In a food processor or blender, combine the pears, buttermilk, honey, sugar, and lemon juice and zest and purée until smooth. Transfer the purée to an airtight container and refrigerate for at least 8 hours, or for up to 24 hours.

Transfer the mixture to an ice-cream maker and freeze according to the manufacturer's instructions. Pack the sherbet into a plastic container and press a sheet of plastic wrap directly onto the surface. Seal with an airtight lid and place in the freezer until firm, about 3 hours. You can thaw and respin this sherbet as needed.

TO MAKE THE CHESTNUT CREAM: In a blender or food processor, combine the milk, chestnuts, and honey and purée until thick and smooth. Transfer the purée to an airtight container and refrigerate for up to 4 days.

CONTINUED

TO MAKE THE RYE POUND CAKE: In a stand mixer fitted with the paddle attachment, combine the sugar, Kamut flour, rye flour, baking powder, and salt and mix on low speed just until combined. Add the butter, increase the mixer speed to medium, and beat until smooth, 5 to 7 minutes. Add the eggs, one at a time, mixing well after each addition. Stop the mixer and scrape down the sides of the bowl. Turn the mixer to low speed and slowly add the vinegar, mixing just until combined. If using Kamut flour, cover the bowl tightly with plastic wrap and refrigerate overnight to allow the flours to hydrate. You can bake the cake immediately, but the texture will be lighter if the batter rests overnight.

Remove the batter from the refrigerator and bring to room temperature. Preheat the oven to 350°F/180°C. Lightly grease a 6-by-3½-in/15-by-7.5-cm loaf pan.

Spoon the batter into the prepared pan. Bake until the cake springs back when lightly pressed with a fingertip or a toothpick inserted into the center of the cake comes out clean, 30 to 45 minutes. Transfer to a wire rack and let cool for 10 minutes, then turn the cake out of the pan and let cool completely. The cake will keep well wrapped at room temperature for up to 4 days.

TO MAKE THE BUTTERMILK CRÈME ANGLAISE: Prepare an ice bath. Set a fine-mesh sieve over a medium bowl. In a small saucepan, combine the cream and buttermilk and heat over medium-high heat to just below a boil. At the same time, bring about 2 in/5 cm water to a simmer in a medium saucepan. Transfer the hot cream mixture to a medium heatproof bowl. In a separate medium bowl, whisk together the egg yolks and honey until blended. Whisk a few large spoonfuls of the warm cream mixture into the yolks to temper them. Then slowly whisk in the remaining warm cream mixture.

Set the bowl over (not touching) the simmering water and cook the custard, stirring constantly with a spoon or whisk, until the custard is thick enough to coat the back of a spoon and holds a line when a finger is drawn through it, about 7 minutes. Do not allow the custard to boil. Pour the custard through the sieve into the bowl, then press a sheet of plastic wrap directly onto the surface of the custard to prevent a skin from forming. Nest the bowl in the ice bath and let the custard cool completely. The crème anglaise can be prepared up 4 days in advance and stored in an airtight container in the refrigerator.

To serve, preheat the oven to 300°F/150°C. Cut the pound cake into slices ½ in/12 mm thick and arrange the slices in a single layer on a sheet pan. Warm for about 5 minutes in the oven. Place a pound cake slice in the bottom of individual bowls and spread a spoonful of the chestnut cream on top. Spread a spoonful of the meringue on top of the chestnut cream. With a kitchen torch, toast the meringue until gently charred (if you don't own a torch, the soft meringue is still delicious). Place a scoop of sherbet on top of the meringue and spoon crème anglaise over the sherbet. With a mandoline, shave the pears directly over the sherbet to cover it. With a fine-tooth grater, grate the chestnuts over the top, blanketing the pear. Serve immediately.

KEFIR ICE CREAM FLOAT

All of the ice cream at the restaurant begins with a kefir base. The kefir adds a layer of acidity to an otherwise sweet dish—along with an infusion of probiotics. We love its tart edge, and think it works well as a base for almost any ice cream flavor.

One of our favorite ways to enjoy ice cream is in ginger burns water kefir → 133 as a float. It reminds Nick of the Vernors floats he drank as a kid.

Serves 6 to 8

2 cups/480 ml heavy cream

1 cup/240 ml whole milk

1 tbsp kefir grains

3 tbsp buttermilk powder

7 egg yolks

3 tbsp fermented honey → 121, or honey

3 tbsp sugar

2 tsp kosher salt

2½ tsp cold water

1 tsp powdered plain gelatin

2 qt/2L ginger burns water kefir → 133, or any good ginger beer

Pour the cream and milk into a medium non-reactive container. Wrap the kefir grains in cheesecloth, tie securely, and add the bundle to the cream mixture. Let stand at room temperature (68° to 72°F/20° to 22°C) until gently soured and noticeably thicker, 24 to 48 hours. Remove the kefir grains and reserve for future batches → 74.

Bring about 2 in/5 cm water to a boil in a large saucepan. Pour the cultured cream mixture into a large heatproof bowl, stir in the buttermilk powder, and set over (not touching) the boiling water. Warm the mixture to 178°F/81°C. The acidity of the kefir may react with the heat and cause the mixture to look broken. It's not; it'll come back together during cooking.

While the base is warming, prepare an ice bath. In a medium bowl, whisk together the egg yolks, honey, sugar, and salt.

When the cream mixture is at 178°F/81°C, whisk a few large spoonfuls of it into the yolks to temper them. Then pour the yolk mixture into the warm cream mixture in the saucepan while whisking constantly. Return the saucepan of water to a simmer and return the bowl to sit over the simmering water. Cook the custard, stirring constantly, alternating between a whisk and a spatula, until the custard is thick enough to coat the back of a spoon and holds a line when a finger is drawn through it, 15 to 20 minutes. Do not allow the custard to boil. Remove from the heat.

Put the water in a small bowl, add the gelatin across the top, and let stand for 5 minutes to bloom. Stir the gelatin mixture into the warm custard. Set a fine-mesh sieve over a medium bowl and pour the custard through the sieve, then nest the bowl in the ice bath and let the custard cool completely. Cover, pressing plastic wrap directly on the surface, and refrigerate for 24 hours.

Transfer the chilled custard to an ice-cream maker and freeze according to the manufacturer's instructions. Pack the ice cream into a plastic container and press a sheet of plastic wrap directly onto the surface. Seal with an airtight lid and place in the freezer until firm, about 4 hours, before serving. This is best served the same day. You can thaw and respin this ice cream as needed.

To serve, scoop ice cream into glasses and pour ginger water kefir over it.

CAROB SEMIFREDDO WITH GOAT CHEESE, BLACK WALNUTS & EUCALYPTUS

The combination of carob and eucalyptus may seem unusual, but it was actually inspired by Thin Mints, Cortney's favorite childhood cookie. When she was a kid, she and her dad would eat them straight from the freezer, standing over the sink to keep the crumbs off the floor. The cold hit of the mint is also something we experience hiking all over Northern California. Eucalyptus, which is naturally mentholated, can be refreshing and cooling, even in the forest. The goat cheese brings more earth to the dish, which gets rounded out with the funky flavor of the black walnuts.

Serves 8

CAROB CUSTARD

1 cup/240 ml heavy cream

1 cup/240 ml goat or cow milk

¼ cup/60 ml fermented honey → 121, or honey

½ tsp dried powdered eucalyptus leaves or dried powdered mint leaves → 30

6 egg yolks

2 tbsp water

2 tsp powdered plain gelatin

1¼ cups/280 g sweetened carob chips

BLACK WALNUT TUILES

1½ tbsp unsalted kefir butter

2¼ tsp water

2¼ tsp fermented honey → 121, or honey

¼ tsp kosher salt

⅓ cup/35 g confectioners' sugar

1 tbsp buckwheat flour

3 tbsp/20 g black walnuts, toasted and finely chopped

CAROB CRUMBS

½ cup/65 g black walnut pieces

⅛ tsp dried powdered eucalyptus leaves or dried powdered mint leaves → 30

3 tbsp light brown sugar

Pinch of kosher salt

1½ tbsp kefir butter → 76, at room temperature

3 oz/85 g dark chocolate, at least 75 percent cacao

4 tbsp/30 g toasted carob powder

2 tbsp parsnip powder → 50 or
confectioners' sugar

MILK GRANITA

1½ cups/375 ml whole milk

1 tbsp fermented honey → 121, or honey

1½ tsp dried powdered eucalyptus leaves or
dried powdered mint leaves → 30

Pinch of kosher salt

1 cup/220 g goat cheese → 68, at room
temperature

1 tsp fermented honey → 121, or honey

Pinch of kosher salt

½ cup/115 g black walnut butter → 83

Dried powdered eucalyptus leaves → 30

Finishing salt

½ cup/65 g black walnut pieces, toasted

Torn fresh mint leaves for garnish

TO MAKE THE CAROB CUSTARD: In a medium
saucepan over medium heat, combine the cream,
goat's milk, honey, and eucalyptus and heat,
stirring, until warmed through, 5 to 7 minutes.
Remove from the heat and set aside to steep
for about 1 hour.

CONTINUED

Set a fine-mesh sieve over a medium bowl. In another medium bowl, whisk together the egg yolks until well blended. Remove the eucalyptus leaves and gently rewarm the cream mixture. Temper the yolks by slowly pouring the warm cream mixture into the yolks, whisking constantly. Return the combined mixture to the saucepan, place over low heat, and cook, stirring constantly, until the custard is thick enough to coat the back of the spoon and holds a line when a finger is drawn through it, 10 to 12 minutes. Do not allow the custard to boil. Remove from the heat and pour through the fine-mesh sieve set into the bowl.

Put the water in a small bowl, add the gelatin across the top, and let stand for 5 minutes to bloom. Add the gelatin mixture to the strained custard and stir until incorporated. Put the carob chips in a large bowl and pour the warm custard over them. Let stand, without stirring, until the carob begins to melt, about 5 minutes. Whisk slowly until the carob is completely melted and blended into the custard. Use a rubber spatula to scrape down the sides of the bowl.

Line the bottom and sides of an 8-by-4-in/ 20-by-10-cm loaf pan, with a sheet of plastic wrap, extending it about 3 in/7.5 cm over the sides of the dish. Pour the carob mixture into the prepared dish and freeze, uncovered, until set, at least 8 hours or for up to 1 week (cover after 8 hours).

Cover a cutting board with a sheet of parchment paper. Cover a small baking sheet or plate that will fit into your freezer with another sheet of parchment paper. Remove the custard from the freezer. Pull on the edges of the plastic wrap to loosen the custard from the mold, lift it from the pan, and invert it onto the parchment-covered

cutting board. Peel away the plastic wrap and discard. Run a long-bladed knife under hot water and wipe it dry with a towel. Use to cut the custard into 4-by-2-in/10-by-5-cm rectangles, then halve each rectangle. Transfer to the prepared sheet pan and return to the freezer to reset, about 2 hours, or up to 3 days ahead of time.

TO MAKE THE BLACK WALNUT TUILES: In a small saucepan over medium heat, combine the butter, water, honey, and salt and warm until the butter has melted and the honey has dissolved. Remove from the heat and let cool.

Into a medium bowl, sift together the confectioners' sugar and buckwheat flour. Whisk in the cooled butter mixture and stir in the nuts. Cover and refrigerate overnight.

Preheat the oven to 325°F/165°C. Line a sheet pan with a silicone baking mat or parchment paper. Using a small spoon, spoon the batter onto the prepared sheet pan, spacing the mounds about 4 in/10 cm apart. Dampen your fingertips and gently push the batter into flat disks. Don't fuss over the shape. These will be broken into pieces. Bake until crisp, about 9 minutes. Remove from the oven and transfer to a wire rack to cool. Store the tuiles in an airtight container in the freezer for up to 1 week.

TO MAKE THE CAROB CRUMBS: Preheat the oven to 300°F/150°C. Line a sheet pan with a silicone baking mat or parchment paper. Toast the black walnut pieces until fragrant, 7 to 10 minutes. Let cool to room temperature.

In a food processor, pulse the cooled nuts into small pieces. Transfer to a medium bowl and whisk in the eucalyptus powder, brown sugar, and salt. With a fork, mix in the butter to make coarse crumbs.

Spread the mixture onto the prepared sheet pan in an even layer. Bake just until crisp on the edges, about 10 minutes, stirring halfway through baking. Watch carefully to make sure the crumbs don't burn. They are dark to begin with, which can make it challenging to tell when they are done. Remove from the oven and let cool on the pan on a wire rack. When cool, break up the crumbs into a medium bowl.

Line a sheet pan with a silicone baking sheet or parchment paper. Prepare an ice bath. Place the chocolate in a medium heatproof bowl. Bring 2 in/5 cm water to a simmer in a medium saucepan. Set the bowl of chocolate over (not touching) the simmering water and heat, stirring occasionally, until melted and smooth. Remove from the heat, fold the cooled nut crumbs into the melted chocolate, and nest the bowl in the ice bath. Using a rubber spatula, toss the crumbs with the chocolate until the chocolate has set. (You may need to use your hands to break it into

large pieces.) Spread the chocolate-covered crumbs on the prepared sheet pan and refrigerate until completely chilled, about 20 minutes.

In a large bowl, whisk together the carob powder and parsnip powder. With your hands, break the chilled crumbs into the carob-parsnip mixture. Transfer to a sieve and shake off any excess powder. Transfer to an airtight container and refrigerate for up to 7 days or freeze for up to 1 month.

TO MAKE THE MILK GRANITA: In a small saucepan over medium heat, combine the milk, honey, powdered eucalyptus leaves, and salt and bring just to a simmer. Remove from the heat and let steep until the milk is infused with the flavor of the eucalyptus, at least 1 hour at room temperature or overnight in the refrigerator. Strain through a fine-mesh sieve into a shallow pan and discard the eucalyptus. Place the pan in the freezer and freeze the milk mixture, stirring it with a fork every hour to break up the large shards of ice, until the mixture is completely frozen and is a mass of icy flakes that look like snow, about 6 hours total. Leave in covered pan. It will keep for 1 week. Shave as needed.

In a medium bowl, combine the room temperature goat cheese, honey, and kosher salt and mix well to combine. If not using immediately, cover and refrigerate for up to 3 days. Bring to room temperature 1 hour before serving.

To serve, spread 2 tbsp of the sweetened goat cheese on the bottom of each individual plate, add a spoonful of black walnut butter, and top with two frozen carob squares. Dust with powdered eucalyptus and sea salt. Garnish with shards of tuile, milk granita, the toasted walnuts, carob crumbs, and torn mint. Serve immediately.

RICE PUDDING WITH AMAZAKE & CITRUS

This dessert is all about the sweetness of koji. Here we use koji to make amazake, a sweet, nonalcoholic style of sake. The amazake is an ingredient in the pudding, as well as a sauce to accompany it. One could simply cook rice koji to make pudding, but instead we use sticky rice, also known as glutinous or sweet rice, as the base so that the grains remain individual and retain their chewiness. It's all about creating layers of rice flavor and texture.

Serves 4 to 6

AMAZAKE

1²/₃ cups/300 g white sweet rice, also known as glutinous or sticky rice, or short-grain white rice

3¼ cups/780 ml water

Pinch of kosher salt

1¼ cups/200 g rice koji → 123

2 cups/480 ml whole milk

PUDDING

½ cup/105 g white sweet rice, or short-grain white rice

3 cups/720 ml whole milk

1 cup/240 ml amazake

1 tbsp fresh ginger juice

1 tsp kosher salt

3 tbsp black sesame paste

3 eggs, separated

3 lb/1.4 kg mixed citrus fruits, such as blood oranges, Cara Cara oranges, and grapefruits, peeled and segmented, juice reserved for garnish

Toasted black sesame seeds for garnish

Amazake for garnish

TO MAKE THE AMAZAKE: Put the rice in a medium bowl, add cold water to cover, and swish the rice with your hand until the water becomes cloudy. Drain and rinse the rice, cover with fresh cold water, and repeat the swishing and draining. Repeat until the water is clear, five or six times. Transfer the rice to a medium heavy-bottomed saucepan, add the 3¼ cups/780 ml water, and let stand for 30 minutes.

Add the salt to the rice, place the saucepan over medium heat, and bring to a boil. Cover, turn the heat to low, and cook until the water is absorbed, about 20 minutes. Alternatively, cook the rice in a rice cooker according the manufacturer's instructions.

Transfer the cooked rice to a bowl and let cool to 160°F/71°C. Crumble the koji, stir it into the rice, and continue cooling the rice to 140°F/60°C.

Create a holding tank/warm environment. Put the cooled rice-koji mixture in a sealable container and hold in your dehydrator or low oven (130°F/54°C) for 10 hours, stirring once after 6 hours, until very sweet with a rich, dense smell. Alternatively, place the rice-koji mixture in a rice cooker set on warm. Cover with a clean kitchen towel and then top with the lid; the towel will

keep the lid ajar. It is important that the temperature not rise above 140°F/60°C. After 6 hours, open the rice cooker, stir, and continue to hold warm until the mixture is very sweet with a rich, dense smell.

Transfer the rice mixture to a blender, add the milk, and purée until smooth. You should have about 4 cups/960 ml amazake. Let cool completely, transfer to an airtight container, and refrigerate for up to 1 week.

TO MAKE THE PUDDING: Put the rice in a medium bowl, add cold water to cover, and swish the rice with your hand until the water becomes cloudy. Drain and rinse the rice, cover with fresh cold water, and repeat the swishing and draining. Repeat until the water is clear, five or six times.

Pour the milk over the rice and let soak for 30 minutes.

In a medium heavy-bottomed saucepan over high heat, combine the milk-rice mixture, the amazake, ginger juice, and salt. Bring to a boil, stirring constantly, then reduce the heat to low, cover, and simmer gently for 15 minutes, stirring occasionally. Uncover and continue to simmer, stirring frequently, until the rice is tender and the mixture is reduced to about 3½ cups/840 ml, 8 to 10 minutes. Make sure that the heat is low and that you stir frequently to prevent scorching on the bottom. Remove the pan from the heat and stir in the sesame paste.

In a small bowl, whisk the egg yolks, then whisk in a few spoonfuls of the hot rice mixture to temper the yolks. Pour the tempered yolks into the rice mixture while stirring constantly with a rubber spatula. Set the pan over medium heat and cook the custard, stirring constantly, until it is thick enough to coat the back of a spoon and holds a line when a finger is drawn through it, about 5 minutes. Transfer the mixture to a large bowl.

In a stand mixer fitted with the whip attachment, beat the egg whites on low speed for 5 minutes. Increase the speed to medium-high and continue to beat until the whites hold stiff peaks, about 5 minutes. Do not overbeat; the whites should not look dry or clumpy. Using a rubber spatula, gently fold the beaten egg whites into the warm rice custard in three additions. The pudding can be served warm or chilled. Cover and refrigerate for up to 4 days.

To serve, spoon the pudding into small bowls and pour in amazake, allowing it to pool around the sides. Garnish with citrus segments and sesame seeds and serve.

RHUBARB SOUP WITH CHAMOMILE MILK CUSTARD

Caramelized onions may seem like an unusual ingredient in a dessert, but here we cook them long and slow to coax out all their sweetness and add richness to the base. The kombu dashi is another ingredient that may take you by surprise, but it goes a long way to enhance the flavor of the soup. The acidity of rhubarb makes this a refreshing early-summer treat.

In eastern Europe, fruit soups are served as desserts as well as first courses. At Bar Tartine, they play both roles as well. To make a dessert version of our sour cherry soup → 150, use this rhubarb soup method. We often steep fresh or dried stone-fruit leaves → 59 in the custard base for these versions as well.

We love to serve this soup with rugelach → 356.

Serves 6 to 8

CANDIED FENNEL SEEDS AND SYRUP

¼ cup/60 ml water

¼ cup/60 ml fermented honey → 121, or honey

¼ cup/25 g fennel seeds, toasted → 31

CHAMOMILE MILK CUSTARD

3 cups/720 ml heavy cream

3 tbsp dried chamomile flowers → 31

½ cup/120 ml milk kefir → 76 or whole milk

2½ tsp powdered plain gelatin

¼ cup/60 ml fermented honey → 121, or honey

½ cup/120 ml sour cream → 71

¼ tsp kosher salt

RHUBARB SOUP

1 tbsp unfiltered grapeseed oil, plus ½ cup/120 ml

¼ sweet white onion, sliced

2 lb/910 g rhubarb, trimmed and chopped

1-in/2.5-cm piece fresh ginger, peeled and finely chopped

1 fennel bulb, cored and julienned

3 cups/720 ml kombu dashi → 137

½ cup/90 g firmly packed light brown sugar

1 tbsp fennel seeds, toasted and ground → 31

1 tbsp anise seeds

2 tbsp dried chamomile flowers → 31

Kosher salt

¼ tsp freshly ground black pepper

Dried powdered chamomile flowers for garnish → 31

Fennel oil → 90 for garnish

Rugelach → 356 to accompany

CONTINUED

TO MAKE THE CANDIED FENNEL SEEDS AND SYRUP: In a small saucepan over low heat, combine the water and honey, stirring to incorporate the honey. Add the fennel seeds, simmer for 5 minutes, and remove from the heat. Let infuse at room temperature for at least 6 hours, or up to 24 hours. Strain the syrup, reserving the liquid and seeds separately. Spread the seeds on a dehydrator tray and dehydrate at 120°F/48°C until brittle, about 12 hours. Store the syrup in the refrigerator and dried seeds covered at room temperature until ready to use.

TO MAKE THE CHAMOMILE MILK CUSTARD: In a small saucepan over medium heat, combine the cream and dried chamomile flowers and bring to a simmer. Remove from the heat and let stand at room temperature for 1 hour, or cover and refrigerate overnight.

Pour the kefir into a large bowl, add the gelatin across the top, and let stand for 5 minutes to bloom.

In a medium saucepan over medium heat, combine the infused cream and honey and warm, whisking to combine. Remove from the heat, strain through a fine-mesh sieve, and pour into the kefir, whisking constantly. Whisk in the sour cream and salt.

Oil six to eight ¼-cup/60-ml ramekins or a baking dish. Divide the custard evenly among the ramekins or pour it into the baking dish. Cover and refrigerate until set, about 8 hours.

TO MAKE THE RHUBARB SOUP: Warm a large saucepan over medium-low heat. Add the 1 tbsp grapeseed oil and, when warm, add the onion and cook, stirring occasionally, until soft, sweet, and golden brown, about 30 minutes. Increase heat to medium and add the rhubarb, ginger, and fennel. Cook, stirring occasionally, until the rhubarb is soft, about 15 minutes. Add the dashi and simmer for 10 minutes. Stir in the brown sugar, ground fennel seeds, and anise seeds, stirring to dissolve the sugar. Enclose the chamomile in a piece of cheesecloth and secure with kitchen twine. Add the chamomile sachet to the saucepan and let steep over low heat for 25 minutes, or until the chamomile aroma is detectable. Season with salt and the pepper. Remove from the heat and let cool slightly. Remove the sachet and discard.

Transfer the soup to a blender, and, working in batches if necessary, add the remaining ½ cup/120 ml oil, and purée until smooth. Pass the purée through a fine-mesh sieve into an airtight container. Cover and chill for at least 4 hours, or for up to 1 week.

To serve, chill individual bowls in the refrigerator for 15 to 30 minutes. If the custard is in ramekins, run a hot knife around the edge of each custard and unmold one into the center of each bowl. If the custard is in a baking dish, scoop it into the bowls, dividing it evenly. Pour ½ to 1 cup/120 to 240 ml of soup around the custard. Garnish with the candied fennel seeds, fennel syrup, powdered chamomile, and fennel oil. Serve with the rugelach.

RYE PORRIDGE WITH HAZELNUT CUSTARD, APRICOT & FLAX

Day-old bread cooked with beer or milk is a popular dish all over northern Europe. It's served either as a loose porridge or baked in birch vessels as a cake. Our lunch menu features an assortment of *smørrebrød*, Danish open-face sandwiches, served on a dense sprouted-rye bread that Chad learned to make in Denmark. It's packed with sprouted rye berries that remind us of raisins and inspired us to make this *øllebrød*, a Danish porridge to match Chad's inspiration for the bread. We use the leftover rye bread here, and we make it with a beer (that has been raised on Chad's sourdough starter) brewed by Linden Street Brewery in Oakland, California. It's a reciprocal feast.

Serves 8

RYE PORRIDGE AND APRICOT PURÉE

8 oz/225 g dried apricots → 56

4 to 6 cups/480 to 720 ml unhopped beer, such as a saison, lambic, or wheat, or hard cider

1 lb/455 g dense rye bread, torn into small pieces

1 cup/240 ml heavy cream

HAZELNUT CUSTARD

4 oz/115 g well-drained farmer's cheese → 67, or well-drained ricotta

6 oz/85 g hazelnut butter → 83

1 cup/240 ml sour cream → 71

1¼ cups/300 ml kefir buttermilk → 76

1¼ tsp agar powder

½ cup/95 g granulated sugar

1 tbsp plus 2 tsp lecithin

7 egg yolks

½ tsp kosher salt

FLAX CROQUANT

1 cup/140 g granulated sugar

1 tbsp water

1 cup/165 g golden flaxseeds

1½ tsp kosher salt

DRY MERINGUE

2 egg whites

⅔ cup/130 g superfine sugar

¼ tsp fresh lemon juice, plus grated zest of 1 lemon

CONTINUED

2 tbsp brown butter → 77

1 tbsp kefir butter → 76

3 tbsp whole milk

Kosher salt

TO MAKE THE RYE PORRIDGE AND APRICOT PURÉE: If the apricots still have a bit of moisture in them, use the smaller amount of beer; if they are very dry, use the larger amount. In a medium saucepan over low heat, combine the apricots and beer and cook gently until the apricots have softened and absorbed some of the beer, about 15 minutes. Remove from the heat and let cool slightly.

Transfer the contents of the pan to a blender, adding only as much liquid as needed to get the mixture to move. Purée until smooth. Reserve 1 cup/240 ml of the purée for garnish. The purée can be prepared up to 1 week in advance and stored in an airtight container in the refrigerator.

In a large heavy-bottomed saucepan over low heat, combine the bread, any leftover apricot liquid, and remaining apricot purée. Cook, stirring every few minutes and mashing the bread as it cooks, until the bread is evenly moist and broken up, about 10 minutes. Add the cream and continue to cook until all of the liquid has been absorbed and the mixture looks like thick oatmeal, 30 to 45 minutes. Be sure not to let the porridge scorch on the bottom of the pan. Let cool completely. The porridge can be made up to 4 days in advance and stored in an airtight container in the refrigerator.

TO MAKE THE HAZELNUT CUSTARD: Preheat the oven to 325°F/165°C. Line the bottom and

sides of an 8-by-4-in/20-by-10-cm loaf pan with parchment paper.

In a blender, purée the cheese and hazelnut butter until smooth. Add the sour cream and pulse to combine. Transfer to a large bowl and set a fine-mesh sieve over the bowl. In a medium saucepan over medium heat, bring the buttermilk and agar powder to boil, and cook for 2 minutes to activate the agar, whisking constantly. Remove from the heat and stir in the sugar to dissolve.

In a medium bowl, whisk the lecithin into the egg yolks. Whisk a few spoonfuls of the warm buttermilk mixture into the eggs to temper the eggs. Pour the tempered egg mixture into the warm buttermilk mixture in the saucepan while whisking constantly. Set the saucepan over low heat and cook the custard, stirring constantly, until it is thick enough to coat the back of a spoon and holds a line when a finger is drawn through it, 5 to 7 minutes. Pour the custard through the fine-mesh sieve into the cheese mixture and whisk until well blended. Whisk in the salt.

Pour the mixture into the prepared loaf pan. Put the loaf pan in a baking dish and pour hot water into the dish to reach halfway up the sides of the custard. Bake until just set around the edges, 1 to 1½ hours. Remove from the oven and let cool in the water bath for 1 hour.

Remove the custard from the water bath, cover, and refrigerate until well chilled, at least 6 hours or for up to 36 hours.

TO MAKE THE FLAX CROQUANT: Line a sheet pan with a silicone baking mat or parchment paper.

In a medium saucepan over medium heat, combine the sugar and water and bring to a simmer

to dissolve. Remove from the heat, fold in the flaxseeds and salt, distributing them evenly, and then let cool until the mixture crystallizes and the seeds begin to separate from the sugar, about 5 minutes. Return the pan to low heat and cook, stirring, until the mixture has caramelized, about 10 minutes. Transfer the mixture to the prepared sheet pan and spread in an even layer. Let cool completely, then break into small pieces. The croquant can be stored in an airtight container at room temperature for up to 1 week.

TO MAKE THE DRY MERINGUE: Preheat the oven to 250°F/95°C, or set a dehydrator to 165°F/75°C. Line a sheet pan or dehydrator tray with a silicone baking mat or parchment paper. Bring about 2 in/5 cm of water to a simmer in a medium saucepan. Combine the egg whites and sugar in the bowl of a stand mixer and set the bowl over (not touching) the simmering water. Whisk continuously until the sugar dissolves and the mixture registers 120°F/48°C on an instant-read

thermometer. Remove from the heat and whisk in lemon juice and zest.

Fit the stand mixer with the whip attachment and beat the warm egg white mixture on low speed for 5 minutes. Increase the speed to medium-high and continue to beat until the meringue is very stiff and shiny and the bowl feels cool to the touch, about 10 minutes.

Transfer the meringue to the prepared pan. Using an offset spatula, spread the meringue in an even layer about ½ in/12 mm thick. Transfer the meringue to the oven and bake for 15 minutes. Turn off the oven and allow the meringue to dry overnight. Alternatively, place in the dehydrator until completely dry and brittle, about 24 hours. Break the meringue into pieces. The meringue can be stored in an airtight container in the freezer for up to 1 month. The freezer helps the meringues to remain very dry.

Remove the custard from the refrigerator. Lift the parchment from the pan and transfer the custard to a cutting board. Heat a long-bladed knife with hot water and wipe the blade dry. Cut the custard in half lengthwise, then cut crosswise to yield eight squares total.

To serve, in a medium saucepan over medium heat, combine the rye porridge, brown butter, cultured butter, and milk. Season with salt and stir until warm. Spoon 2 tbsp of the reserved apricot purée in the bottom of each of eight small, deep bowls. Place one custard square on top of the purée, then spoon warm porridge over the custard, dividing it evenly among the bowls. Garnish with flax croquant and grate meringue over the top. Serve immediately.

CANDIED BEET & SUNFLOWER FRANGIPANE TART

Native California bay laurel grows wild all over the Bay Area, but for culinary uses we choose locally grown Mediterranean bay. Beets and bay leaves may not be known as a classic combination, but the inherent sweetness and earthiness of the beets play well with the loamy, nutty qualities of the bay.

Makes one 9-in/23-cm tart

BEET JELLY

2¼ cups/525 ml syrup from candied beets → 125

2¼ tsp agar powder

Pinch of kosher salt

BAY LEAF MERINGUE

2 egg whites

⅔ cup/130 g superfine sugar

¼ tsp fresh lemon juice, plus grated zest of 1 lemon

1 tsp powdered bay leaf → 30

FROZEN YOGURT

½ cup/110 ml milk kefir → 76 or whole milk

1 tsp powdered plain gelatin

½ cup/100 g granulated sugar

½ cup/120 ml fermented honey → 121 or honey

½ cup/125 ml well-drained farmer's cheese → 67 or well-drained ricotta

½ cup/100 ml kefir buttermilk → 76

½ cup/120 ml drained yogurt → 74

½ cup/55 g buttermilk powder

3 tbsp fresh lemon juice

2 tsp powdered bay leaf → 30

1 tsp kosher salt

SUNFLOWER SEED FRANGIPANE

¾ cup/110 g sunflower seeds → 81

6 tbsp/85 g kefir butter → 76, at room temperature

½ cup/100 g granulated sugar

2 tsp Kamut flour

1 tsp rice powder → 48 or rice flour

1 whole egg, plus 1 egg white

SALTED SHORT CRUST

1 cup/125 g all-purpose flour

¾ cup plus 1 tbsp/100 g Kamut flour

¼ cup/20 g light rye flour

2¼ tsp baking powder

½ tsp kosher salt

¾ cup/165 g kefir butter → 76, at room temperature

⅔ cup/120 g firmly packed light brown sugar

6 egg yolks

3 lb/1.4 kg candied beets → 125, sliced into thin rounds

¼ cup/35 g sunflower seeds, toasted, for garnish

TO MAKE THE BEET JELLY: In a blender, combine the beet syrup, agar powder, and salt and process until combined, about 1 minute. Transfer to a small saucepan over medium heat and bring to a boil. Remove from the heat and pour into a shallow baking dish. Refrigerate until firmly set, about 1 hour.

Transfer the jelly to the blender and purée until smooth, stopping to scrape down the sides of the blender as needed to ensure that the jelly is evenly blended. The jelly will keep in an airtight container in the refrigerator for up to 1 month.

TO MAKE THE BAY LEAF MERINGUE: Preheat the oven to 200°F/95°C, or set a dehydrator to 165°F/75°C. Line a sheet pan with a silicone baking mat or parchment paper. Bring about 2 in/5 cm of water to a simmer in a medium saucepan. Combine the egg whites, sugar, and lemon juice in the bowl of a stand mixer and set the bowl over (not touching) the simmering water. Whisk continuously until the sugar dissolves and the mixture registers 120°F/48°C on an instant-read thermometer.

CONTINUED

Fit the stand mixer with the whip attachment and beat the warm egg white mixture on low speed for 5 minutes. Increase the speed to medium-high and continue to beat until the meringue is very stiff and shiny and the bowl feels cool to the touch, about 10 minutes. Using a rubber spatula, fold in the lemon zest and powdered bay leaf.

Transfer the meringue to the prepared pan. Using an offset spatula, spread the meringue in an even layer about ½ in/12 mm thick. Transfer the meringue to the oven and bake for 15 minutes. Turn off the oven and allow the meringue to dry overnight in the oven. Alternatively, place it in the dehydrator until completely dry and brittle, 24 to 48 hours. Break the meringue into pieces and store in an airtight container at room temperature for up to 4 days or in the freezer for up to 1 month. The freezer helps the meringues to remain very dry.

TO MAKE THE FROZEN YOGURT: Put 4 tsp of the milk kefir in a small bowl, add the gelatin across the top, and let stand for 5 minutes to bloom. Meanwhile, in a small saucepan over medium heat, combine the remaining milk kefir, the sugar, and honey and bring to a simmer, stirring until the sugar has dissolved. Add the gelatin mixture, stirring to make sure that it dissolves completely.

In a blender, combine the milk kefir mixture, cheese, buttermilk, yogurt, buttermilk powder, lemon juice, powdered bay leaf, and salt and process until well blended. Transfer to an airtight container and refrigerate until well chilled, for at least 8 hours or up to 3 days.

Transfer the chilled mixture to an ice-cream maker and freeze according to the manufacturer's instructions. Pack the frozen yogurt into a container and press a sheet of plastic wrap directly onto the surface. Place in the freezer until firm, about 3 hours. You can thaw and respin the frozen yogurt as needed.

TO MAKE THE SUNFLOWER SEED FRANGIPANE: Preheat the oven to 300°F/150°C. Spread the sunflower seeds on a sheet pan and toast in the oven until lightly browned and fragrant, 20 to 30 minutes. Let cool to room temperature. In a food processor or spice grinder, pulse the seeds until reduced to a coarse meal.

In a stand mixer fitted with the whip attachment, combine the butter and sugar and mix on medium-high speed until light and fluffy, about 3 minutes. Add the Kamut flour, rice powder, whole egg, and egg white and mix on medium-high speed until very light, about 10 minutes. Fold in the sunflower meal. Refrigerate until well chilled. The frangipane will keep in an airtight container in the refrigerator for up to 3 days.

TO MAKE THE SALTED SHORT CRUST: Into a medium bowl, sift together the all-purpose flour, Kamut flour, rye flour, baking powder, and salt. In a stand mixer fitted with the paddle attachment, combine the butter and brown sugar and beat on medium-high speed until light and airy, about 4 minutes. Add the egg yolks one at a time, then continue to beat until well combined, about 1 minute. On low speed, add the flour mixture to the butter-egg mixture and mix just until the dough comes together. Gather the dough into a ball, flatten into a disk, wrap in plastic wrap, and refrigerate until well chilled, at least 4 hours.

Preheat the oven to 325°F/165°C. Oil a 9-in/23-cm fluted tart pan with a removable bottom, then dust with flour, tapping out the excess.

On a lightly floured work surface, roll out the dough to a round at least 10 in/25 cm in diameter and about ¼ in/6 mm thick. Carefully drape the dough around the rolling pin, position the pin over the center of the prepared tart pan, and unfurl the dough round into the pan. Gently push the dough onto the bottom and into the fluted sides, taking care not to tear it. Trim off the excess by running the rolling pin over the rim of the pan to cut away extra dough. Cover with plastic wrap and freeze for at least 30 minutes, or up to 24 hours. This dough is very tender, and if you're having difficulty getting it into the pan, just press it in patches. It'll bake up fine.

Dock the dough with a fork by piercing through the surface to allow air to escape and prevent bubbles. Don't get crazy here; too many holes can cause the filling to leak out. Next, line the shell with a round of parchment, a coffee filter, or aluminum foil and add dried beans, pie weights, or rice to weight the dough down (you can use the rice after toasting for rice powder → 48). Bake

for 20 minutes. Remove the weights and bake for 10 minutes more, until the crust is lightly golden. Remove from the oven and let cool on a wire rack for at least 2 hours.

When fully cooled, fill with the chilled frangipane, smoothing the surface. Starting at the outside edge of the tart, arrange the candied beet slices in concentric circles over the filling, overlapping the slices slightly and finishing at the center. Leftover beets can be diced and used for garnish. Bake until the frangipane filling is firm to the touch, about 45 minutes. Remove from the oven and let cool on a wire rack for at least 2 hours. Remove the tart from the pan by placing your hand on the bottom of the pan and carefully pushing upward, letting the sides fall away around your arm. Slide the tart onto a serving plate or cutting board and leave at room temperature until ready to serve. (If serving the next day, refrigerate and bring to room temperature 2 hours before serving.)

To serve, cut the tart into eight pieces and place a slice on individual plates. Put a spoonful of beet jelly next to each slice, and then place a scoop of frozen yogurt on the beet jelly. Garnish with the sunflower seeds and diced beets, if using. Grate the meringue over the top or serve small shards of it on the plate. Serve immediately.

CREPE CAKE WITH APPLE BUTTER, FARMER'S CHEESE & PECANS

In Hungary, crepes are called *palacsinta*. Hungarian cooks stuff them with savory and sweet fillings and roll them, fold them, layer them, and fry them. Here, we stack crepes into a cake with alternating layers of fresh cheese and preserved apple butter. We include a bit of apple brandy in the crepe batter to pay homage to the fruit spirits so widely imbibed throughout eastern and central Europe.

Make this cake the night before or early the same day you plan to serve it, then chill it. Chilling the finished cake makes it easier to cut.

Serves 8 to 10

CREPES

5 tbsp/70 g brown butter → 77

2 cups/255 g all-purpose flour, sifted

½ cup/60 g buckwheat flour, sifted

1 tsp yogurt powder → 48, or grated zest of 1 lemon

1 tsp kosher salt

3¾ cups/900 ml whole milk

1¼ cups/300 ml heavy cream

5 eggs, lightly beaten

2 tbsp apple brandy

Unsalted butter for cooking the crepes

2 cups/650 g well-drained farmer's cheese → 67, or well-drained ricotta

3 tbsp creamed honey → 122 or honey

Kosher salt

4 cups/450 g pecans

2 cups/455 g apple butter → 126, or store-bought apple butter

¼ cup/60 ml apple cider syrup → 130

2 cups/480 ml sour cream → 71

TO MAKE THE CREPES: In a small heavy-bottomed saucepan, melt the brown butter over medium heat. Set aside to cool.

In a large bowl, combine the all-purpose flour, buckwheat flour, yogurt powder, and salt and stir to mix well. Make a well in the center of the flour mixture. In a medium bowl, whisk together the milk, cream, eggs, brandy, and cooled yet still fluid browned butter. Pour the milk mixture into the well in the flour mixture. Then, using a rubber spatula, gradually mix the dry ingredients into the wet ingredients, working carefully to avoid forming clumps. Do not overmix, as you do not want to develop the gluten. Some small lumps may remain; they will hydrate as the batter rests. Cover the bowl and refrigerate for at least 3 hours, or for up to 3 days.

CONTINUED

Have ready a flat dinner plate and a small off-set spatula. Place an 8-in/20-cm crepe pan or nonstick skillet over medium heat and add ½ tsp unsalted butter. When the butter melts, swirl the pan so the butter covers the bottom evenly. Using a paper towel, wipe the excess butter from the pan. To test the heat level of the pan, drop a small spoonful of batter into it; if the batter quickly spreads and bubbles soon form around the edges, the pan is ready. Holding the pan handle with one hand, ladle 2 tbsp/30 ml of the batter into the pan with your other hand. Immediately rotate your wrist so the batter evenly coats the bottom of the pan. Cook, shaking the pan from time to time to prevent sticking, until bubbles begin to form on the surface and the bottom is golden brown, about 1 minute. Using the spatula, lift the edge of the crepe, grasp it, and flip it over. Cook until the second side is just set, about 30 seconds. Transfer the crepe to the plate. If your first crepe does not turn out well, adjust the heat and try again. You want the pan hot enough for the batter to begin cooking right away but not so hot that it burns. After the first coating of butter, the pan should be self-seasoning from the batter, but if the crepes begin to stick, add a little more butter.

Once you have the right temperature, proceed to make crepes with all of the batter, stacking the crepes as you go in stacks of ten. As each stack is ready, transfer it to the refrigerator. You should have thirty crepes in all. If you plan to build the cake the same day, let the crepes cool completely and leave uncovered. If you plan to build the cake the next day, let cool completely, then cover tightly and refrigerate.

Preheat the oven to 300°F/150°C. Spread the pecans in a single layer on a sheet pan and toast until fragrant, 8 to 10 minutes. Let cool completely.

Put all but ½ cup/55 g of the nuts in a food processor and process to a creamy, smooth butter. Chop the remaining nuts into small pieces and reserve for garnish.

About 1 hour before you begin to build your cake, put the farmer's cheese in a medium bowl and bring to room temperature. Fold in the creamed honey and season with salt.

To build the cake, place a crepe on a large, flat serving plate or cake stand. Using an offset spatula, spread a thin layer of the cheese mixture evenly over the crepe, extending it to the edges, then top with a second crepe, pressing gently. Spread a thin layer of the apple butter over the second crepe, extending it to the edges. Continue this way, alternating the cheese and apple butter fillings and pressing down as you go to create a nicely balanced cake, until you have used up all of the crepes. Do not spread filling over the top crepe. Cover the cake with plastic wrap and chill for at least 4 hours, or for up to 24 hours.

Heat a long, sharp knife with hot tap water and wipe dry. First cut the cake into quarters, then cut it into eight to twelve slices. Transfer the slices to individual plates, standing them upright. Drip a spoonful of the pecan butter over the top. Then, using a quick back-and-forth motion, cover the slice with a spoonful of the apple syrup, allowing it to drip down the sides with the pecan butter. Place a scoop of sour cream next to each slice and garnish with the chopped pecans.

STEAMED PARSNIP CAKE WITH CIDER, KEFIR, HONEY & BEE POLLEN

This is an ode to steamed Japanese mochi (rice cakes). We are on a never-ending quest to utilize the natural sweetness in ingredients to flavor desserts. We don't look down on refined white sugar; we just try to use it in moderation. Here, we use parsnip, honey, and rice koji powder, all of which have inherent sweetness. In autumn, when parsnips begin to show up in the markets, the apple season coincides and the last of the bee pollen is collected before the winter. We highlight these ingredients together here as a way to move us into a new season.

Serves 8

1½ lb/680 g parsnips, peeled and left whole

½ cup plus 1 tbsp/130 g kefir butter → 76, at room temperature, plus 2 tbsp, chilled

2 tbsp fermented honey → 121, or honey

1½ cups/240 g rice koji powder → 48 or rice powder → 48 or rice flour

Kosher salt

1 cup/240 ml apple cider syrup → 130

½ cup/120 ml kefir cream → 76

Parsnip powder → 50 for garnish

Bee pollen for garnish

Finishing salt

Freshly ground black pepper

Pour water into a steamer pan, place the steamer rack above the water, and put the parsnips on the rack. Cover the steamer, bring the water to a boil over medium heat, and steam until the parsnips are quite tender, about 30 minutes. Remove the parsnips from the steamer and let cool slightly, then coarsely chop.

Transfer the parsnips to a blender, add the ½ cup plus 1 tbsp/130 g butter and the honey and process until smooth. Pour the purée into a medium bowl. In a small bowl, stir together the rice koji powder and ½ tsp kosher salt, add to the puréed parsnips, and mix until combined. Taste and add more salt if needed.

Using some of the chilled butter, grease a 9½-by-6½-by-1-in/24-by-16.5-by-2.5-cm sheet pan. You may have to get creative, depending on the size of your steamer; the important thing to note is that you will want to release the steamed cake in one piece and you do not want the cake any thicker than 1 in/2.5 cm or it will not cook evenly. Using a spatula, spread the puréed parsnip mixture evenly in the prepared pan. Knock the pan on the countertop a few times to rid the mixture of any air bubbles.

Pour water into a steamer pan, place the steamer rack above the water, and bring the water to a boil. Place the sheet pan on the rack, cover the steamer, and steam until the cake has puffed and

is set in the center, about 40 minutes. You know it is done when it springs back into place when you prod it with your finger and it begins to pull away from the sides of the pan. Remove from the steamer. Let cool to room temperature. Run a knife around the edge and invert the cake from the pan onto a sheet of parchment paper, being careful not to break it. Cover and refrigerate until well chilled, for at least 4 hours, or for up to 36 hours; it is much easier to cut when cool.

Cut the chilled cake into eight pieces. Put the pieces on a small pan, making sure they are not touching, and warm in the steamer until heated through, 4 to 6 minutes.

In a small saucepan over medium heat, warm the apple cider syrup until bubbling around the edges, about 4 minutes. Remove from the heat and whisk in the remaining chilled butter. Taste and season with salt if desired.

To serve, put two spoonfuls of the warm syrup in the bottom of each of eight individual bowls. With a small offset spatula, transfer a slice of warm cake to each bowl. With the back of a spoon, make a small indentation in the center of each slice. With a spoon, drop about 1 tbsp of the kefir cream into each indentation. Finish with parsnip powder, bee pollen, finishing salt, and one turn of the pepper mill. Serve warm.

FARMER'S CHEESECAKE WITH RHUBARB, SORREL & CARAWAY HONEY

When we think about pairing flavors, we often think about families—about foods related to one another. It only makes sense to us that foods that share a common DNA would be compatible on the plate. That's the train of thought that brought us to combine rhubarb, sorrel, and buckwheat, all members of the Polygonaceae family, with this no-bake cheesecake. The rhubarb and sorrel both have tart, vegetal flavors, while the buckwheat is earthy and nutty. Buckwheat, which is actually a fruit seed and not a grain, plays a double role here: first in the crust and again in the caraway honey.

You can top the cheesecake with macerated strawberries in place of the rhubarb compote. You will need 4 cups/560 g

strawberries. Remove the stems, then leave the small berries whole and cut the large berries into halves or quarters. Toss the berries with ½ cup/100 sugar and ¼ cup/60 ml fresh lemon juice and let stand at room temperature until they release their juices, about 2 hours.

Makes one 9-in/23-cm tart

BUCKWHEAT "GRAHAM" CRACKER CRUMBS

¼ cup/60 ml whole milk

3 tbsp fermented honey → 121, or honey

1¼ cups/150 g buckwheat flour

¾ cup/120 g rice powder → 48 or rice flour

6 tbsp/85 g firmly packed light brown sugar

¾ tsp baking soda

½ tsp kosher salt

Pinch of ground cinnamon

4 tbsp/55 g unsalted butter, cut into cubes and chilled, plus more if needed

CRUST

¾ cup/170 g unsalted kefir butter → 76

2 tbsp plus ½ tsp/35 g firmly packed light brown sugar

2¾ cups/350 g buckwheat "graham" cracker crumbs or graham cracker crumbs

¼ tsp kosher salt

½ tsp ground ginger

¼ tsp ground cinnamon

CONTINUED

RHUBARB COMPOTE

2 lb/910 g red rhubarb, trimmed and cut into ½-in/12-mm dice

½ cup/120 ml fermented honey → 121, or honey

2 tbsp light brown sugar

Grated zest and juice of 2 lemons

1 tsp kosher salt

¼ tsp caraway seeds, toasted and ground → 31

⅛ tsp coriander seeds, toasted and ground → 31

CARAWAY HONEY

½ cup/120 ml fermented buckwheat honey → 121, or honey

2 tsp caraway seeds, toasted and ground → 31

Sorrel petals for garnish

Freshly ground black pepper

TO MAKE THE BUCKWHEAT "GRAHAM" CRACKER CRUMBS: In a small saucepan over medium-low heat, combine the milk and honey and heat just until the honey has dissolved. Remove from the heat and let cool to room temperature.

In the bowl of a stand mixer, combine the buckwheat flour, rice powder, brown sugar, baking soda, salt, and cinnamon and stir to mix. Scatter the butter evenly over the surface. Mix on low speed just until the mixture resembles coarse meal. Add the cooled milk and honey and mix just until combined. Gather up the dough, shape into a ball, wrap in plastic wrap, and chill for at least 1 hour, or for up to 3 days.

FILLING

1 lb/450 g well-drained farmer's cheese → 67 or well-drained ricotta

8 oz/225 g cream cheese, at room temperature

3 tbsp fermented honey → 121, or honey

Grated zest and juice of ½ lemon

Pinch of kosher salt

Pinch of ground ginger

Preheat the oven to 325°F/180°C. Line a sheet pan with a silicone baking mat or parchment paper. Break the dough into golf-ball-size pieces and arrange them about 3 in/7.5 cm apart on the prepared pan. Lightly oil the palm of one hand and press down on each mound of dough to flatten it into a disk about ⅛ in/3 mm thick. Don't worry too much about how they look. Remember, you are making crumbs.

Bake until well browned, about 15 minutes. Remove from the oven and break up with a metal spatula or dough scraper to expose the interiors. Return the pan to the oven and bake until the crumbles are crisp and dry, 10 to 15 minutes longer. Let cool completely, then put the crumbles in a food processor and process to fine, uniform crumbs. You should have 2¾ cups/350 g of crumbs. The crumbs will keep at room temperature for up to 2 weeks as long as they are completely dry.

CONTINUED

TO MAKE THE CRUST: In a small saucepan over low heat, melt the butter, add the brown sugar, and stir until the sugar has dissolved. Remove from the heat. In a medium bowl, combine the cracker crumbs, salt, ginger, and cinnamon and stir to mix. Pour in the butter mixture and stir until the crumb mixture is evenly moistened. It should weep a bit of butter when squeezed; if it feels dry, melt another tablespoon of butter and stir it in.

Transfer the crumb mixture to a 9-in/23-cm tart pan with a removable bottom and press the mixture evenly over the bottom and up the sides of the pan. Freeze for at least 1 hour, or up to overnight.

TO MAKE THE FILLING: In a stand mixer fitted with the paddle attachment, combine the farmer's cheese, cream cheese, honey, lemon zest and juice, salt, and ginger and mix on medium speed until all of the ingredients are evenly combined. The mixture should be very thick. Alternatively, mix by hand in a large bowl.

Transfer the filling to the chilled tart shell, spreading it into a thick, even layer. Freeze the tart, uncovered, for at least 2 hours to ensure that it can be easily removed from the pan. If not using right away, wrap the frozen tart in plastic wrap, and return to the freezer until ready to serve.

TO MAKE THE COMPOTE: In a medium heavy-bottomed saucepan over medium heat, combine the rhubarb, honey, brown sugar, and lemon zest and juice. Bring to a simmer, stirring to dissolve the sugar. Simmer until the rhubarb is tender and the liquid is reduced by half, about 10 minutes. Stir in the salt, caraway seeds, and coriander seeds. Remove from the heat and let cool to room temperature.

TO MAKE THE CARAWAY HONEY: In a small saucepan over low heat, combine the honey and caraway seeds and warm to infuse the honey with the flavor of the caraway, about 10 minutes. Remove from the heat and let cool to room temperature.

At least 2 hours before serving, remove the frozen tart from the pan by placing your hand on the bottom of the pan and carefully pushing upward, letting the sides fall away around your arm. The tart must be frozen for this step to ensure the crust lines remain clean. Let the tart stand at room temperature until it is halfway thawed (the filling will be not quite as soft as cream cheese). Cut into eight pieces using a sharp knife and slicing assertively. It will want to crumble a bit if you saw and hesitate. Refrigerate until ready to serve, or for up to 2 days.

To serve, place a scoop of compote on individual plates, top with a tart slice, and garnish with the caraway honey, sorrel petals, and pepper.

HAZELNUT BUTTER AND STRAWBERRY JAM COOKIES

This cookie is an ode to our love of peanut butter and jelly sandwiches. We use hazelnut butter here because we enjoy the subtle nuttiness and rich mouthfeel that it has. Feel free to use any nut butter and jam flavor, but we like to make a preserved strawberry jam for the filling.

Makes 12 sandwich cookies

COOKIES

3¼ cups/840 g hazelnut butter → 83

1 cup/200 g granulated sugar

1 cup/180 g packed light brown sugar

1 tsp baking soda

½ tsp kosher salt

⅛ tsp freshly cracked black pepper

2 eggs

PRESERVED STRAWBERRY JAM

2 lb/910 g dried strawberries → 58

½ lb/225 g fresh strawberries, juiced → 129

TO MAKE THE COOKIES: Preheat the oven to 350°F/175°C. Line a sheet pan with parchment paper. In a stand mixer fitted with the paddle attachment, mix the hazelnut butter, granulated sugar, brown sugar, baking soda, salt, and pepper until well combined. Add the eggs and beat until thoroughly combined. Spoon 2-tbsp/30-g balls of dough onto the prepared pan and pat them down into flat disks. Alternatively, press into a cookie mold to create a more uniform shape. The shaped cookies can be covered and refrigerated for up to 4 days, or frozen for up to 1 month. They bake up perfectly directly from the refrigerator or freezer. Add a few minutes to baking time for frozen dough.

Bake for 12 to 14 minutes, turning the pan once halfway through baking, until the cookies are brown around the edges. Let cool on the sheet pan. The baked cookies will keep in an airtight container at room temperature for up to 4 days.

TO MAKE THE PRESERVED STRAWBERRY JAM: Combine half of the dried strawberries and half of the strawberry juice in a blender and purée until a thick paste has formed. Transfer to a bowl. Purée the remaining juice and berries and combine with the first batch. Cover and refrigerate until ready to use.

Spread 1 to 2 tbsp of jam on one side of a cookie. Top with a second cookie to create a sandwich. Repeat until the cookies are used up. The sandwich cookies are best eaten the day they are filled.

RUGELACH

In Yiddish, the word *rugelach* translates to "little twists." Cortney grew up craving these cookies. Here, we alter the shape a bit from the traditional cookie, which is often formed into a crescent. Many fillings can be used for this (see rhubarb compote → 350 or strawberry jam → 354). We use poppyseeds here for their texture and nutty aroma.

Makes 24 cookies

POPPYSEED PASTE

¾ cup/115 g poppyseeds

⅛ cup/30 g kefir butter → 76

½ cup/120 ml whole milk

¼ cup/50 g sugar

¼ cup/85 g fermented honey → 121, or honey

Juice and grated zest of 1 lemon

½ tsp kosher salt

1 egg

DOUGH

½ cup/60 g all-purpose flour

½ cup/60 g light rye flour

1 cup/110 g Kamut flour

1 tbsp sugar

1½ tsp dried fennel flowers → 33, powdered

1½ tsp kosher salt

⅛ tsp freshly ground black pepper

½ lb/112 g kefir butter → 76, cut into ½-in/12-mm dice and chilled

½ lb/225 g cream cheese, at room temperature

⅛ cup/30 ml sour cream → 71, at room temperature

TO MAKE THE POPPYSEED PASTE: In a spice or coffee grinder, pulse the poppyseeds in batches for 15 to 20 seconds until broken up and powdery. In a small saucepan, melt the butter over medium heat. Whisk in the milk, sugar, honey, lemon juice and zest, and salt, and simmer, stirring occasionally, until the sugar and honey are fully dissolved. In a medium nonreactive bowl, whisk the egg. Gradually pour the hot liquid into the egg, whisking constantly. Add the egg mixture back to the saucepan and set the pan over low heat. Cook, whisking constantly, until the mixture turns yellow, is thick enough to coat the back of a spoon, and holds a line when a finger is drawn through it, 3 to 5 minutes. Remove from the heat and whisk the poppyseeds and salt into the warm mixture. Let cool completely before using. The paste can be stored in an airtight container in the refrigerator for up to 1 week.

TO MAKE THE DOUGH: In a food processor, combine the all-purpose flour, rye flour, Kamut flour, sugar, fennel pollen, salt, and pepper and process briefly to combine. Scatter the butter over the flour mixture and pulse until the mixture is crumbly. Transfer to a large bowl, add the cream cheese and sour cream, and mix with a wooden spoon until a smooth dough forms. Cover with plastic wrap and refrigerate until well chilled, at least 4 hours, or for up to 24 hours.

On a floured work surface, roll out the dough to a rectangle about ¼ in/6 mm thick. Spread the poppyseed paste in a thin layer over the dough. Starting from a long edge, roll up the dough into a log. Wrap tightly in plastic wrap and chill until firm, at least 2 hours or for up to 24 hours. You can also freeze for up to 2 weeks, either in logs or cut into cookies. They will bake up nicely directly from the freezer.

Preheat the oven to 350°F/180°C. Line a sheet pan with parchment paper. Cut the log crosswise into pieces 1 in/2.5 cm thick. Arrange the pieces cut-side down on the prepared pan. Bake until dark golden brown, 15 to 20 minutes.

Remove from the oven, transfer to a wire rack, and let cool completely. The cookies taste best when eaten the day they are made, but they can be stored in an airtight container at room temperature for up to 2 days.

INDEX

ACKNOWLEDGMENTS

Just as most writers shouldn't open restaurants, most cooks shouldn't write books. We apologize to our staff, guests, families, and each other for the past year and a half.

This project wouldn't have been possible without:

CHAD ROBERTSON and **LIZ PRUEITT**, for giving us this opportunity. Thanks, too, for the many reshoots, reassurances in times of extreme anxiety, and the constant trust and generosity.

KATHERINE COWLES, our agent, for answering all our calls, for forcing us to write a book, and for the honesty and patience.

JAN NEWBERRY, who pushed us to get it done. Thanks for all of your help.

JULIETTE CEZZAR, for making our food, so seemingly incongruous and unclassifiable, into something clean, concise, and beautiful. Thank you for moving photos around dozens of times, and back again, with a smile and a sense of humor.

SARAH BILLINGSLEY, our editor at Chronicle books. We can't imagine managing this process for a living. We can't imagine managing us. You do it well. In addition: publisher **CHRISTINE CARSWELL**, publishing director **LORENA JONES**, managing editor **DOUG OGAN**, editor **DAWN YANAGIHARA**, copyeditor **SHARON SILVA**, production manager **TERA KILLIP**, publicist **DAVID HAWK**, and marketing manager **PETER PEREZ**.

MINDY AND JUSTON ENOS, for destroying their backyard for us. For having full-time jobs and also growing incredible vegetables and raising seriously cranky chickens. We are your biggest fans.

SHERI CODIANA, LAUREN GODFREY, STEPHANIE HUA: Your recipe tests often tasted better than actual dishes on the menu at Bar Tartine. Thank you all for your humor, insight, and ability to interpret unreadable recipes. Sorry about the rice poisoning and for making you eat tripe, clams, etcetera. We hope you are rehydrated.

KAREN LEBOVITZ, ANTHONY MYINT, KYLE CONNAUGHTON, DAN FELDER, ALI BOUZARI, AND PHIL BALLA: Thanks for putting extra eyes on this.

HARRY KONGVONGXAY, SAM SHIRE, CAITLIN KOETHER, MOLLY FRITZ, and **MARY CHRISTIE**, who made up the management team at Bar Tartine while we wrote this cookbook. Thanks for picking up our slack during this bookmaking process.